THE STATE OF DISUNION

THE STATE OF DISUNION

REGIONAL SOURCES OF MODERN AMERICAN PARTISANSHIP

NICOLE MELLOW

THE JOHNS HOPKINS UNIVERSITY PRESS
BALTIMORE

The Johns Hopkins University Press
2715 North Charles Street
Baltimore, Maryland 21218-4363
www.press.jhu.edu

Library of Congress Cataloging-in-Publication Data

Mellow, Nicole.
The state of disunion : regional sources of modern American partisanship / Nicole Mellow.
    p. cm.
Includes bibliographical references and index.
ISBN-13: 978-0-8018-8812-0 (hardcover : alk. paper)
ISBN-13: 978-0-8018-8816-8 (pbk. : alk. paper)
ISBN-10: 0-8018-8812-3 (hardcover : alk. paper)
ISBN-10: 0-8018-8816-6 (pbk. : alk. paper)
    1. Political parties—United States. 2. Political culture—United States.
3. Political participation—United States. 4. Opposition (Political science)—
United States. 5. Divided government—United States. 6. United States—
Politics and government—2001– I. Title.
    JK2261.M46 2008
    324.273—dc22
                                2007034000

A catalog record for this book is available from the British Library.

Special discounts are available for bulk purchases of this book.
For more information, please contact Special Sales at 410-516-6936 or specialsales@press.jhu.edu.

CONTENTS

ACKNOWLEDGMENTS

Many individuals contributed to the development of the ideas that are expressed in these pages, and I owe all of them a great debt for what they have taught me about politics. My deep gratitude goes to Peter Trubowitz and Walter Dean Burnham for nurturing my interest in political geography while I was a graduate student at the University of Texas at Austin. It was also they who taught me the value of roaming widely through the toolbox to find whatever is necessary to best answer the interesting questions. Before them, Sidney Plotkin ignited my interest in politics at Vassar College when he put a copy of E. E. Schattschneider's book in my hand and helped me understand its insights. I owe thanks, also, to Ralph Nuñez, president of New York City's Homes for the Homeless and my first boss, for opening my eyes to the marvels of real-world politics.

Individuals at several institutions have been kind enough to read parts or all of the manuscript and to offer useful critiques along the way. In particular, the following scholars provided invaluable advice and insights: Brian Balogh, Richard Bensel, Catherin Boone, James K. Galbraith, Bryan Garsten, Gary Jacobsohn, Farid Kahhat, Tse-Min Lin, David Mayhew, Sidney Milkis, James Morone, Michael Nelson, Benjamin Page, Howard Reiter, Gretchen Ritter, Bartholomew Sparrow, Anand Swamy, Jeffrey K. Tulis, Tamara Waggener, and Margaret Weir. Special credit goes to Sid Milkis, who asked hard questions at critical junctures. Anand Swamy helped me think through the methodological issues. Jeff Tulis was particularly influential in the development of this project, and I am deeply grateful for his willingness to read and reread my work. Tim Sullivan's close read immeasurably improved the manuscript. Finally, the strong support and useful suggestions from the anonymous reviewers at Princeton University Press and at the Johns Hopkins University Press were simply terrific, especially for one's first book. The book is stronger as a result of the advice of all of these scholars; any shortcomings that remain are not for want of their efforts.

Colleagues at Williams College have contributed to this project through their willingness to read my work, offer suggestions, and engage in lively and thoughtful conversation about American politics. I would especially like to thank Monique Deveaux, Cathy Johnson, Michael MacDonald, Jim Mahon, George Marcus, Darel Paul, and Mark Reinhardt for their ideas and inspirations, and Sharron Macklin for her technological mastery. Fellows at the Oakley Center for the Humanities and Social Sciences at Williams provided valuable comments on my work and helped expand my intellectual horizon across disciplinary boundaries. Bright students at Williams regularly challenged me to refine my thinking about parties, politics, and geography. I particularly want to thank Jacob Eisler and Alex Matthews for their painstaking research assistance and their abundant curiosity about politics.

A number of institutions and individuals helped make possible the research and writing of this book. A fellowship from the Miller Center for Public Affairs at the University of Virginia enabled me to make substantial headway with my work and introduced me to a wonderful group of political historians. Fellowships from the University of Texas allowed me to devote uninterrupted time to the project, as did an Oakley Center Fellowship from Williams College. Both the Carl Albert Congressional Research Center and the Dirksen Congressional Center provided valuable financial support and access to their archival holdings. I am also grateful to Alan Burns at the Clemson University Libraries for his assistance in tracking down documents in the Harry S. Dent Papers in the library's special collections. The Political Science Department at Williams College provided generous support for research assistance. I am also thankful to the following individuals for generously sharing their data: Keith Poole, Howard Rosenthal, Kenneth Meier, and Deborah McFarlane.

Many people associated with the publication process at the Johns Hopkins University Press put time and effort into this book, and it is a better product for their efforts. I am grateful to my editor, Henry Tom, whose support throughout helped make this book a reality. I also extend my appreciation to Anne Whitmore, whose copyediting abilities are simply phenomenal. And I am deeply and profoundly grateful to my good friend, Henk van Assen, a gifted book designer, who generously gave his time to this project to make my ideas come alive visually.

This book would not have been completed without the support of my family and many friends. In particular, my parents, Richard Mellow and Gail Mellow, instilled in me a desire to keep learning, and they seem never to tire of listening to my ideas. My friendship with Sunila Kale afforded the opportunity for endless spirited discussions, while Christian Novetzke provided sane advice and necessary comic relief. Jeff Tulis was tireless in his support and encouragement, and I have deep gratitude for his friendship. The arrival of Rafael Henry was all the incentive I needed to finish the book, and his presence makes the imperative of improving democratic politics ever more clear to me. And most of all, Paige Bartels offered patience, wisdom, humor, and good daily counsel, without which I would not have persevered.

THE STATE OF DISUNION

INTRODUCTION

THE 2000 U.S. presidential campaign began as a relatively forgettable season, not nearly as exciting as the parties' respective primary seasons, but by its end it had become a drama that transfixed the nation—the world, really—for five weeks beyond election night. At its center were the major party candidates, Democrat Al Gore, the sitting vice president, and Republican George W. Bush, the governor of Texas. The voting on election night was close. By the end of the night, the race had come down to Florida. With that state's votes still undecided, neither candidate was willing to concede the election. Over the next few days, a dispute erupted over the state's vote returns, and the election saga expanded over weeks to include the full battalions of the parties, legions of lawyers, various Florida officials, and judges at both the state and the federal level. In the end, the disagreement over the vote count was resolved, in unprecedented fashion, by the intervention of the U.S. Supreme Court—a decision hardly without its own controversy. Florida's electoral votes, and with them the presidency, went to Bush.

Having won the election, President-elect Bush faced a difficult political landscape. His was a victory clouded by ambiguity and contestation, and he could claim no electoral mandate as he prepared to move into office. Congress, his partner in lawmaking, was hardly a source of reassurance. Republicans had a remarkably slim majority in the House—just five seats—and the Senate was evenly split. Bush, who had campaigned on the promise of being "a uniter, not a divider," now faced a country almost perfectly divided between the parties. Delivering on his campaign promise, especially after the rancor of the election, would not be easy.

For his first official appearance as president-elect, Bush chose to speak to the nation from a podium in the chamber of the Texas State House. The setting was symbolic. Democrats controlled the Texas House, and Bush's campaign had cited his work as governor with both Democrats and Republicans as evidence of his ability to unite across divides. The Democratic Speaker of the House, Pete Laney, introduced the new president to the country. Bush, citing the "spirit of cooperation" he had seen in that very hall, insisted that the "nation must rise above a house divided." For his part, the president promised, "Whether you voted for me or not, I will do my best to serve your interests, and I will work to earn your respect."[1]

Despite the president's optimistic call for unity, it did not take long for the country's deep divisions to manifest themselves. In the 2004 presidential election, as in 2000, the electorate was polarized. Election day produced higher turnout, fewer independents, and greater party unity in ballot casting than any election in recent decades, signaling the intensity of voter passions. Two years later, in the midterm elections, Democrats gained control of Congress for the first time in twelve years, yet the division of seats between the parties remained as close as it had for the prior decade. Partisan clashes on legislation still rule in Washington as well. Party-line voting in Congress has been the norm for years, and both parties have resorted to any number of rule manipulations in their efforts to defeat their opponent. Even the normally cordial Senate became embroiled in a virulent partisanship in 2005 when Republicans threatened to derail Democratic opposition to President Bush's judicial nominees with a parliamentary maneuver nicknamed the "nuclear option." Left and right interest groups regularly trade accusations of obduracy and malfeasance through a proliferating number of blogs, books with sensational titles, 527-sponsored advertisements, even documentaries.

To describe this partisan rift, the phrase "red state–blue state divide" was coined, in reference to the geographic distribution of party support in the presidential elections of 2000 and 2004.[2] In both elections, Bush drew his support from the states of the South and the interior West, the so-called red states. His Democratic opponents, first Al Gore and then John Kerry, won in the North, including the Northeast and parts of the Midwest, and in the Pacific Coast states, dubbed the blue states.

The combination of geographic division and partisan acrimony has led pundits to marvel that politics in the new millennium appear to be taking on "the coloration of the Civil War."[3] The resurrection of this potent image—of a country torn apart geographically by its political beliefs and party attachments—raises the question What is the relationship between geography and partisanship? Why, 150 years after the Civil War, with globalization linking far-flung places and undermining local differences, do distinct subnational identities still exist, and how do they inform partisan conflict? How have Republicans come to dominate in the South and interior West, and why have Democrats prospered in the North and Pacific Coast states?

This book tackles these questions through an analysis of geography and party in the post–World War II era. Regional conflicts were common in the nineteenth century, as the different sections of the country battled over issues including slavery, tariffs, and the strength of the central government. National industrial development and widespread acceptance of the modern administrative state in the first half of the twentieth century collapsed many of the regional differences that had fed these earlier conflicts. For most scholars, though, it was the civil rights achievements of the 1960s, especially the enfranchisement of African Americans in the South, which finally put an end to the political significance of regional differences. National political consolidation was achieved once all citizens could exercise the full rights of citizenship, including selecting the national government.

My analysis shows that regional disputes continue to inform American politics. Submerged during the New Deal years, geographic divisions returned in the late 1960s and 1970s across a broad spectrum of issues. Politicians' responses led to a regional reorganization of the two-party system and the resuscitation of party conflict. The following chapters trace the post–World War II evolution of regional economic, racial, and cultural divisions, and show the effects these have had on national party building and interparty conflict. The story encompasses the demise of the multiregional New Deal Democratic political order and the rise of a new regionally divided party system. Bipartisanship gave way to partisanship as Republicans dominated the South and West and as Democrats found themselves displaced to the North and Pacific Coast states.

In this book I make three primary claims. First, the geographic regions within the United States are potent and unique fusions of their inhabitants' material and cultural experiences. Second, regional differences are translated into political significance in part because ambitious politicians exploit them for partisan gain. Third, ambitious politicians' exploitation of regional differences is largely responsible for today's partisan conflict. I found that it is the political parties' abilities or inabilities to develop cross-regional interests which has determined their fate on the national stage. By closely examining three cases—the creation of policy surrounding trade, welfare, and abortion—I hope to both illuminate the past and shed light on the prospects for overcoming current divisions.

Ironically, President Bush's attempt to steep himself in bipartisanship that night in Austin, Texas, itself reveals the importance that regions play in national politics. Demonstrating cooperation with Texas Democrats is not the same as showing an ability to cooperate with Democrats from New York, Massachusetts, or California. While of the same party and sharing many of the same general principles, Democrats in different parts of the country are shaped by the prevailing politics of their region, as are Republicans. Georgia Democrat Zell Miller does not share all of the views of Massachusetts Democrat Ted Kennedy, just as Rhode Island Republican Lincoln Chaffee does not share the same views as Kansas Republican Sam Brownback. While it would be inaccurate to say that all Texas Democrats are conservative, the state's history of Democratic dominance points to a legacy of conservatism within the Texas Democratic Party that is different from that in other parts of the country. So, while the Texas legislature may have been the best site from which to signal an ability to work with members of both parties, the real significance of Bush's claim may have been that he had been able to work well with other Texans. How those affiliations play out in national policy debates is the point of this book.

THE WAR BETWEEN THE PARTIES: ALTERNATIVE INTERPRETATIONS

Geography shapes American politics. The Federalists and anti-federalists anticipated it. Politicians profit from it (and pay for it). Citizens live through its consequences. Despite this, geography has not been a significant factor in scholarly explanations for today's partisanship.

Two social science interpretations dominate explanations for the intensity of current party conflict. The first focuses on the interests of key actors—elected officials, party activists, and core interest groups—and the actions they take to achieve their desired goals. The second concerns the ideas that have animated politics in recent decades. These two explanations, while drawing from different intellectual traditions, establish important parts of the story of rising conflict. Yet, lacking systematic analysis of the country's regions and their very different developmental paths, neither provides a fully satisfactory account of rising partisanship.[4] Not only is the role of contemporary regions in party politics a crucial explanatory factor in the wholesale shift from mid-century bipartisan cooperation to today's partisanship, it is one that accommodates both interests and ideas.

The explanation that focuses on the effects of rational actors pursuing their interests points to two developments as contributing to the growth in party conflict. The first is the proliferation of single-issue interest groups, which began in the 1960s. Typically more ideologically extreme than the average voter on the issues around which they organize, these groups are significant electoral actors because they bundle funds, votes, and other resources to lawmakers' campaigns in exchange for legislative support. Lawmakers have responded to the proliferation of groups by using the party less as a vehicle for mass mobilization and more to convey their credibility and to organize themselves to achieve the legislative outputs desired by their interest group constituents.[5] Second, to facilitate collective action, lawmakers changed the internal operation of Congress, and participated in the "nationalizing" of their party organizations.[6] For scholars like David Rohde, this institutional reorganization had a profound influence on party conflict. Rohde argues that by the 1970s parties were more ideologically homogeneous; because of the increasingly similar interests of their constituents, party members in Congress instituted reforms that strengthened party leadership, thinking this the best way to achieve the members' now collective goals. Under the directorship of discipline-enforcing leaders, the parties have come into increasing conflict with each other.[7] This account has been elaborated and generalized by Rohde and John Aldrich in their theory of "conditional party government."[8]

This explanation is useful for its description of the decisions made by key political actors that facilitated the increase of conflict, yet the fundamental, substantive reasons for debate are still unclear. Why was voters' electoral behavior creating increasingly homogeneous parties in the first place? To what conditions, or changes in conditions, were voters responding? For Rohde, it was a growth in the number of liberal Democrats in Congress that led to the push for House reforms. But what caused these numbers to grow across successive elections? Rohde argues that the reforms then contributed to an increasingly liberal national party as southern Democrats became more like northern liberals in their party. But, if reforms helped drive internal homogeneity, they did so among Democrats in large part because many southerners left the party. Rohde leaves the significance of this shift unexplored. What effect did the departure of southerners have on the nature of the party's ideological homogeneity (on what it meant to be "liberal") or on the nature of the subsequent conflict with Republicans?

These questions cannot be fully answered unless the larger historical environment within which the parties were operating is understood. Explanations that focus narrowly on interest pursuit and institutional structure leave us with too cursory a treatment of what drives conflict. More attention is needed to the larger social context that shapes how actors articulate and prioritize their interests and that, ultimately, leads them to choose one set of actions over another in any given moment. Because changing the context can change the logic of actors' choices, which then leads to different outcomes, a close examination of the historical setting with which political actors contend is needed.

Examining this setting is the terrain of political historians, and their accounts, especially those that focus on changing political ideas, provide the second common explanation for today's partisanship. Scholars have long pointed to a tradition of ideological division between American parties that extends back to founding era debates between Hamilton, Jefferson, and their compatriots over core political values, economic organization, and the proper conception of governmental authority.[9] As one analysis puts it, "American party history, and by extension American political history at large, has been irreducibly ideological."[10] From this perspective, the key to understanding today's conflict is to understand how older disputes have been refashioned by new conditions.

For those working in this tradition, the current conflict arose out of efforts by public intellectuals and party leaders on the right to develop and impose a "public philosophy" alternative to the reigning, though increasingly unpopular, New Deal philosophy. While the country had largely endorsed the New Deal's agenda of government activism in pursuit of public welfare, the social tumult and economic woes of the late 1960s and 1970s caused a growing number of voters to question Democratic commitments and solutions. Fueled by the country's problems at home and abroad and by a negative reaction to the activism of the left, strands of conservatism that had been percolating separately converged with the growing neoconservative movement, which began to articulate its rejection of the path taken by New Deal liberalism. Newly energized, the conservative movement's preference for private sphere, individual, and market solutions to the nation's ills clashed with liberals' continued belief in government activism to tame inequalities.[11]

But, more than the parties' renewed debate over economic policy, the "culture wars" have become the real focus of most analysts' attention. John Kenneth White, for example, has described post-1960s politics as centered around a "values divide" in which the very definition of "good" and "bad" is debated—a result of the upending of traditional norms of white Anglo-Saxon Protestant culture by growing recognition of the country's racial and ethnic diversity and

the acceptance of new family patterns.[12] Samuel Huntington has similarly described the effect of those years as invoking the country's "creedal passions" and
pulling a new generation of citizens into debate about core values.[13] James
Ceaser writes that more fundamental even than a conflict over values, left and
right disagree on the foundational ideas, deriving from "nature, History, and
faith," that underlie values; the two sides even disagree over whether foundational ideas should play a role in politics.[14] For these and other authors, today's
political conflict reflects differences in deeply held moral and ontological beliefs that are often manifested in battles centering on race, gender, religion,
and various "post-material" concerns. Representing these conflicting ideas in
government, the political parties are inevitably drawn into battle.[15]

These historical accounts help explain the substance of today's conflict.
They identify the principles that have unified each of the parties as well as
the source of the divisions between them in ways that the accounts of interest-
seeking actors do not. But they have their own limitations. Changes in values
occur neither spontaneously nor randomly; there are patterns to the support
and development of ideas. These patterns need careful explication if we are to
make sense of why ideological consensus fell apart as it did and why the challenges that arose took the precise form they did. For example, when stagflation
fostered skepticism of Keynesianism, why did conservative solutions become
the more viable competitor than radically left solutions? How did Republican
Party ideology come to fuse libertarian, moralistic, and laissez-faire capitalist
ideas, given that they appear to contain clear tensions? How did feminist ideals
come to be more associated with Democrats than Republicans, given that the
Democratic Party was long dominated by conservative southerners and was
closely tied to labor, which was initially resistant to many feminist demands?
But perhaps most importantly, why does the appeal of individual ideas appear
to be geographically based, at least sufficiently so to generate solidly red states
and solidly blue states? These sorts of questions cannot be answered by reference to the intrinsic nature of the ideas themselves. Needed is attention to the
way national trends have affected various regions, along with examination of
how these effects shifted the electoral motivations of the political actors who
suffused those ideas with particular meanings and fashioned them into broad
party ideologies.

REGIONS, PARTIES, AND CONFLICT: AN OVERVIEW OF THE ARGUMENT
V. O. Key, the eminent scholar of both regions and parties, wrote in the early
1940s that "[s]ectional interests have constituted important building blocks for
the American parties. Each party has had its roots deep in sectional interest and

each has sought to build intersectional combinations powerful enough to govern."[16] My study begins with the New Deal Democratic Party of the early 1960s, a party whose electoral strength derived from the accord brokered between its two regional halves, in the North and South. The premise of this accord was that national policy was tailored to accommodate the interests dominant in each region: organized labor and manufacturers in the North and agriculturalists and labor-intensive industry in the South. Issues that defied tailoring, such as civil rights for African Americans, were suppressed. Making sustained allies of North and South had been one of Franklin D. Roosevelt's chief accomplishments, and so attractive were the regional benefits of New Deal policies that they tended to induce the cooperation of northern Republicans as well.[17] The result was the classic bipartisanship of the late New Deal decades, often described as the consensus era in American politics.[18]

Yet, the very social and economic developments that the governing Democratic regime put in motion brought regional distinctions to the fore and frayed the North-South accord. In his analysis of presidents and partisan regimes, Stephen Skowronek has argued that presidents who are "regime articulators" inherit the regime's governing commitments yet must manage its increasingly contentious coalition partners.[19] As New Deal regime articulators, John Kennedy and Lyndon Johnson were confronted with the dilemma of holding together a fractious coalition, and they made political decisions that further weakened the longstanding regional accord of the Democratic Party. Republican leaders of the late 1960s and early 1970s were quick to exploit the emerging fissures in the New Deal coalition—perhaps most obviously in the area of civil rights.[20] But, as later chapters of this book show, Republicans fractured the Democratic Party regionally with a host of other policy ideas as well.[21] Because of the history of antagonisms between North and South, the dissonance between the two regions at the time, and the increasingly similar socioeconomic experiences of the South and West, Republican efforts to splinter Democrats on a regional axis were powerfully effective.

During his presidency, Richard Nixon consistently promoted policies that split the New Deal interregional alliance, even forgoing Republican unity at times to do so. With the country awash in political turmoil, regional strife in the 1970s was especially intense. Congressional Democrats turned repeatedly to economic policy—an area in which the two halves of the party had long been most in agreement—for a salve. But, as the United States' position in the global economy changed, so too did regional relationships to that economy, and southern and northern Democrats found themselves in disagreement. Republican advantage at this time lay in appealing to southern Democrats, not just on racial issues but on other social issues and economic and foreign policy matters as well. The result was the peak of the "conservative coalition" of Republicans and southern Democrats of the late 1960s and early 1970s. While different in form from the bipartisanship of the early postwar years, the conservative coalition's legislative activity nonetheless represented a new high-water mark of bipartisanship.

The regional discord of the late New Deal years led to a wrenching reorganization of the geographic bases of the party system. The most transparent outcome of Republican efforts to destabilize Democratic geography was an acceleration of the Republicans' capture of the South, but Republican Party leaders concentrated on the West as well, a region with fewer House seats than the North and South (though disproportionately large in the Senate and electoral college) but, like the South, containing states with fast-growing economies and populations. Also as in the South, the farming states of the interior West had a political history of antagonism toward a perceived domination by northern financial and political elites. These economic, social, and symbolic similarities were fodder for a growing Republican Party.

With the regional cracking of the Democratic Party, the New Deal regime, long assumed to be a solid fixture of twentieth-century politics, was revealed as a unique and ultimately unstable sectional fusion in American party history. Two new parties replaced the New Deal party system in the 1970s: the "emerging Republican majority," centered in the fast-growing suburbs and small towns of the South and West, and a refashioned Democratic Party, developing its electoral muscle in the historically urbanized, more densely populated, and commercially developed states of the North and the Pacific Coast.[22] As the demands made by the South and West on the national government began to clash with those of the North and Pacific Coast, the parties responded. The early postwar electoral geography of both parties disintegrated, and partisan conflict intensified as their geographic bases shifted.

Not only has regional conflict driven oppositional party politics, but the logic of regional incentives points to the eventual return to bipartisanship. The first party to effectively crack the other's regional stronghold with geographically targeted policy inducements will not only begin to redefine the geographic bases of the parties but will also help introduce the next era of consensus politics.

My argument that conflict between today's national parties is built on regional differences is made by examining three fundamental axes of conflict—

foreign economic, social welfare, and cultural political. Using representative cases of trade, welfare, and abortion policy making in the U.S. House of Representatives, respectively, the following chapters trace the impact of economic and social change in the South, interior West (hereafter "West"), North, and Pacific Coast on the parties' issue stances and coalition building efforts.[23] The influence of these developments on the level of interparty conflict becomes clear, and charting them reveals a narrative of party system evolutions, regime change, and the rise of geographically based party conflict that spans nearly half a century and the major dimensions of contemporary political debate. Appendix A describes the logic of my case selection in more detail, while Appendix B describes my method for analyzing House vote data.

Chapter 1 defines the regions. The insights of multiple theoretical traditions, including political economy and political culture perspectives, provide a useful starting point for developing a new interpretation of region and its political significance. This recasting not only provides the most leverage for understanding contemporary politics but also clarifies why regions are enduring political phenomena despite continual social and economic change.

With regions firmly defined, Chapter 2 describes the breakdown of the New Deal regime and the bipartisan consensus that it generated as well as the emergence of a new era of national party competition and conflict. This chapter presents an overview of key national party developments since World War II, highlighting their regional dimensions. Party support shifted in, and among, each of the regions as Democrats and Republicans worked to define the key issues and strategies that helped establish their regional bases in the new, post–New Deal era.

Chapters 3, 4, and 5 provide in-depth analyses of the relationship between regions and party since the 1960s in the policy arenas of trade, welfare, and abortion, respectively.[24] The resurgence in trade policy partisanship reflects the conflicting imperatives of an economically declining industrial belt in the North and a growing, export-oriented Sun Belt in the South and West. Chapter 3 illustrates clearly the role that continuing differences in the material conditions of the regions have played in party politics, though it also highlights northern disillusionment with Cold War security solutions, which fed regional ambivalence about the modern defense state.

Chapter 4 examines the increasing partisanship surrounding welfare policy through the lens of the now-defunct program Aid to Families with Dependent Children (AFDC). Like trade, AFDC is embedded in regional political economies, revealing the political and party consequences of material change.

But more importantly, welfare has served as a venue for the parties to engage racial politics, which became particularly pertinent in the context of the South's resistance to civil rights. New Deal Democrats first used welfare policy to build a northern urban constituency while simultaneously placating the labor and racial management demands of the white South's Cotton Belt. In the aftermath of civil rights, Republicans used welfare to break that cross-regional coalition of the New Deal regime. By the end of the 1960s, the infrastructure of the welfare state was concentrated in the urban North and Pacific Coast, where support for continuing and expanding the entitlement program was greatest. Opposition to welfare centered in the South and West, where racial politics and the rhetoric of "traditional family values" converged with the "devolution revolution" to foster support for the state level and private solutions to poverty backed by the Republican Party. Bearing significant political stakes for the parties' abilities to build and break regional coalitions, efforts at welfare reform through the 1990s generated increasing partisanship.

Chapter 5 focuses on growing party conflict over abortion. The 1960s and 1970s saw widespread social change, but in the South and West, rapid economic modernization and population mobility generated additional social dislocations, and the combination stimulated social conservatism: the traditional mores of religious conservatives became the ballast for rapid economic change and the focus of new demands on government. In response, the Republican Party forged an alliance with religious conservatives, criticizing Democrats' support for abortion rights and other policies favoring social change as a product of the cultural imperialism of states in the Northeast and, especially, the Pacific Coast. This facilitated Republican success in attracting new voters in the Bible Belt and elsewhere. Changing material conditions and social identities have been forged, in sometimes paradoxical ways, within the crucible of regions.

Chapters 3 (trade) and 4 (welfare) each examines three episodes of policymaking: First, the early 1960s, during the Kennedy administration, the classic period of postwar consensus and decline in party conflict; second, Nixon-era legislation, which occurred during the lowest period of partisan conflict; and, third, the height of partisanship in the mid-1990s during the Clinton administration. Settlements on trade and welfare policy during both the Kennedy and Nixon administrations were bipartisan, but the coalitional differences between the two periods illustrate why the Nixon administration inaugurated the rise in conflict that characterizes today's politics. Chapter 5, on abortion, examines only two periods, since Congress did not begin legislating on the issue until the

1970s: bipartisan legislation on abortion funding from the 1970s and partisan legislation from the late 1990s on the "partial birth" abortion ban.

Both parties have used policy to alternately build new cross-regional coalitions, fortify the geographic footprint of existing regimes, and divide the opposition along geographic lines, and these strategic activities are the subject of the concluding chapter. The result is a party system made dynamic by politicians' exploitation of regional changes. Geographic incentives explain New Deal bipartisanship, the Republican-sponsored bipartisanship of the early 1970s, and the current era of partisan conflict. If past patterns hold true, this contentious phase will give way to bipartisanship when one party successfully penetrates the other's regional stronghold and both parties compete for the same geographic audience.

CHAPTER 1

RECASTING REGION

GEOGRAPHY HAS been both the promise and the challenge of American union since the founding. While advocates of the Constitution saw the size and diversity of the territory they proposed to incorporate as the best way to secure liberty, many were critical of the effort to create a strong centralized government that would displace the power of the individual states. Prominent among the skeptics was the anti-federalist Cato, who voiced his concerns in a series of letters in the *New-York Journal*. One of his chief worries was that the citizens of the different states and the different regions were simply too dissimilar for harmonious collective self-governance.

> The strongest principle of union resides within our domestic walls. The ties of the parent exceed that of any other; as we depart from home, the next general principle of union is among citizens of the same state, where acquaintance, habits, and fortunes, nourish affection, and attachment; enlarge the circle still further, and, as citizens of different states, though we acknowledge the same national denomination, we lose the ties of acquaintance, habits, and fortunes, and thus, by degrees, we lessen in our attachments, till, at length, we no more than acknowledge a sameness of species.[1]

While Cato lost the argument against ratification, his fundamental insight was prescient. Geography does produce politically significant differences.

This chapter explains why, advancing a conceptualization of "region" that departs from conventional academic treatments. Most scholars consider regions to be products of either economic processes or cultural practices, but if Cato is correct, regions cannot be so simply reduced to either "fortunes" or "habits." Rather, regions are politically significant precisely because they fuse the material and ideational experiences of their inhabitants. This fusion, deeply informed by history, is what makes them potent and enduring.

Geography's significance to American politics is, at one level, self-evident. The political system is premised on geographic representation. Congressional districts send representatives to the House who are charged with making claims on behalf of the locale that elected them. Each state, regardless of its territorial or population size, is accorded two senators to represent it in national government. The president wins election through electoral-college votes predicated on state boundaries. And in the modern administrative state, many of the benefits and encumbrances of fiscal policies are apportioned according to the geography of state and district. Aside from their role in national government, states have their integrity preserved constitutionally, through the Tenth Amendment and the federal system. In short, geography is of fundamental structural importance to American politics.

While the interests of states are formally protected by the Constitution, representatives to national government have long organized informally along regional lines to help promote common interests. This has had the effect of simultaneously minimizing the importance of some state differences and elevating others. For example, members of early congresses lived, ate, and socialized in regionally segregated boardinghouse fraternities, and these affiliations were often mirrored in lawmakers' voting alignments.[2] The stances taken in battles over foreign policy, finance, capital projects, and the scope of the national government that divided Jeffersonian Republicans from Federalists fell largely along regional lines. Regions then quickly became a central organizing principle of the mass-mobilizing two-party system. After the Civil War, Democrats and Republicans were firmly sectional parties.[3] It was not until the election of 1932, when party politics were nationalized along class lines, that the regional significance of the two-party system receded. Mid-twentieth-century observers of American politics predicted that the real end of regional party politics would come with the undoing of the Jim Crow South. Scholars such as V. O. Key and E. E. Schattschneider argued that southern industrialization and urbanization would equalize conditions throughout the country and aid the eradication of racial hierarchies in the region, clearing the way for debates over issues, such as labor-business relations, to become national in scope.[4]

Given the history of regionalism in America's past, it is hardly surprising that "red state" and "blue state" are the reigning descriptors of contemporary national politics. Only from the context of the New Deal era, which normalized a national politics for the better part of the twentieth century, does regional division appear anachronistic. But, understanding why regions have continued to define party politics, even after the break-up of the solidly Democratic South, is more elusive.

THE MATTER OR THE MIND: EXISTING EXPLANATIONS OF REGIONS

Grasping why regions contribute to national party conflict requires some sense of what defines a region. Understanding the salient features that differentiate one region from another helps clarify the sources of geographic conflict and makes clearer how this conflict relates to political parties. Two theoretical traditions offer some insight.

The first is rooted in political economy. Following Frederick Jackson Turner's path-breaking work on American sectionalism, a body of scholarship emerged that attributed regions' continued political differences to their uneven economic development. The economies of different regions in the country have historically varied, not just in the natural resources upon which they have relied but also in production factors, access to capital and markets, and their degree of integration into the national and global economy.[5]

While regional categories vary slightly, all political economy analyses agree on a basic difference between those regions that industrialized earlier and those historically more dependent on agricultural production. Among these, Richard Bensel's division of the country into "core" and "periphery" regions is an especially well-known taxonomy and a useful example of the genre.[6] The core consists of the areas that industrialized earliest, including the states of the Northeast and parts of the upper Midwest and the Pacific Coast states, which developed slightly later.[7] Relative to the rest of the country (Bensel's periphery), states in core areas were defined by a high degree and concentration of urbanization, proximity to ports and the byways of commercial activity, and formation of and reliance on their own financial sectors.[8]

Cities such as New York, Pittsburgh, and San Francisco are quintessential examples of core urban centers. Yet, for political economists, these and other industrial centers are significant because they dominated their regional landscapes, serving as the hubs that drew together and directed the larger, economically integrated geographic areas that surrounded them. As one analyst describes it, industrial regions were distinctive because of their "extensive 'systems' of cities—great urban masses [that] highlight the key manufacturing zones of the nation."[9] It was the urban manufacturing zones of New England, the Mid-Atlantic, and Great Lakes and Pacific Coast states that drove the twentieth-century national economy. By 1910, these four subregions were mostly urban, and within another ten years their states had the highest average per capita incomes.[10] By the end of World War II, the industrial, financial, and commercial centers of this core economy dominated not only domestic markets but the international economy as well.

In sharp contrast, the states of the South and the interior West have functioned as distinct halves of the traditionally agrarian economic periphery. States in these areas were historically dependent on subsistence farming and cash crop cultivation, resource extraction (especially to the west), and inexpensive labor. Settled earlier, the South was defined by its large cotton, tobacco, and rice farms, and maintenance of the region's social and economic structure was predicated first on the institution of slavery and then on sharecropping and tenant farming. Organized later, in the nineteenth century, the states of the western frontier constituted the country's debtor region. They depended primarily on the production of foodstuffs (ranging from cattle to wheat and soybeans) and were rich in minerals and other natural resources, including fossil fuels such as oil. It was not until well into the twentieth century, and specifically until after World War II, that the states of the South and West began to develop and diversify their economies. Since then, both regions have been sites of rapid economic development and population growth, largely as a result of growth in tourism, agribusiness, business services, and defense and related high tech industries.

Party conflict historically has intensified when the parties have hailed from different regions.[11] For political economists, this is because fundamental economic differences between the regions lead parties in those circumstances to fight for control of the nation's resources. The logic is that the more members of a party hail from the same region, the closer their interests, and therefore their policy preferences, will be. Members of Congress conveniently find that what is good for their district is good for their party and vice versa. In this view, regional, and by extension party, conflict focuses on whether the resources of the national government will be used to promote industrial core or agricultural periphery activity. Because the interests are typically opposed and the resources are fixed, the conflict is zero-sum. Conversely, from this reasoning, the more diversified a party's geographic base, the less likely it will be that its members will have common preferences and, under these conditions, regional factionalism within the party is likely to flourish.[12]

To the extent that economic modernization lessens sectional economic differences, regions, for political economists, lose their significance—a loss tempered, though, by the uncertain impact of globalization on the U.S. economy. Scholars have demonstrated that, despite nationwide industrial and post-industrial development in the last half-century, American regional economies still differ and translate into divergent policy preferences. John Agnew, Richard Bensel, Anne Markusen, and Peter Trubowitz, among others, have shown that Sun Belt states, states in the South and West, experienced the recent global economic changes differently from states in the deindustrialized, or Rust Belt, North, and this difference led to conflicts between the regions over policies that had economic ramifications, including foreign defense, domestic spending, and tax policy. The matter of which region's industries and constituencies benefit from government largesse and which region pays the costs continues to sustain some degree of sectional friction.[13]

By this reading of regions, economic disputes drive contemporary party conflict. Yet, while economic matters are an important part of contemporary party divisions, they are hardly the sole axis of partisan conflict. The post-1960s "culture wars" between the parties have garnered the most scholarly and popular attention.[14] The dominant scholarship on political geography, which reads regions as proxies for political economy, cannot easily accommodate the social and religious disputes at the heart of so much of today's partisan conflict. Existing political economy theory cannot, for example, easily explain contemporary divisions over gay marriage, prayer in school, or stem cell research. The causal link between different economies and differing opinions on gay marriage or the Pledge of Allegiance is not immediately apparent. One popular contention is that these high profile issues are election-year ploys used by Republicans to distract and mobilize working-class voters to their party—that class conflict is still the driving (though hidden and subverted) dynamic in party fights.[15] This interpretation fails to explain, though, why politicians believe cultural issues (or attendant moral beliefs and intimations of "ways of life") are useful for mobilizing votes in the first place. More important, recent scholarship has demonstrated that, contrary to popular belief, cultural conservatism is not solely the province of low-income and working-class voters but rather receives substantial support from segments of the middle class.[16] It cannot be simply that social class values have come to stand in for underlying economic class grievances, as some suggest.

An alternative theory explains regional divisions as rooted in cultural differences. Since the writings of Alexis de Tocqueville, observers of American politics have noted distinct regional cultures that have resulted from patterns of ethnocultural migration, variations in race relations among regions, differing religious orientations, and timing of settlement.[17] For example, while Puritan settlements were concentrated in New England states, Presbyterian Scots (or Scotch-Irish) expanded to the south and west of the Mid-Atlantic. Catholic and Jewish immigration in the nineteenth and twentieth centuries was concentrated in the big cities of the Northeast and Midwest. After the Civil War, African Americans remained heavily concentrated in the southern states. Even in the late twentieth century, some of the most politically potent socioreligious trends have distinct geographic patterns. The country's fast growing Mormon and Christian evangelical populations are concentrated in states in the West and South. Secularism, which has increased simultaneously, is concentrated in the Northeast and Pacific Coast states.[18]

On the cultural reading, population and group differences, especially as they contributed historically to the settling of different areas and the establishment in those places of dominant ideas and values, are an important source of regional distinctiveness. But, simply equating culture with demographics is a serious mistake that is both overly reductive, ignoring the diversity of views within groups, and ahistorical, ignoring the conditions that influence or change ideas. Rather, culture, as Lisa Wedeen writes, is better understood as "practices of meaning-making" that stem from the interaction of what people do with their language and symbols. When applied to a geographic territory, this notion of culture suggests, "a variable, contested, incompletely integrated way in which the inhabitants of a specific territory share a set of semiotic practices."[19] The significance of regional culture, then, is the web of meanings, symbols, foundational principles, and interpretive frameworks that have broad political effects independent of any given group or population.

The most powerful version of the cultural argument about regions suggests that regional identities—bound to, yet larger than, the traits, associations, and objective conditions that inform them—are relational and, through symbolic reference and rhetoric, operate as battles over political priorities, even over the very meaning of America. As Anne Norton has written in describing antebellum regional cultures, "the Puritans were praised in the North, derided in the South. They served, in antebellum political culture, not as the symbol of a common cultural origin, but as a shibboleth for regional disparity."[20] Because regional identities and cultures reflect what inhabitants believe about themselves or aspire to, oftentimes codified into laws or authenticated by local mores, they have a residual power that surpasses and outlasts the material facts that informed their creation. Thus, despite the replacement of New England's traditional "Yankee" stock with an increasingly heterogeneous population, historian George W. Pierson could conclude as late as the mid-1950s that, "as a region of the heart and mind, New England is still very much alive."[21]

Key to understanding regions as cultural entities is the recognition of the substantiating role of history in the formation of place. Kent Ryden describes American regions as "collaborative, imaginative cultural constructions built out of history," a history that includes both the "big" episodes and personages of the past as well as the "little" events, the "distinctive local patterns of work, economy, and social life." While historically constituted, regional identities and cultures are never unproblematic but rather are regularly contested and reconstructed by those inside and outside the region.[22] The South, as both a coherent and yet intensely contested culture, is perhaps the most commonly accepted region in this regard, for reasons that writers such as W. J. Cash and C. Vann Woodward have made clear.[23] Yet, while perhaps less self-conscious about it, each region has its own historically informed identity and culture.[24]

Understanding how the culture of a region is evolving requires knowledge of specific material and demographic changes that have occurred within the region. For example, the racial attitudes of the white South have changed dramatically in the last half-century. The civil rights movement and civil rights laws were crucial, but explaining this transformation also requires reference to the impact of the region's economic modernization on social relations, the efforts by southern boosters to showcase a new South to northern investors, and the arrival of new migrants who held different attitudes about race. Invoking Wedeen's definition of culture, comprehending shifting attitudes about race among southern whites requires knowledge of practices such as work habits, patterns of education, and political mobilization and their interaction with prevailing symbols, including those signifying race, tradition and modernity, northern capitalism, and regional identity.

Moreover, culture, especially as it evolves within a region, is too indeterminate to predict the precise form and tenor of regional responses to current policy debates. Understanding how cultural currents will inform real policy positions requires a clear grasp of ongoing regional material changes. To use the South as an example again, the region's longstanding resistance to a strong central state ("big government") is most directly evident in policy debates such as those over social welfare; yet, in apparent contradiction, the region favors increased government activity and federal spending in areas such as defense, aerospace, and transportation.[25] This variation in policy preferences cannot be resolved by reference to culture alone. It requires knowing that the region, as political economists explain, is economically dependent on military bases and defense contracts and on highways and airports. Those forms of big government thus become defensible: among other benefits, they provide a means to release economic growth and thereby, theoretically at least, to foster independence and freedom from the state.

Existing analyses of political geography, whether they emphasize economy or culture, run aground on contemporary party politics.[26] Political economists fail to explain the contemporary cultural divisions that are paramount in political debate, and the cultural accounts that could help explain today's divisions cannot be sufficiently leveraged until they are made to respond to geography-specific economic and demographic changes. To understand why and how both traditions inform the current partisanship, we need a better understanding of region and its political significance.

THE MATTER *AND* THE MIND: NEW DETERMINANTS OF REGION

Regions remain powerful in American politics precisely because they fuse economic and cultural experiences. In both a literal and theoretical sense, region is the site where concrete material interests merge with prevailing local symbols and interpretive patterns to inform and create experience. To try to divorce material from ideal and establish one as primary for understanding regional identity is akin to the mistake made in early debates about whether class or gender, gender or race is more politically formative and consequential. Multiple identities are nearly always at work, often in complex and sometimes conflicting ways. More useful is an attempt to understand how interaction generates political response. Regional material differences continue to exist, as the political economists have made clear. Yet, as regional cultural historians have made clear, American regions differ in how they understand themselves and how they apprehend their objective realities, especially vis-à-vis other regions. This is particularly true when politicians activate these interpretations, as a long history of southern and western populists have done in railing against northern financial and political elites. The unique patterning of material life and cultural traditions informs regional experience and generates distinct regional developmental paths. Our task is to understand how it does so.

The way "nation" is characterized helps elucidate my claim about the determinants of region. The nation and a sense of national unity are formed by a shared set of values (such as those associated with classical liberalism) as well as imperatives, like security, and goals, like material prosperity. In writing of the nation as an "imagined community," Benedict Anderson describes it as limited and sovereign, suggesting a defined territory, the material elements of which are to be secured against the encroachment of outsiders. Just as important in generating the human resources to protect that material or territorial entity, the nation, according to Anderson, "is imagined as a *community*, because, regardless of the actual inequality and exploitation that may prevail in each [state], the nation is always conceived as a deep, horizontal comradeship. Ultimately it is this fraternity that makes it possible, over the past two centuries for so many millions of people, not so much to kill, as willingly to die for such limited imaginings."[27] Thus, more than the real conditions that generate a sense of loyalty among citizens, it is the perception of shared connections that conjures such dedication. This perception may be fortified by certain material realities (e.g., national wealth, natural resources, manmade products such as monuments), but the sense of connection is likely contrary to the lived experience of social relations and material conditions. Such is the power of the symbols and ideas.

This fraternity, especially in the face of outsiders or threats, is powerfully linked to the idea of cultural purification and a sense of "chosenness," often ethnically based.[28] In the American context, nationalism and national coherence are fraught with the built-in tension between the nation's construction on a set of universal ideals open to any and all and its founding largely by Anglo-Saxon Protestants.[29] While universal, the ideas of American nation are open to interpretation; the reigning interpretation both was established by the politically dominant and has often been challenged by the politically subordinate. This quality of being interpretable has a paradoxical effect: in some instances, the broadly interpretable nature of American ideals is what makes them powerful tools for uniting a diverse population; yet, in other instances, the recognition of different interpretations has led to internal conflict and division, even civil war.[30]

Recognizing the general properties of nations and the particular attributes of the American nation is useful for thinking about regions, which exist as "subnations" of a sort. While regions don't have strong institutional and constitutional forms to bind them (though there are muted versions of these, for example, the Northeast-Midwest Congressional Coalition and the Congressional Sun Belt Caucus), they cohere through a history of shared values and symbols as well as material realities. This is especially true in the American case because of its history of regional differentiation. As Anderson points out, young Americans are taught to remember the Civil War as a conflict between "brothers," but at the time, the war was considered a conflict between two sovereign nation-states.[31] Although the militarily enforced end to slavery, the passage of time, broadly shared experiences (e.g. the Depression, World War II), and an active agenda of Americanization have certainly weakened the constitutive elements of the northern and southern regional communities from their 1860s nation-state incarnation, it would be hasty to assume that no residue of their status as imagined communities exists.

In an era of globalization that both combines and fragments the traditional political geographies of nation-states, political scientists are already beginning to explore the ways that the material and the ideal interact to carve out new politically relevant geographies, both smaller than and larger than the nation. James Gimpel and Jason Schuknecht offer an account of political sectionalism within the states of the United States. They explain persistent party identification of areas within states as the outcome of both "compositional" and "contextual" factors. Compositional factors are politically significant social groupings, including economic, racial, ethnic, ideological, and religious.[32] This alone indicates the significance of both material and nonmaterial factors in ways that suggest an interaction of traditional economic and cultural readings of geography, though it does so in a way that reduces culture to measurable characteristics and demographics. The contextual element, though, goes beyond demographics and "adds something extra to . . . communities through the instrument of political socialization."[33] As these authors describe it, a person's political sensibility and partisan leaning derive not just from the person's group identifications but also from the conversations and influences of people who are geographically proximate to her or him. Noting that sphere of influence taps the vein of regional political culture. While Gimpel and Schucknecht are concerned with local communicative context and, indeed, with partisan differences between localities, my claim is simply that the general partisan patterns that are observed across the larger geography of region (i.e., North, South, West, and Pacific Coast) similarly reflect material and nonmaterial influences.

The process of political socialization described by Gimpel and Schucknect is one of the ways that a sense of region, like a sense of nation, is reinforced and sustained over time. (The process, in both cases, can also generate challenge.) Political socialization in the United States has created deep histories of often antagonistic regional identity and mythmaking, and it continues to nurture and transmit distinct regional worldviews and related political commitments. As an indirect example of this, consider the Massachusetts vehicle that sports a

Confederate flag bumper sticker. Regardless of the precise message the owner intends to signify (if specificity is even consciously intended), the displaying of such an historically embedded reminder of southern antagonism to the North signals the owner's own sense of alienation (and rebellion?) from the surrounding environment into which he or she is being socialized—the cultural context of the North. Drawing on past symbols to signal current discontent is made meaningful because of generations of regional political socialization.

For Peter Katzenstein, global regions are similarly constituted by both material and ideational elements; they are defined by both territorial and material realities and by the symbolic meaning attached to that geography. Katzenstein points out that regions' precise boundaries are often in dispute and that a strict territorial definition of a region might be somewhat different from its cultural definition. Yet, as he points out, border confusion does not stop political actors from using and exploiting regional references. An obvious example is the evolution, still ongoing and contested, of the definition of "Europe."[34] The example of the bumper sticker illustrates this in the American context. Regardless of whether the South includes Florida or not (or Texas, or Virginia), the bumper sticker's evocation of southern rebellion is meaningfully exploited by the vehicle's owner.

Katzenstein's point about the fluidity of regional borders applies in any context, including that of American regionalism. To facilitate conversation, I rely on conventional, fixed boundaries as labels for my primary regions (North, South, West, and Pacific Coast). The boundaries themselves, however, should not be regarded as fixed. If regions are politically powerful because they are the sites of both cultural and material experiences, then, as Katzenstein argues, they cannot be defined by reference to a single, unchanging line of geographic demarcation. To assert such a line would be to claim a single experience (early industrialization or rebellion against the Union, for examples) as the sole determinant of a region's character. For understanding politics, regions should be thought of as to some extent mutable or as having "variable edges."[35] What distends or contracts a region's boundaries is the number of shared experiences among its inhabitants, given the political issues and events of the moment. To the extent that the centers of concentration of cultural and material experiences overlap, a region's boundaries become more rigid and the potential for political mobilization more profound. Thinking about boundaries as inherently flexible rather than rigidly defined by some earlier political act makes it possible to better apprehend politically consequential phenomena.

The changing definition of the American "West" over time makes this clearer. At the turn of the twentieth century, Frederick Jackson Turner wrote: "The West, at bottom, is a form of society, rather than an area." Describing Americans' westward push, Turner noted, "The wilderness disappears, the 'West' proper passes on to a new frontier, and in the former area, a new society has emerged from its contact with the backwoods. Gradually this society loses its primitive conditions, and assimilates itself to the type of the older social conditions of the East; but it bears within it enduring and distinguishing survivals of its frontier experience."[36] For Turner, the West's differentiation from the rest of the nation comes from the adaptation of existing social forms to areas previously unsettled by white Americans; by definition, the region evolves as a geographic form. The West's older areas are closer to, yet nonetheless still different from, the East. To define the West as a particular set of states or a particular set of territories is meaningful only for a moment in time.

Geographic dynamism intertwines with temporal change. Political economists have shown how regional economies change and evolve: material conditions are manipulated and altered. Cultural historians have documented demographic change within regions as well as groups' evolving interpretations of events and relationships: culture is not static, either. Thus, regions are inherently dynamic, but their dynamism is constrained nonetheless. A region's cultural predisposition bounds its economic change in ways that distinguish it from other regions. At the same time, the elements of economic change provide a limited set of objective conditions for the interpretive project. Through this interaction between subjective and objective, each region derives its own historical identity, a composite of past economic arrangements and the meanings that those elements have been given by prevailing cultural interpretations. In this way, each region is, at any moment, a product of its history yet still retains its temporal dynamism. As Katzenstein writes, in a global context, "[r]egions are not simply physical constants or ideological constructs; they express changing human practices. Economic development, military expansion, and symbolic identification with particular places all can shift over time, and with them the boundaries and salient features of particular regions."[37]

To recognize that the United States can be characterized by reference to its values (liberalism) and its material practices (industrialism) is not to deny the complexity and heterogeneity of its internal life. That advocates of illiberal, republican, and communist ideas exist within the nation and that agriculture and services exist alongside traditional industry does not detract from a description of the *dominant* tendencies of the United States. It is the politics within the country, between the discordant interests, that give rise to those prevailing characterizations. Similarly, characterizing regions through reference to their dominant material and cultural practices disguises (as any aggregation does), yet does not deny, the internal diversity that exists within them. A discussion of the interface of region and nation allows insight into the politics that help establish some regional ideas and interests over others. Yet, it is the heterogeneity within regions, along with their temporal and geographic malleability, that allows for change.

Since World War II, three especially consequential developments have fueled regional political differences: the relocation of companies and jobs from the Northeast, Midwest, and, most recently, Pacific Coast states to the interior West and South; the migration of African Americans from the South to the cities of the North and Pacific Coast, culminating in the passage of civil rights legislation in the South; and the growth of secularism in the cities of the Northeast and Pacific Coast states and simultaneous rise of Christian evangelicalism, largely in the South and Southwest. These three developments have each generated geographically based political divisions, loosely and popularly characterized as the politics of the Sun Belt, Cotton Belt, and Bible Belt (and their related regions of contrast).

The party politics and legislative battles associated with the changes in each of these belts are the topic of Chapters 3 through 5. Because the geographies of these belts overlap to no small degree, the cumulative and intertwined effects of the changes within them have transformed the geography of the national party system and generated intense policy conflict. For example, the loss of jobs and tax revenue in the North (deriving from industrial departures) strained the public welfare capacity of states in the region and exacerbated local demands for increased federal compensation as a way to ameliorate social divisions (related to social group migration). Also, a rising Christian right (a collection of regionally based religious changes) mobilized in the mid-1990s to reduce federal welfare expenditures and limit the provision of cash disbursements; the effects of this reform were disproportionately borne in central cities and among minority communities because of their disproportionate poverty (related to social group migration). Red versus blue cannot be reduced simply to the politics of economic change or the politics of race or the politics of religious division. I aim to show how all three have contributed to the nation's current party conflict.

ANALYZING REGION: A PRACTICAL NOTE

Based on the insights of political economy and cultural interpretations of region, I have designated four primary regions for analysis: North, South, Pacific Coast, and interior West.[38] The composition of the regions (their constituent

Figure 1.1
Regions of the United States

states) is constant throughout the book and is illustrated in Figure 1.1.[39] In the course of the analysis, the regions are often themselves disaggregated to illustrate the nuances of change within them. I use these four geographically fixed regions not only for consistency but because my theory is that the geographic realignment of the parties and the rise in party conflict are owing to a combination of cultural and economic issues. To the extent that cultural and economic factors appear within each of the four geographic units that I have defined, region as a fusion of culture and economy gains potency.

Maintaining, throughout the book, consistent regional boundaries for North, South, West, and Pacific Coast imposes some costs in that each chapter's findings could potentially be made more robust if geographic demarcations for the regions were allowed to vary slightly according to the issue being examined, but any marginal loss is compensated for by a significant gain in analytic leverage on the larger question of how regions have fed partisanship. If one issue shows stronger effects than another in a particular region, the sources of party strength and the potential for party change in that region can be better understood. From the standpoint of electoral strategy, party advancement of an issue position (e.g., advocacy of free trade or opposition to abortion) constitutes a success only to the extent that it helps bring in new territory (and thus greater party representation in Congress or in winning electoral votes). A party's capture of a territory is solidified by the extent to which it speaks to the multiplicity of geographically embedded experience and related issue concerns (e.g., free trade *and* pro-life), and it is weaker to the extent to which it is driven by partial responsiveness (e.g., free trade *but not* pro-life).

By using the same regional categories for each issue, it is possible to see not only the varied ways that Republicans and Democrats have built their respective geographic bases but, as importantly, where each party is weak. For example, the Democratic Party's pro-choice position on abortion has hurt it in some areas of the North, such as the states of the East North Central subregion, while the party's generally more protectionist position on trade has tended to help it in those areas. By using the same regional categories for all issues (for example, by not altering the demarcation lines to accommodate the differences in geography between the Bible Belt [abortion] and the Rust Belt [trade]), while simultaneously discussing the variation within regions on each issue, the location of the parties' geographic strengths becomes clear.

Each of these four primary regions is distinct, yet the South and West, where Republicans now prevail, share key similarities, as do the North and Pacific Coast states, where Democrats tend to dominate. Understanding the link between regional differences and partisanship requires some attention to how politicians have attended to those differences. In his farewell address to the nation, President George Washington warned citizens that enterprising politicians would exaggerate regional differences for their own partisan ends.[40] True to this warning, contemporary politicians continue to excite local attachments to further their partisan agenda. "Texas conservative" and "Massachusetts liberal" are terms bandied about at election time because they are politically meaningful labels capable of conjuring a host of regional differences and animosities.

The similarities among geographic places (within regions and occasionally across regions) have provided opportunities for the parties as they seek to build coalitions large enough to secure national power. Both parties use issues and policies for this purpose: to build new coalitions, to sustain existing ones, and to divide the opposition. Chapters 3 through 5 show the effects of policy decisions on party coalitions in these different ways. Taken together, they produce a picture of a Republican order that owes its rise both to the success of its leaders in using policy to break the cross-regional lock of the New Deal Democratic party and to their use of policy stances to fashion a new cross-regional alliance of their own in the South and West. Acquiring real estate, figuratively speaking, and building geographic empires is at the heart of both the struggles between the parties and the peace that prevails, however briefly, when one of them triumphs.

CHAPTER 2

REGIME CHANGE

FROM THE NEW DEAL STATE TO THE REPUBLICAN REVOLUTION

FROM THE 1930s to the mid-1960s, the public philosophy of the New Deal Democratic Party defined American politics. National institutions reflected the ideas and served the key interests of the Democratic coalition. The regime produced Keynesian fiscal policy, the bureaucratic welfare state, a social contract between labor and capital, and containment of Soviet communism, results that a majority of Americans around the country regularly reauthorized. Simply put, Democrats prevailed at mid-century by using government activism to promote economic security at home and national security abroad, and Republicans were hard-pressed to compete. The sole Republican to win the presidency in that era, Dwight Eisenhower, was a moderate whose governance marched more in step with New Deal dictates than with the conservatives in his own party. And Republicans hardly ever won control of the House or the Senate. Between 1933 and 1971, they controlled Congress only twice, for a total of four years. As E. J. Dionne has written, "To many in the late 1940s, it appeared that conservatives were doomed . . . to crankiness, incoherence, and irrelevance."[1]

By the 1970s, this Democratic dominance had disappeared. The social disruptions of the 1960s from the civil rights and feminist movements, dissension over the war in Vietnam, and economic deterioration that resulted in unemployment and rising prices upended the regime. The Democratic Party was at war with itself, often pitting northerner against southerner, as the subsequent chapters on trade, welfare, and abortion make clear. In 1968, Richard Nixon became the first Republican to successfully capitalize on this Democratic weakness; and by 1980, the country seemed poised to embrace a new governing philosophy—one that stressed a strong military but a limited government.

A revitalized national defense became a Republican pillar in the aftermath of Vietnam and the Iranian hostage crisis. In response to the moribund economy of the 1970s, Republicans stressed the benefits that would accrue from unfettering capital, and they countered Keynesianism's apparent failures with deregulation, tax cuts, and monetary policy solutions to economic woes such as inflation. To counter the volatile effects of their approach to economic management, Republicans offered new ballast—conservative social values. Churning economic and social changes, they argued, were best navigated with the stability and security of traditional values. Claiming fidelity to the Constitution and Judeo-Christian precepts, the party argued for race-neutral individual rights, a resurrection of "traditional family values," support for law and order, and greater respect for religious beliefs.

Unlike the establishment of the New Deal order, however, the new Republican majority emerged slowly and faced considerable resistance. Whereas voters nationwide had endorsed the New Deal Democratic regime, the public was more ambivalent about the emerging Republican state. Although the party dominated the presidency in the 1970s and 1980s, Republicans could not gain complete control of Congress; they captured the Senate for the better part of the 1980s, but not the House. When they finally became the majority party in both houses of Congress, in 1994, largely through the party's increasing success in the growing states of the South and West, the national electorate chose a Democrat, Bill Clinton, as president. From Nixon's presidency until George W. Bush's election in 2000, dividing the government between the two parties had been the norm. And, although Bush enjoyed several years of unified government, in 2006, divided government was restored.[2]

THE ERA OF INCREASING PARTISANSHIP: 1970s TO THE PRESENT

As Republicans tried to wrest control of the national government from Democrats, conflict between the two parties increased. From the 1970s to the present, Republicans more frequently and with greater unity rejected Democratic solutions for governing in favor of their own policy remedies. They were in turn met by increasing Democratic unity in defense of those policies. This growth in conflict is especially striking because it reversed a long trend toward less parti-

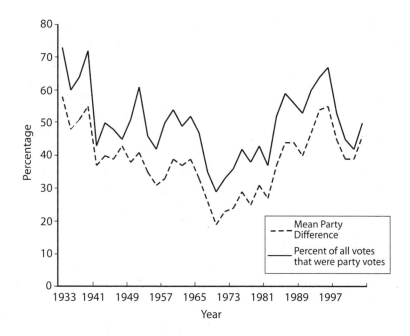

Figure 2.1
Party Conflict in the House of Representatives, 73rd through 108th Congresses, 1933–2004
Source: Calculated from roll call data.

sanship. The trend was most apparent in Congress, where the frequency with which members voted with their party can be tracked and aggregated over time to get a more systematic sense of changes in partisanship. With the notable exception of the congresses held just before and after the New Deal realignment, party conflict decreased steadily from the turn of the century until the 1970s, when partisanship reemerged.

Records of roll call votes in the House of Representatives are useful for assessing changes in the degrees of party conflict over time. Indices of *party voting* show how frequently party majorities vote against each other, while *party difference* shows how unified the parties are on average in their opposition to each other.[3] Tracking these measures across congresses from the 1930s until 2004 illustrates the decline in party conflict from the 1930s to the 1970s and then the resurgence in conflict that followed.

The degree and trend of partisanship is evident in shifts in party voting and party difference lines, which mirror each other. Using either measurement, party conflict declined until 1969, the opening of the 91st Congress and the beginning of President Nixon's first term. From that point on, party conflict has risen, reaching a high point in the 104th Congress after the Newt Gingrich–led "Republican Revolution." Conflict then dropped off slightly for the next three congresses before rising again.

These same trends in party conflict and party difference also mark the individual policy areas of trade, welfare, and abortion, as the following chapters reveal. Because these very different policy areas represent the variety of conflicts in which the parties were engaged—foreign, economic, social—the similarities in the shift from bipartisanship to partisanship are noteworthy and suggest a systemic source. This source is the geographical shifts in the party system.

THE CHANGING GEOGRAPHY OF THE PARTY SYSTEM

For Republicans, the battle to defeat Democrats may still rage and their new order may have arisen gradually, even haltingly; but the tide, they claim, has turned steadily in their favor. William Kristol declared in the aftermath of the 1994 Republican takeover of Congress, "The nation's long, slow electoral and ideological realignment with the Republican party is reaching a watershed."[4] Kristol was partially correct. Republicans did increasingly dominate elections for the next twelve years, yet it was not because of a national realignment. Republican realignments in the South and West were responsible for the party's successes in gaining control of national institutions—first Congress and then the presidency. In contrast, the North and Pacific Coast shifted away from Republican control. Because Democrats performed better in these densely populated though geographically smaller regions, they were able to maintain a close electoral parity with Republicans. The result in 2000–2006 was a country divided, with power precipitously balanced between the regions and the parties.

These trends in national party strength are apparent regardless of whether one examines the electoral outcomes for the presidency or for Congress. Figure 2.2, for example, shows the percentage of major-party (Republican or Democratic) voters in the four primary regions of analysis—the North, South, West, and Pacific Coast—who supported the Republican presidential candidate from 1960 until 2004.

Voters around the country behaved similarly at the beginning of the period being examined in this book and then gradually diverged. This behavior accentuates the uniqueness of the New Deal regime; the elections from the 1930s to the late 1960s represent the only sustained period since the Civil War in which northerners and southerners voted for the same party. Although the trend lines

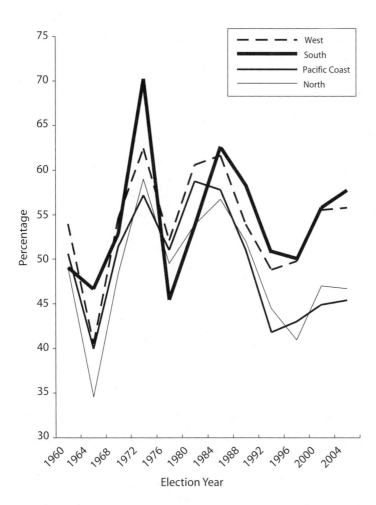

Figure 2.2
Percentage of Major Party Voters Selecting Republican Presidential Candidate, 1960–2004, by Region
Source: Calculated from data in *Presidential Elections, 1789–2000* (Washington DC: Congressional Quarterly Press, 2002) and www.cnn.com (2004 data).

tend to shift in the same direction, reflecting the idiosyncrasies of each presidential election, clearly, voters in the South and West have become more regular supporters of the Republican candidate, and national party philosophy, than voters in the North and Pacific Coast. The only exception was in 1976, when Jimmy Carter, a Georgian, ran on the Democratic ticket and brought southern voters back to the party fold. By the 1990s, the red-blue partisan division among the regions that has become famous in the next decade was already

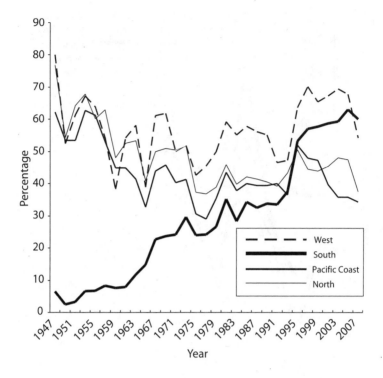

Figure 2.3
Percentage of House Seats Held by Republicans, 80th to 110th Congresses, 1947–2007, by Region
Source: Calculated from data provided by Keith Poole and Howard Rosenthal at voteview.com (Congresses 80–106) and New York Times (Congresses 107–110).

visible. Democrat Bill Clinton won easily in the North and Pacific Coast but, despite being a southerner, struggled in the South and West.

This trend has translated into the clear red state–blue state divide of the electoral college that has been the subject of so much contemporary media coverage. The composition of Congress has also changed, in ways that will likely have a more enduring impact on national policy making. Figure 2.3 shows the changes in the delegations sent to the House by each of the four regions from 1947 to 2007. While the southern and western delegations have become more Republican, northern and Pacific Coast delegations have become less Republican over that time.

Most stark, of course, is the growth in the percentage of House seats held by Republicans in the South. Although Democrats controlled virtually every southern seat from the time of the states' postbellum readmittance to the

Union until the end of World War II, Republicans captured a majority of these seats by the mid-1990s. By 2005, Republicans held 63 percent of southern seats in the House. The party's gains are also apparent in the West, where Republicans controlled as much as 70 percent of seats in the 1990s and early 2000s. The West has historically vacillated between the two parties to a greater degree than other regions, but Republicans have largely controlled it since the 1970s.

In contrast, Democrats have done increasingly well in the North and Pacific Coast states, the regions with the greatest population and the most House seats. Democrats began the postwar era controlling just 23 percent of northern House seats. In 1964, the party captured a majority of the region's seats and by 1973 were regularly controlling a majority of those seats. Although this majority has often been a slim one (52 percent of northern seats in 2005, for example), because of the region's overall number of seats, the Democratic majority there has translated into a significant voting bloc. After the 2006 election, this became especially significant: Democrats captured 63 percent of the seats in the North, and these large numbers helped them win back control of the House. Democrats have found even greater success in the Pacific Coast states. The party gained a majority of seats here in 1959 and has not relinquished it since then. In recent years, Democrats have controlled 66 percent of Pacific Coast seats, rivaling Republican control of the South and West.

Attributes of the political system make these trends toward divergent regional dominances in the House more profound. One is the "incumbency effect," or the increasing tendency for incumbents to retain their seats with ease.[5] The combination of the incumbency effect with the secular party growth trends in each region likely means that when seats do open up, they are being captured by the "new" or ascendant party in the region.[6] A powerful attribute is decennial reapportionment. The North has been steadily, rapidly losing population—and therefore House seats—to the South and West (including some of the Pacific Coast states). Because the gains have mostly been in the areas of the country where Republicans have been successful, that party has continued to benefit from reapportionment.[7]

The reasons for these shifts are the topic of the next chapters, but the result has been a secular realignment of the party system. From a century-long perspective, the parties have completely reversed their traditional regional bases.[8] Republicans lost their moorings in the North but are now the majority party in the South and West, while Democrats have seen their losses in the formerly solidly Democratic South offset by gains in the North and Pacific Coast. As this has occurred, the geographic centers of the two parties have traded po-

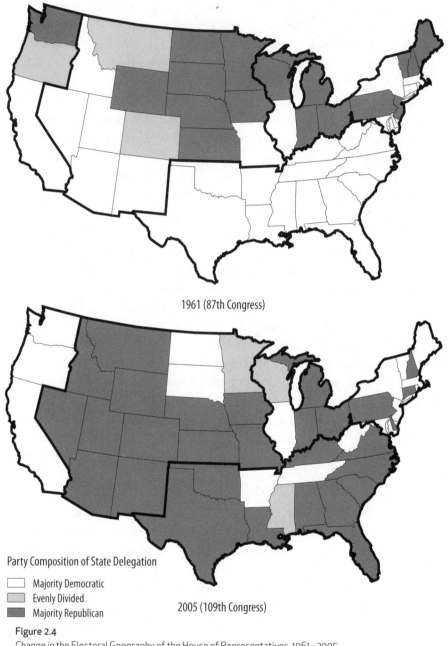

1961 (87th Congress)

Party Composition of State Delegation

- ☐ Majority Democratic
- ☐ Evenly Divided
- ■ Majority Republican

2005 (109th Congress)

Figure 2.4
Change in the Electoral Geography of the House of Representatives, 1961–2005

sitions. The maps of the electoral geography of the House of Representatives in 1961 and in 2005, shown in Figure 2.4, reveal the shifts in the party system that occurred in just those four and a half decades.

In 1961, Democrats controlled every state in the South. Republicans had a majority in most northern states, though Democrats were the majority party in several of the states with big urban areas, including New York, Massachusetts, and Illinois. Together, the urban North and the South represented the backbone of the New Deal Democratic Party regime. Both the Pacific Coast and the West were mixed in their representation, with Republicans faring better in the north of these regions and Democrats in the southern parts. Forty-four years later, this pattern is largely reversed. In 2005, Republicans were the majority in most southern states, with only 3 of the region's 14 states still majority Democratic. The Republican Party was also the majority party in 12 of the West's 15 states. In contrast, Democrats were the majority in all Pacific Coast states. In the North, 8 states, including the most urbanized, most populous ones, were majority Democratic, 7 states were majority Republican, and 1 was evenly divided between the parties. In the 2006 "blue sweep" elections, Democrats picked up 5 states in the North (CT, NH, PA, IN, WI), solidifying their hold of the region. The party also picked up 1 state in the South (NC) and 3 in the West (IA, MN, CO). Democratic gains in the North are not surprising and are in keeping with the long-term secular trends of the region. The party's gains in the South and especially the West indicate interregional tensions within the Republican coalition. The political implications of these inroads into Republican territory are explored in the book's conclusion.

At the end of World War II, nearly 70 percent of Democrats in Congress came from the South or the West. This changed in 1964. Since then, a majority of House Democrats have hailed from the North or Pacific Coast states. Today, nearly two out of three Democrats in the House come from one of these two regions, and this sets the policy direction for the national party. Conversely, only 24 percent of the Republican Party was located in the South and West at the end of World War II, but by 1996, a majority of Republicans were from one of these two regions, and the size of this majority has only grown with elections since then. The picture that emerges is of an increasingly partisan southern and western Republican pitted against an increasingly partisan Democrat from the North or Pacific Coast—in other words, a Tom DeLay against a Nancy Pelosi, a Trent Lott against a Teddy Kennedy, or a George Bush against a John Kerry. These are the partisan poles of contemporary politics.

STRATEGIES AND ISSUES OF THE EMERGING REGIONAL PARTY BATTLES

As the strategic focus of the parties has shifted from navigating the cross-regional coalitions of the New Deal years to cultivating interests in their new growth regions, bipartisanship has given way to partisanship. The mechanisms of this shift are the subject of the next three chapters, which trace regional change, regional party alignments, and party conflict over foreign, economic, and social policies. Here we review some of the key national developments and a suggestion of their regional implications.

In the aftermath of the Great Depression, the centerpiece of the New Deal Democratic Party's success was its ability to convince voters that it could "put America back to work" and that government was both responsible and able to ameliorate the vicissitudes of capitalism. Liberal Keynesian growth at the end of World War II allowed Democrats to flourish, appealing to both labor and business throughout the long boom economy of the 1950s and 1960s. Yet, as the position of the United States in the global economy began to change in the 1970s and 1980s, the negotiated arrangement among labor, business, and the Democrats fell apart. With plants shutting down, jobs being relocated, and capital becoming mercurial, the leverage that government and unions were once able to exercise over business weakened.

For the New Deal Democratic Party, which had benefited politically from the relationship, the breakdown in the arrangement between business and labor presented problems, forcing a choice. In this environment, it did not help Democrats that Americans, rather than maintaining or strengthening their support for labor and thus their connection to the party, were losing their working-class consciousness. Asked in 1960 to choose whether they were working class or middle class, 66 percent of Americans said "working class."[9] By 2000, this percentage had fallen to 46 percent, despite increasing income inequality.[10]

The drop-off in working-class identity is undoubtedly related to the simultaneous decline of unions, long a bulwark of working-class consciousness and a key partner in the Democratic coalition, especially in the North. Although there remains significant regional variation, overall membership in unions declined from 25 percent of the labor force in the late 1960s to just 11 percent in 2000.[11]

As Chapter 3 makes clear, the economic changes that were hurting the North were helping the South, presenting the Democrats with a dilemma. Companies began leaving the unionized North for the non-union South and

West as well as for other countries, further hastening labor's decline. A business-friendly climate and civic boosterism made the attraction of these new regions much the same as that which eventually drew companies to less-developed countries: a cheaper workforce, no unions, fewer regulations, and lower taxes.[12] And in the aftermath of the 1973 oil crisis, these cost savings became especially attractive for businesses operating in the energy-dependent regions of the North. *Fortune* magazine declared in 1977, "Northerners are missing the key point about the Sunbelt's boom. It's booming in great part because it's pro-business—and Northern cities, by and large, aren't."[13]

Through the early 1970s, as other regional divisions (such as those over race) began to surface, Democratic leaders continued to focus on economic issues. With economic problems mounting and with regional relations strained, economic policy proved a rallying point against Republican advances. Democratic leaders called economic policy "wonderful Democratic medicine" for their ability to unite North and South.[14] Yet, with the growing divergence of the regions' economic fortunes, this medicine lost its potency. Northern Democrats continued to proffer New Deal economic solutions for their union constituencies as well as for the less mobile industries and the state organizations that had developed with and around them during the height of industrial development. But for southern Democrats, that message had less appeal; and if Democrats were unwilling to facilitate the economy-growing inducements their states were offering to migrating industry and capital, Republicans were ready to take their place.

Increasingly in the 1980s and 1990s, Republicans did just that. The party's pro-business economic messages resonated with southern and western boosterism, and Republicans increased their presence in the fast developing suburbs of the Sun Belt. Speaking at a regional conference of the Republican National Committee in Idaho in 1981, Minority Whip Robert Michel described the party's compatibility with the West: "This part of Idaho and the West is just like the Republican Party in the western states: filled with fresh air and fresh ideas, rugged, tough, independent, dependable, a bit wild, always ready to go, and always eager to grow! The solid West is the cornerstone upon which our Republican Party is going to build America's future!"[15] Although Michel's flattery of the region is characteristically political, the strategy was long term. Republicans were well aware of the growth potential of the region and the implications this had for the region's percentage of Congressional seats.[16]

After the 1994 Republican takeover of Congress, institutional control of rule-making privileges allowed them to drive home the message of their pro-growth interests. As conservative strategist Grover Norquist explained after the 1996 election, in which Republicans retained control of Congress,

> When they [Democrats] couldn't take the House and the Senate, they couldn't change the rules. They couldn't change the campaign finance laws to kneecap Republican donors and raise union dues and go back to financing the big-city machines, which we've begun to defund. They would take over our committees and increase franked mail and try to make themselves invulnerable. The secular trend continues: today there are more self-employed people and small business owners than there are labor union members. The secular trend is every year more people are self-employed. That tends to make them Republicans.[17]

The Republican message of laissez-faire capitalism now successfully competed with the Democrats' emphasis on managed economic growth in a way not seen since before the 1930s. While Hoover's defeat in 1932 and the resilience of the New Deal realignment had forced the Republican Party to tone down its unabashed pro-business rhetoric, the party has found a new home for that message in the New Economy states of the South and West.[18]

Economic issues had proved potent for Democrats after World War II because key industries, and the labor force that worked for them, benefited from the country's emerging Cold War foreign policy. As Harry Truman and subsequent presidents argued, fighting communism required fostering the liberal capitalism of allies and potential allies. Policies such as the Marshall Plan and other provisions of foreign aid helped allies rebuild their economies and simultaneously expanded markets for American goods. But this foreign policy also required a strong, modern military, and one of the biggest beneficiaries of the ever-deepening attention to containing communism was the defense industry. Beginning with the North Atlantic Treaty Organization (NATO) and extending to alliances in the Third World, the increasing military commitments made by American political leaders put a premium on the development of military equipment, delivery systems, and men and women to run them.

Just as economic policy eventually failed as glue for the Democratic coalition, so too did containment policy. In the aftermath of Vietnam, a regional split on the direction of American foreign policy upended the anticommunist consensus. Liberals argued that the United States had overextended itself and that funds dedicated to an unwinnable and unnecessary war in Southeast Asia would be better spent on domestic needs. This message appealed to more than just young people anxious about military service. It had enduring appeal in the cities of the North, both because the older military industries there were in decline and because aging infrastructure and overtaxed services were increasingly in need of an injection of public resources. As Ronald Reagan escalated the country's efforts to roll back communism with stepped-up military spending in the 1980s, Democrats, especially in the North, opposed this prioritization of national resources and demanded that the country pull back from its military commitments.[19]

In contrast, southern Democrats and Republicans, especially in the West, continued to provide congressional support to presidents' Cold War foreign policy initiatives. While the Northeast and Midwest had been the primary sites of military production during World War II, the center had shifted to states in the South and West, such as Florida, Texas, North Carolina, and Missouri, in the early 1970s, and the shift accelerated into the 1980s. Military contractors, like other types of manufacturers, were increasingly relocating to Sun Belt states, and much of the research and development that provided the new high-tech weaponry prized by military strategists was concentrated in these two regions. Military bases were also disproportionately located in these same states. With the economies of the so-called Gun Belt regions thus linked to the military and with the South's cultural history of sympathy for the military, southern Democrats continued to promote a strong defense state. So, too, did Republicans, both in Congress and in the presidency, especially as promoting a revitalized national security became an avenue by which they could compete with Democrats in the South and West.[20]

The Keynesian domestic state and Cold War internationalism had been central elements of the New Deal Democratic order. When northern and southern Democrats divided over the merits of these policies, the national party suffered. At the same time, Republican leaders relentlessly pressed other, regionally divisive social and cultural issues to their advantage.

Fueled in part by the decisions of the Democratic leadership in the early 1960s, long-suppressed tensions between the two regional halves of the Democratic Party emerged on several fronts, especially on issues related to race. The party's commitment to spending on domestic social programs, combined with its support for African American civil rights, helped northern lawmakers court blacks who had migrated to the region's cities from farms in the Cotton Belt. But, as the national party committed itself to racial equality, white southern discontent, evident since the Dixiecrat revolt in 1948, grew.[21]

Beginning in the 1950s, Republicans sought to benefit from this schism. As early as the 1952 presidential race, Republican national chairman Guy Gabrielson pitched the party to Dixiecrats in an effort to attract southern whites. "Our friends call themselves States' Righters," Gabrielson said, "and we call ourselves Republicans. . . . The Dixiecrat Party believes in states' rights. That's what the Republican Party believes in."[22] Barry Goldwater's states' rights message and its success in the Deep South twelve years later demonstrated the logic of this approach. Richard Nixon then carefully, and not always successfully, incorporated racial wedge issues, including efforts to slow civil rights enforcement, into his "southern strategy."[23] As Kevin Phillips, a Nixon campaign consultant and the author of the southern strategy, explained during the 1972 presidential campaign, "Negro-Democratic mutual identification" hurt Democrats and helped Republicans in 1968, and exploiting this would be critical to future Republican advances.[24]

In the 1970s, conservatives encoded race in their attacks on social welfare spending. By the time Ronald Reagan denounced "welfare queens," Republicans were regularly using racially charged stereotypes for political and electoral benefit. Merging neoconservative critiques of social welfare programs with rhetoric, often subtly racialized, that polarized taxpayers and program beneficiaries, Republicans launched an attack on the welfare state; this tactic helped the party grow in suburbs around the nation but especially those being built in the South and West.[25] The divisions over race supplanted the class divide that had earlier benefited New Deal Democrats. Since passage of the Voting Rights Act in 1965, for example, the gap in party support between black and white voters in presidential elections has been far greater (on the magnitude of 40 to 50 percentage points greater) than the gap between low- and middle-income white voters.[26] In other words, racial groups are more coherent and politically opposed than class groups among whites, which has compounded the erosion of union strength and declining class-consciousness to the great detriment of Democratic Party's attempts to build a multiracial working- and middle-class coalition.

Race was not the only issue the Republicans used to divide Democrats and to construct a new geographic majority. By 1963, in meetings of the congressional Republican leadership, Senator Thruston Morton, Republican from Kentucky, was already urging his fellow party members to think about issues other than race in appealing to the South: "There are other areas than civil rights in which we can make our pitch to the Southern voter. The Southern voter today is more closely allied—philosophically—with the center of the Republican Party than he is with the present leadership of the Democratic Party. I urge candidates for Congress, Senate, to stand firmly on that position, because you go out and try to get to the right of the Southern Democrat on civil rights, you can't do it, for one thing, it's impossible."[27]

Most of the "other areas" the Republican Party focused on have fallen within the broad arena of cultural and religious politics. Issues such as abortion, school prayer, gun control, gender equality, and homosexuality offered new material with which Republicans could construct a larger and enduring coalition. For strategists such as Phillips, the center of this coalition would be located in the South and the West: "Who needs Manhattan when we can get the electoral votes of eleven southern states? Put those together with the Farm Belt and the Rocky Mountains, and we don't need the big cities. We don't even want them." In using race and cultural issues, Republicans often relied on the anti-elitism that had long been a tradition in the South and West. (As Phillips explained, "The whole secret to politics is knowing who hates who.")[28] Republican strategist Lee Atwater explained the logic of a generic populism as it related to social issues in 1984: "Populists have always been liberal on economics. So long as the crucial issues were generally confined to economics—as during the New Deal—the liberal candidate would expect to get most of the populist vote. But populists are conservatives on most social issues. . . . As for race, it was hardly an issue—it went without saying that the populists' chosen leaders were hardcore segregationists."[29]

Thus, while race was a potent issue for dividing Democrats during the 1960s and 1970s, other social issues, especially those related to maintaining traditional family structures, have since become more important to Republican strategists. "Culture war" issues like abortion and prayer in school began their rise to national political prominence in response to the feminist and gay liberation movements of the 1960s and 1970s. These movements concentrated on college campuses and in urban areas, yet expressions of equality and demands for social progress radiated outward through American society, were reflected in the medium of popular culture, and were instituted nationally through key Supreme Court decisions, such as *Roe v. Wade* in 1973.[30]

An increasingly diverse and highly educated professional class concentrated in the North and Pacific Coast demanded that the government pay attention to civil rights issues and inequalities among groups and also to "quality of life" issues such as the environment, and northern Democrats became vocal advocates of these socially progressive goals.[31] For Democratic strategists such as Pat Caddell, it was this group that held the future of the party. As Caddell argued to Jimmy Carter in 1976, not only did college-educated, white-collar professionals want something different from the traditional economic message of the Democrats, so too did Baby Boomers (the groups overlap). These voters, he said, "perceive a new cluster of issues—the 'counterculture' and issues such as growth versus the environment—where the old definitions don't apply."[32] These voters were also concentrated in the cities and suburbs of the North and Pacific Coast states. "Blue staters" tend to have higher levels of educational attainment. In recent census data rankings of the percent of a state's population that is over the age of 25 and has at least a college degree, 10 of the top 15 states are in the North or Pacific Coast regions, while 12 of the bottom 15 are in the South or West.[33]

When the early institutional successes of groups demanding greater rights sparked resistance from religious conservatives, especially among those who had long been removed from political affairs, the potential for a new Democratic cleavage became apparent. President Nixon identified as the "Silent Majority" these voters and those generally ambivalent or opposed to social change. Conservative animosity was directed at the activism on college campuses and in cities, the "judicial activism" of the Warren and Burger courts, and the increasingly northern-dominated Democratic Party that, Republicans argued, "inflicted" activism upon the nation. By 1972, the success of this strategy was clear: George McGovern became one of the first prominent Democrats to be tarred with the social activist connection when he became the "acid, amnesty, and abortion" candidate in 1972.

Although Catholic voters in the North were early targets for the Republican message of social conservatism, the party found increasing success among white evangelicals, a growing population concentrated in the South and West.[34] Ralph Reed, Republican operative and former executive director of the Christian Coalition, argued, "The religious conservative movement was the only hope to build a Republican Party in the South."[35] And, as Reed explained in an interview in the mid-1990s with journalist and author Elizabeth Drew, religious conservatives have increasingly focused their attention on Congress: "The long-term interests of the movement do not reside at 1600 Pennsylvania Avenue. A realignment on the Hill will affect U.S. policy for the next ten to twenty years."[36] Legislative activity since 2000, such as "right to live" proposals, bills to restrict abortion, and Constitutional amendments to ban gay marriage, suggest that fulfillment of his prophecy is well under way.

Social issues (including race) combined with economic and foreign policy issues to force the dissolution of the Democratic Party regional bloc and to nurture the new regional combinations of the party system. As the parties have used these issues to create new geographic coalitions, their rhetoric has become increasingly partisan. Throughout this process, the regions have remained central because of their ability to subsume and combine economic and cultural factors.

Seen from this angle, the regional divorce in the Democratic Party that be-gan in the late 1960s was not simply the break-up of another party coalition. The North-South alliance that had sustained the New Deal regime for the prior thirty years was a post–Civil War novelty in American politics. Incorporating a majority of the nation's citizens, the New Deal's strength was national, giving control to Democrats and demanding accommodation by northern Republi-cans. It defined what was "normal" for American politics for a large portion of the twentieth century.

When Republican and southern Democratic bipartisan activity replaced the New Deal norm, Democratic leaders grew anxious to find issues and opera-tional strategies that would reinvigorate the old coalition. Watching the North-South coalition unravel, Majority Leader Carl Albert pleaded with the Demo-cratic Caucus in 1970 to fortify their defenses in the face of Republican opportunism: "Let us not fall into the trap our political enemies lay for us. Let us disagree, but let us resolve our disagreements in our own house, not in the arena where our political opponents find it to their distinct advantage. For Democratic divisiveness is their only hope."[37]

Albert's plea for partisan unity signifies the dire nature of the Democrats' circumstances. The party was growing in the North, but, despite the size of the region's population, that growth was not enough to ensure future governing control. The party depended on the South for that, even as its policy directions shifted in ways that were distancing the party from the South. Conversely, while Republican *opportunity* depended on dividing the Democratic Party, its *success* depended on building a new coalition. Given regional economic and demo-graphic trends, and given the country's long history of regional animosities and cultural differences, Republicans banked on a coalition of the country's new growth areas. With Democrats concentrated in the older industrial areas of the North and Pacific Coast, Republicans solidified their hold in the growing metropolises of the South and West, and today the two parties find themselves competing on behalf of different geographic audiences.

CHAPTER 3

SUN BELT RISING

GLOBALIZATION AND REGIONAL CHANGES ON TRADE POLICY

INTENSE CONFLICT over tariffs and trade defined much of nineteenth-century regional and party politics, but after Franklin D. Roosevelt secured passage of the Reciprocal Trade Agreements Act in 1934 and with the rise of the Cold War, serious dispute receded and free trade became the norm. Following Roosevelt, New Deal Democrats continued to author the country's free trade regime into the 1960s, and broad sections of both parties regularly authorized trade liberalization and greater executive authority over trade agreements. The logic seemed clear: trade liberalization contributed to the booming postwar economy and was part of the Cold War foreign policy effort to stabilize existing allies and entice new ones in the fight against the Soviet Union. For Democrats, this policy stance became a powerful tool for party building, uniting North and South. The regional benefits of trade liberalization were sufficiently strong, though, to lure the cooperation of northern Republicans as well. Trade as a coalition builder for Democrats collapsed in the late 1960s. By then, the United States was undergoing profound industrial and demographic restructuring and the national consensus on communist containment was eroding. The implications varied across regions, and as regional trade incentives diverged, northern and southern Democrats found themselves on opposite sides of the issue.

Under President Richard Nixon, the Republican Party became the new home of free trade. Economic developments made the West the emerging center of free trade promotion, uniting western Republicans with their northern compatriots. Nixon's promotion of trade liberalization not only unified Republicans across regions, but it also provided opportunity for an alliance with southern Democrats. The South's historic attachment to free trade and a mix of material incentives designed to ease the region's economic transformation made southern states hospitable to the administration's trade policy. The country's free trade regime was thus sustained in these years by a new bipartisan coalition of Republicans and southern Democrats. Meanwhile, its former champion, northern Democrats, now opposed it, becoming increasingly protectionist in response to the declining fortunes of manufacturing in their states.

In the following decades, as Rust Belt northerners came to dominate the Democratic Party and as the Republican Party shifted south and westward into the trade-dependent Sun Belt, trade policy became an increasing source of contention between the parties.

PARTY CONFLICT ON TRADE FROM THE END
OF WORLD WAR II TO THE PRESENT

Partisanship regarding trade has declined and then increased. Figure 3.1 shows the average difference in the parties' support for free trade on all trade and tariff votes cast from 1947 to 1998.[1]

In the years immediately following World War II, a unified Democratic Party supported trade liberalization while an equally unified Republican Party opposed freer trade. But, as President Truman and subsequent presidents constructed a new Cold War international order around a bipolar distribution of power between the United States and the Soviet Union, Republicans increasingly joined Democrats in providing presidents with trade-liberalizing authority, resulting in a heyday of trade bipartisanship and foreign policy bipartisanship more generally. The consensus lasted until support for the war in Vietnam began to erode and the the national economy began to decline in the early 1970s.

Party differences on trade reached their lowest levels in the early 1970s, and bipartisanship peaked at this time. Because party difference scores are absolute values, they conceal important changes that were emerging in the parties' orientations toward trade. The national parties' positions were in the process of reversing, which contributed to the subsequent heightening of party conflict. In contrast to the broad consensus of the earlier postwar decades, the bipartisanship of the early 1970s disguised an intraparty cleavage between northern

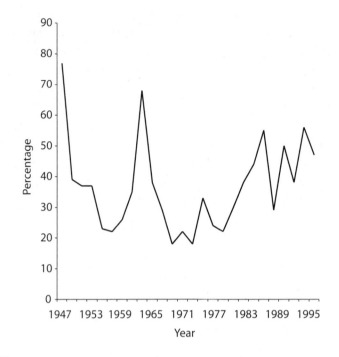

Figure 3.1
Mean Difference between Parties on All Trade Votes, 80th through 105th Congresses, 1947–1998
Source: Calculated from vote data provided by Keith Poole and Howard Rosenthal at voteview.com.

and southern Democrats. While northern Democrats became increasingly dis-
enchanted with free trade as their region's deindustrialization accelerated,
southern Democrats remained largely committed to free trade, joining with
Republicans, who were now increasingly unified in support of free trade. The
effect of this conservative coalition alignment of southern Democrats and Republicans from various regions was bipartisan continuation of the country's
free trade regime. Yet, it was from this point forward that the national Democratic Party became associated with trade protectionism, a position pursued,
promoted, and recalibrated as "fair trade" most forcefully by northern Democrats. Using general trade bills only, Figure 3.2 shows the shift in national party
positions, implying the consequent degree of partisanship.[2]

By the mid-1980s, the parties were almost as far apart on trade as they had
been in the immediate aftermath of World War II. As Table 3.1 makes clear, regional trade preferences had begun to diverge even earlier. Table 3.1 shows the

Figure 3.2

Mean Party Support for Free Trade, 81st through 105th Congresses, 1949–1998

Source: Calculated from roll call data.

Note: Figure represents major trade legislation, as described in note 2. The number of key trade bills voted on each decade varied.

percentage of representatives from each region and subregion voting for free trade on the legislation analyzed in detail in this chapter: the 1962 Trade Expansion Act, the 1974 Trade Reform Act, and the 1998 vote to provide the president with fast-track trade authority. Between 1962 and 1973 (when the 1974 legislation was first voted on in the House), southern and western representatives increased their support of free trade, while northern and Pacific Coast lawmakers, by and large, decreased their support. Regional divergence on trade is most apparent among northern and western lawmakers. From the 1970s onward, the typical western representative stood solidly behind trade liberalization, while support by the average northern representative declined precipitously. Support for free trade from the Pacific Coast and the South stayed split fairly evenly between these two regional poles.

The country as a whole supported trade liberalization in the early 1960s, with resistance only in the isolationist Midwest. Expanding trade expanded

TABLE 3.1. LEVEL OF SUPPORT FOR FREE TRADE BY REGION, 1962–1998

REGION	1962 TEA (%)	1973 TRA (%)	1998 FAST TRACK (%)	CHANGE FROM 1962 TO 1998 (− INDICATES MORE PROTECTIONIST)
North	60	50	28	−32
New England	74	37	17	−57
Mid-Atlantic	70	50	22	−48
East North Central	44	54	38	−6
Pacific Coast	64	59	48	−16
South	61	78	49	−12
Southeast	65	88	45	−20
Southwest	55	60	87	32
West	50	63	67	17
West North Central	45	70	68	23
Mountain	62	50	65	3

Source: Calculated from roll call data.

Note: Based on key votes: 1962 TEA = % voting *against* Mason motion to recommit the Trade Expansion Act (HR 11970), defeated 171-253, 6/28/62; 1973 TRA = % voting *for* modified closed rule for Trade Reform Act of 1973 (HR 10710), passed 230-147, 12/10/73; 1998 fast track = % voting *for* Reciprocal Trade Agreements Authorities Act ("fast track renewal") (HR 2621), motion defeated 180-243, 9/25/98.

markets for U.S. products and economic support for trade allies in the fight against the Soviet Union. Strong support for free trade was still clear in the early 1970s, but regional fissures were emerging. While representatives from emerging Sun Belt states in the West, South, and Pacific Coast staunchly supported the country's free trade regime, northerners were beginning to defect, especially those in New England and the Mid-Atlantic, where manufacturing fortunes were in decline. These regional divisions grew in the 1980s and 1990s, through recession and then recovery. In the late 1990s, the West and Southwest still strongly supported free trade, while opposition to free trade was still greatest in the North; but joining northern lawmakers in resistance were representatives from the Pacific Coast and the Southeast, especially those whose districts were home to older and declining manufacturing industries.

The growing regional differences over trade reflect two phenomena. First, the frequency with which regional representatives voted against each other increased independently of developments in the party system. In the 1980s and 1990s, for example, western Republicans were more likely to support free trade than northern Republicans, while northern Democrats were more likely to support protectionist measures than western Democrats. Part of what was happening, in other words, was strictly about geography. Second, at the same time, the parties were increasingly the vehicles through which regional differences over trade were expressed. The growing opposition to free trade in the North was voiced largely by the growing number of Democrats in the region, while the increasingly numerous Republicans in the West were forceful promoters of trade liberalization there.

As the Democratic Party shifted to the North, the region and the party became the center of trade protectionism. Likewise, as Republican strength grew in the South and the West, that party abandoned its former protectionism and instead increasingly embraced trade liberalization. For both parties, these new policy positions benefited key interests in their growth regions and were thus important in building their coalitions. The debates over the 1962 Trade Expansion Act, the 1974 Trade Reform Act, and the 1998 fast-track trade authority illustrate these changes and how they contributed both to the geographic reorganization of the party system and to increased party conflict.

CLASSIC BIPARTISANSHIP: THE 1962 TRADE EXPANSION ACT

When President Kennedy first proposed the idea that would become the 1962 Trade Expansion Act (TEA), pundits predicted that the trade bill would set off "The Great Debate" of 1962, between liberal trade and protectionism in Congress and the nation.[3] Instead, the most significant piece of trade legislation since the Reciprocal Trade Agreement Act of 1934 passed Congress with little real dissent.

The potential points of contention seemed many. The bill significantly expanded executive authority, giving the president the ability to reduce tariffs by up to 50 percent of previous levels, a far larger tariff-cutting authority than had been granted in recent decades. On some items, the bill empowered the president to eliminate tariffs completely. For the first time, trade negotiations could be conducted over categories of goods instead of simply on an item-by-item basis, again vesting more summary power in the hands of executive negotiators. The bill also removed peril points—minimum acceptable tariffs—which protectionist Republicans had inserted into trade law in the 1950s as recourse to industries threatened by imports. Finally, the bill introduced the controversial idea of trade adjustment assistance, which would provide compensation and retraining to individuals and firms hurt by foreign competition.

Yet, despite plentiful grounds for dispute and four weeks of congressional committee hearings, Kennedy's bill passed with few changes, supported overwhelmingly by Democrats and with little effectively organized opposition from Republicans. On the final vote, nearly half of the Republican House members crossed over to vote with Democrats in support of the bill, making the tally a lopsided 300 votes in favor of more free trade and only 127 against.

Prominent trade scholars have described the early postwar decades as a time of bipartisan consensus on free trade, and in general the 1962 TEA fits this pattern.[4] Mild partisanship existed, however, before the final vote. Typical of trade legislation, the TEA was considered under a closed rule that allowed amendment only to recommit the bill to committee. Republican Noah Mason of Illinois made the motion to recommit, which, if passed, would have effectively killed the legislation. The vote on the Mason motion fell along party lines. Even here, however, Republicans offered far less than a determined opposition. Meeting just two days before the vote, the Republican Policy Committee chose not to formulate a party position on the TEA. Moreover, Republican leaders in the House announced their support for the Mason motion to recommit only in the final moments of debate, hardly a strong signal to the party's membership.[5] As a result, even on this key vote more than a quarter of Republicans sided with the Democrats.

A STRONG ECONOMY, ROBUST COLD WAR IDEOLOGY, AND THE POWER OF THE NEW DEAL REGIME

The alliance between South and North, Democrat and Republican on the issue of trade was driven by economics and strengthened by ideology. The United States had emerged from World War II a superpower and one of the few advanced industrialized nations with its economic infrastructure intact. As the leader in constructing the postwar international order, it initiated a series of policies and programs, including trade initiatives, to rebuild the economies of its allies and strengthen its international presence. The goal was to simultaneously fortify the buttresses against Soviet communism and ensure that, in the aftermath of a wartime economy, demand for U.S. goods did not slake.[6]

From the outset, President Kennedy linked the need for the TEA to both economic and foreign policy objectives, positioning the bill as a logical next step in the effort to maintain a strong economy and in the country's fight against communism. The White House conducted an extensive lobbying campaign, directed at members of Congress as well as at influential groups such as the National Association of Manufacturers and the AFL-CIO.[7] Kennedy even resorted to drawing on wartime patriotism in his campaign for the bill. Firms that contributed to expanding exports were given a pennant emblazoned with the letter "E," similar to the one hung over efficient war plants during World War II.[8] In his message to Congress, Kennedy emphasized the bill's broad appeal.

> This philosophy of the free market—the wider economic choice for men and nations—is as old as freedom itself. It is not a partisan philosophy. For many years our trade legislation has enjoyed bi-partisan backing from those members of both parties who recognized how essential trade is to our basic security abroad and our economic health at home. This is even more true today. The Trade Expansion Act of 1962 is designed as the expression of a nation, not of any single faction, not of any single faction or section.[9]

Kennedy's message fashioned trade liberalization as a logical extension of the country's founding commitment to liberty. With an aggressive public relations campaign emphasizing that the benefits of free trade extended to all regions and both parties, Kennedy made it difficult for any in Congress to resist. As one observer at the time put it, "This bill was wrapped in the American flag. No one dared trample on it."[10] More than this, though, Kennedy's trade liberalization was emblematic of the policy promises that kept the New Deal regime strong, it pledged to provide economic and foreign policy security. It also worked to the benefit of key interests in both South and North.[11]

The breadth of support for free trade reflects the strength of American exports in the early 1960s. With a history of exporting cotton and tobacco, the South had long been and still was a cornerstone of free trade. By the 1960s, with the aid of federal investment and technological developments, the region was shifting away from its traditional agricultural economy and entering a period of rapid industrialization, much of which was based around defense-related industries.[12] Because of the dominant position of American manufacturing in the global economy and because policy that benefited national defense also benefited defense industries, the South's new industrialization tended to reinforce the region's long-standing commitment to free trade. Some of the older southern industries, however, most notably textiles, were under pressure from growing imports. By negotiating a textiles agreement with other exporting nations just before consideration of the TEA, Kennedy was able to secure the support of such powerful textile states as North Carolina, South Carolina, Georgia, and Tennessee.[13]

Also working in Kennedy's favor was the South's ethos of self-reliance. The economic libertarianism and the emphasis on self-sufficiency that was characteristic of the region made it responsive to arguments about increasing free market opportunity, the greater executive authority required to accomplish this notwithstanding. Additionally, the region's historic resistance to external authority, along with its militaristic history, meant that southerners appreciated trade liberalization's role in the fight against communism. The combination of cultural attributes and material benefits paved the way for the South's support of Kennedy's legislation.[14]

As a whole, the still solidly Democratic South provided strong support for Kennedy's bill in terms of both votes and leadership in the House. Wilbur Mills, the Arkansas Democrat who served as chair of the powerful Ways and Means Committee, which introduced the bill, was an ardent supporter of free trade and asked the same of other committee members. Because of the strength of the committee system in Congress at the time, his support, like Kennedy's, made opposition difficult.[15] Under Mills's skillful stewardship, several protectionist amendments were rejected even before the bill was brought to the floor, ensuring that only a clean bill reached the floor.[16] The strength of southern support for the TEA is evident in Figure 3.3, a map of House support for the 1962 free trade bill.

The majority of southern states were above—in some cases well above—the national average in their support of the Trade Expansion Act.[17] Yet, as the map makes clear, the other cornerstone of support for the TEA was the North, where a majority of states also demonstrated above average support for free trade. Since the 1930s, the North had maintained a powerful alliance with the South because of the increasing reliance on trade by the region's industrialists and workers to expand markets for their manufactured goods. In urging lawmakers to support the bill, Hale Boggs of Louisiana invoked this New Deal alliance and the unusual coalition of interests on which it rested. "Who is for this bill?" he asked. "The US Chamber of Commerce is for it. The AFL-CIO is for it. The United States Steelworkers of America are for it. The American Farm Bureau is for it. . . . The people who raise and sell tobacco are for it. The people who represent cotton are for it. Most of the manufacturers are for it."[18] It is relatively rare in American politics for such a broad cross-section of interests to be unified in favor of a particular policy direction, and Boggs made sure to draw attention to the consensus.

In the debate, northern Democrats stood firmly with southerners on the importance of the TEA to the free trade regime. Of the 97 Democrats in the North, all but 4 voted against the Mason motion to recommit and thus kill the bill. Pacific Coast Democrats were even stronger in their support; all of them voted against the Mason motion. The strength of northern and Pacific Coast support was due to the regions' positions as the global providers of manufactured goods. According to administration figures, exports from the North

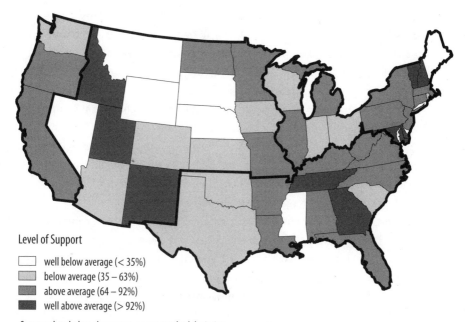

Level of Support

☐ well below average (< 35%)
▨ below average (35 – 63%)
▨ above average (64 – 92%)
■ well above average (> 92%)

Category breaks based on mean ± one standard deviation.

Figure 3.3
House Support for Free Trade, 1962

and Pacific Coast states were worth nearly $13 billion, while the South exported just $5 billion, and the West just under $2.5 billion.[19] In addition, estimates indicated exporting firms employed one out of every three manufacturing workers.[20] With a brisk level of export activity and with little foreign competition, American industry, finance, and, importantly, labor, all favored free trade. New York Democrat Eugene Keogh put it most simply when he said that the greater New York area depended on trade as the "very foundation for its entire economy."[21]

Especially important for northern and Pacific Coast support was union support, which was contingent upon inclusion of the adjustment assistance provision. Because unions were a key regional partner in the Democratic coalition, northern Democrats were vocal in their support of this measure. Using language that was simultaneously pro-capital and pro-labor, Keogh argued that the adjustment program fit "closely into the competitive environment which is essential for the health of our economy. Unlike tariffs which simply erect a protective barrier against outside competition, the forms of assistance which I have just described will assist firms to meet the challenge of this competition and will strengthen their response."[22] The Democratic Party at the time benefited from the mutual cooperation of business and labor, and policies that both supported, such as the TEA, were highly valued.

While the New Deal Democratic coalition of northern labor and industry and southern industry and agriculture provided the backbone of support for the TEA, the legislation gained considerable support (as well as its bipartisan flavor) from the large number of northern Republicans who crossed party lines to vote in support of the legislation. Forty-five percent of Republicans from New England and Mid-Atlantic states voted against the Mason motion, and 63 percent voted for final passage of the trade liberalization bill.

Northern Republicans who lent their support to the TEA comprised the "eastern establishment" wing of the party, and they spoke for the industrial and financial interests that were instrumental in pushing the party toward international activism.[23] The areas they represented had played a large role, for example, in ensuring the victory of moderate internationalist General Dwight Eisenhower over conservative isolationist Robert Taft ten years before, in the 1952 Republican primary.[24] Indeed, northern Republicans' support for the TEA was legitimized by former President Eisenhower's endorsement of the bill, echoed by his secretary of state, Christian Herter. Sounding indistinguishable from many of the bill's Democratic supporters, northern Republicans, such as John Lindsay of New York, urged fellow party members to support the legislation on the grounds that it was crucial to the country's prosperity and security.[25]

In the years between the end of World War II and passage of the TEA, the value of both imports and exports had roughly doubled; but because of the strength of American exports, particularly manufactured goods, the United States consistently maintained a favorable balance of trade. In 1960, the value of exports exceeded that of imports by close to $6 billion.[26] A key goal of Kennedy's trade initiative was to ensure that this advantage, and the domestic economic prosperity it brought, did not erode. Of particular concern was the fact that nearly a third of American trading activity was with the countries of Western Europe, and the emergence of the European Economic Community (the Common Market), with its continental economic cooperation, meant a potential loss of markets for U.S. goods.[27]

In addition, the United States had sustained a balance of payments deficit that, since the late 1950s, was reducing U.S. gold stocks and threatening to destabilize the dollar. One possible outcome was that the country would have to cut back on its overseas commitments—a possibility unpalatable to many for both economic and security reasons. One alternative, Kennedy argued, was to use the new trade initiative to increase exports and in this way reduce the payments deficit.[28] It would also enhance security; many saw trade with allies and with emerging nations in the developing world as a way to promote western political ideals and foster loyalty. By linking trade liberalization to the country's foreign policy strategy of Soviet containment, Kennedy was able to sell the policy to those without great benefits from external markets.

The most unified resistance to Kennedy's trade initiative came from Republicans in the West. Those from the West's mountain states voted unanimously to recommit the TEA to committee, as did 81 percent of Republicans from West North Central states.

The Republican Party in the early 1960s perched upon a regional fault line, one that within several years would rupture and lead to the regional and (therefore) ideological reorientation of the party.[29] While northeastern Republicans benefited from and supported the policies of the New Deal Democratic regime on a range of issues, westerners in the party were typically resistant to New Deal efforts to enhance executive power. Many maintained a Taft-like skepticism of international involvement as well.[30] This was especially true when that involvement was directed toward Europe, as was the case with the TEA. This faction of the Republican Party came from what one analyst has called the "region of isolationism," an area centered in the states of Kansas, Nebraska, and the Dakotas and extending as far west as Wyoming and Idaho.[31] Not surprisingly, the only bloc of Republicans in the North that were opposed to Kennedy's bill were in the region's western half, Ohio, Indiana, and Wisconsin. Ninety-two percent of these East North Central Republicans were opposed to the TEA and voted to recommit the bill.

In debate over the TEA, many western and midwestern Republicans voiced protectionist sentiment, speaking out on behalf of their districts' agricultural interests or the interests of resource-extracting industries, such as coal, oil, and timber, which expected to be hurt by any growth in imports. Western oil interests were particularly unhappy with the plan, and their representatives, led by Oklahoma Democrat Tom Steed, pushed for concessions from the administration to protect domestic producers.[32]

Agricultural interests were in an increasingly paradoxical position. Despite growing reliance on exports, farm leaders and their representatives in the West had long opposed the country's free trade commitments because of their potential to undermine existing domestic agricultural price support and subsidy programs.[33] Of particular concern in House debates on the TEA was the plight of small farmers, who, some argued, would lose doubly with the bill because in addition to being hurt by trade liberalization they would also be ineligible for the workers' adjustment assistance.[34] Differences between sectors were often reflected in regional divisions over trade, and the history of these antagonisms was often implicit in the debates. Drawing on time-honed imagery, Ohio Republican Jackson Betts complained, "The farmer's tax money will go to help pay the unemployment compensation of workers who are dislocated as a result of this."[35]

Calling up more than just the divide between tax-paying rural folk and government-dependent city denizens, protectionist rhetoric also invoked historic western suspicions of discriminatory treatment suffered at the hands of northeastern elites. This, too, relied on historic imagery. In populist tones, Republican Glenn Cunningham from Nebraska argued as much against the northeastern wing of his own party as against the reigning Democratic regime:

> [T]he Madison Avenue approach has been used to try to sell this proposition to the people. International influences have been very active in promoting this legislation and similar plans for closer and closer economic and political links between the United States and certain other countries. . . . I am convinced [this bill] will not do the things the intellectual hucksters claim. . . . I cannot let down the workers and businesses of Nebraska and throughout the rest of the country.[36]

Despite the anti-intellectual populist rhetoric and the very real discontent of some Republicans, especially westerners, the strength of the New Deal Democrat and northern Republican internationalist coalition was too strong for this resistance to be effective. A combination of U.S. economic advantage and a political context focused on the "the brooding menace of Communist imperialism"[37] made widespread bipartisan support for free trade possible. As it turns out, changes along both dimensions would make this particular consensus fleeting.

CHANGING FORTUNES, REORGANIZING PARTIES:
THE 1974 TRADE REFORM ACT

Among the many changes of the 1960s, the end of U.S. economic hegemony carried especially far-reaching implications. Declining rates of relative productivity, greater exposure to competition from foreign goods, increasing investments abroad by U.S.-based multinational corporations, and escalating costs of the war in Vietnam contributed to the strain on the American economy. By 1971, with both a balance of payments deficit and a trade deficit, the era of American global economic dominance that had begun in the closing years of World War II was largely over. Then, when the 1973 oil shocks triggered stagflation, the economic problems that had only loomed on the horizon during discussion of trade in 1962 went front and center in national debate.[38]

In the early 1970s, as the majority party in Congress but without control of the presidency for the first time in a decade, Democrats focused on the country's economic woes in an effort to discredit President Nixon and regain control of government. Party leaders understood the economy to be the most important concern of voters and an area in which their party had traditionally been strong. With the gulf between northern and southern Democrats widening on issues including race and Vietnam, Democratic leaders believed that they could also use the economy as an issue to unite the different factions of their party. John Barriere, executive director of the Democratic Steering Committee, made this logic clear in a 1971 memorandum to House Majority Leader Carl Albert. As he explained, economic issues would provide a way to "attain maximum unity and, at the same time, achieve maximum political mileage." Albert's response to Barriere's proposal was definitive: "This is an excellent idea: Let's do it!"[39]

Most of the Democratic efforts focused on domestic economic initiatives, but trade policy became part of the agenda when, in 1973, Nixon moved forward with a new request for expanded trade authority. Nixon's request came at an inauspicious time. By the early 1970s, manufacturing imports from the rebuilt industrialized economies of Europe and Japan and from newly industrializing countries were beginning to compete with American products. As a share of world trade, American trade declined by 16 percent between 1960 and 1970; and among the countries of the Organization for Economic Cooperation and Development (OECD), the U.S. share of trade dropped by more than 23 percent.[40] In 1971, the U.S. experienced its first trade deficit since 1888, and in 1972, this deficit reached $6.8 billion, two-thirds of which was with Japan and Europe.[41] These unnerving developments inspired a new wave of protectionism in Congress and elsewhere, and it was this with which Nixon had to contend when promoting the Trade Reform Act in 1973.

The president's trade negotiating authority under the 1962 TEA lapsed in 1967, and in 1973 Nixon sought renewed authority, arguing that negotiators in the upcoming Tokyo Round of the General Agreement on Tariffs and Trade (GATT) talks needed credible authority to bargain effectively. While fairly complex, the main points of the trade proposal included extending presidential negotiating authority for an additional five years; granting authority, for the first time, to negotiate the removal of nontariff barriers (the area where most contention now centered); loosening adjustment assistance eligibility; enhancing import relief measures; and granting "most-favored-nation" (MFN) status to imports from Communist nations, with the Soviet Union as the target.

Despite growing Democratic concerns over the events of Watergate and presidential budget impoundments, the bill that was reported out of the Ways and Means Committee gave the president almost all of what he had requested, although it also included new consulting and oversight mechanisms, including provisions that would enable Congress to exercise some veto power over presidential actions. The committee also added stringent restrictions on MFN status. Targeting the Soviet Union's policies toward Jewish emigration, the Jackson-Vanick amendment made MFN status conditional on the recipient country's willingness to implement a policy of unrestricted emigration. Despite these minor limitations, Nixon, like Kennedy ten years before, was given a broad grant of authority to pursue new trade agreements. And, like Kennedy before him, Nixon received this authority from a bipartisan coalition.

Entirely different, however, was the shape of the coalition. Unlike the bipartisan coalition of 1962, Nixon's support came from an alliance of southern Democrats and Republicans from all regions, who were called the "conservative coalition." The most significant changes from ten years earlier were that western Republicans were now strongly supportive of free trade while northern Democrats no longer were. In passing the 1973 Trade Reform Act (the precursor to the 1974 Act), 90 percent of House Republicans voted to support free trade, as did 48 percent of Democrats, the majority of whom were southerners. Eighty-six of the 123 Democratic votes cast against the legislation, or 70 percent of the Democratic opposition, came from northern and Pacific Coast representatives.

More crucial than the final vote, however, was the vote a day earlier over whether to consider the legislation under a "modified closed rule" that limited consideration to three amendments, all of which the Ways and Means Committee had proposed.[42] The House approved the closed rule by a vote of 230 to 147. Had the rule been rejected, there was a strong chance that the Ways and Means Committee would have pulled the entire bill to prevent it from being crippled by protectionist amendments.[43] Indeed, some speculated that the bill's detractors were focused on defeating the rule as a strategy to ensure the defeat of the legislation.[44] Like the final vote, the vote on the rule was passed by the conservative coalition, which in the early 1970s was voting as a bloc more consistently than in the decades before or since. Eighty-four percent of Republicans joined with 44 percent of Democrats in support of the closed rule and free trade. The split in the Democratic Party again fell squarely along regional lines. Seventy-five percent of southern Democrats voted with Republicans in favor of free trade while 80 percent of northern Democrats and 67 percent of Pacific Coast Democrats voted for protection.[45]

In a mere ten years, the political alignments on trade had shifted dramatically. Republicans, historically the party that sought to shelter the domestic economy from free trade, now fully embraced the idea of breaking down trade barriers. Just as startling, the unified Democratic coalition that had instituted and given shape to the country's free trade regime in earlier decades was gone, and it in its place was a party weakened by regional differences. Most pronounced were the differences between northerners and southerners.

REGIONAL ECONOMIC DIVERGENCE AND THE NEW DEAL COALITION

Democratic leaders in 1962 had used trade policy to bolster interests in the regions that mattered most to their coalition, North and South. Ten years later, Republican leaders used trade to the opposite end—to expose the divergent interests within that old Democratic coalition. Trade politics in 1973 were regionally divisive, and the most significant division was between northerners and southerners.[46] In a radical departure from earlier decades, northern Democrats broke from southern Democrats to urge the defeat first of the closed rule and then of the entire Trade Reform Act.

The effect of regional differences on lawmakers' vote choice reflects this schism, which becomes evident when controlling for party affiliation. While Republicans in all regions supported free trade to the same degree, regional differences among Democrats were pronounced and significant.[47] While 80 percent of northern Democrats favored protection, just 25 percent of southern Democrats did. The map of Democratic support for Nixon's Trade Reform bill (Figure 3.4) illustrates this break between northerners and southerners. While the South is still above average in its support of free trade, Democrats in the North are below or well below average.

The root of the problem was not just that the country was facing difficulties as a result of global economic change and that representatives from different regions believed in different solutions. Rather, economic changes were having markedly different effects in the regions. This was the crux of the growing divergence on trade. The regression results of state support for free trade among Democrats, presented in Table 3.2, give some sense of the factors that drove Democrats apart on the issue of trade policy.[48]

In states with prominent agricultural interests and with a high depen-

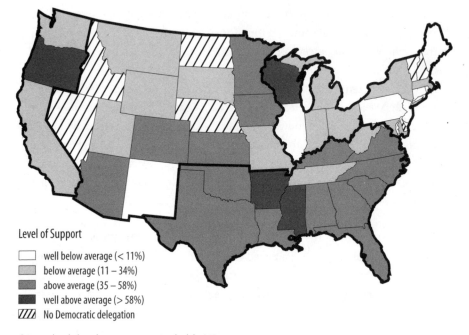

Level of Support

☐ well below average (< 11%)
▨ below average (11 – 34%)
▨ above average (35 – 58%)
■ well above average (> 58%)
▨▨ No Democratic delegation

Category breaks based on mean ± one standard deviation.

Figure 3.4
House Support for Free Trade among Democrats, 1973

dence on exports for revenue, Democrats were still inclined toward free trade. This defines the Sun Belt, which was beginning to prosper, with rapid economic growth in new defense and other high-tech industries. Democrats in the South and, to a lesser degree, the West maintained their commitment to trade liberalization. Conversely, the heavily unionized states of the North and Pacific Coast sent Democrats to Congress who were now protectionist in the face of declining regional fortunes and unemployment. This was especially true of New England and Mid-Atlantic lawmakers, responding to the departing industries and increasing unemployment in their districts. Indeed, a state's unemployment rate had a large effect on its representatives' support for free trade; increasing the unemployment rate by 1 percent results in a 6 percent drop in mean support for free trade. Unemployment was highest in the North (where it ranged from 6.0 percent in East North Central states to 6.9 percent in New England) and Pacific Coast states (8.7 percent) and lowest in the South (from 4.5 percent in the South Atlantic to 5.2 percent in East South Central).[49]

State culture also appears to have played a role in Democratic support for

TABLE 3.2. ANALYSIS OF DEMOCRATIC SUPPORT FOR
FREE TRADE, 1973

	b (se)
Constant	0.243 (0.149)
Unemployment	−6.443*** (2.035)
Export dependence	4.805** (2.054)
Size of agricultural sector	0.010*** (0.003)
South	0.192*** (0.064)
West	0.134* (0.074)
Pacific Coast	0.168 (0.105)

Sources: Free trade vote data calculated by author from the Interuniversity
Consortium for Political and Social Research (ICPSR); exports and unemployment (1972 Statistical Abstract); agriculture (USDA Agricultural Statistics,
1973).
OLS analysis: Adj. R^2: .59; N: 40
*$p \leq$ .10; **$p \leq$ .05; ***$p \leq$ .01
For more details about the OLS analysis, see note 48.

free trade. Once key economic factors are controlled, the West and South were still more likely to support free trade than the North, which probably reflects an independent effect of regional political cultures on lawmakers' trade votes.[50] Despite the federal government's role in the economic development of these regions, both the South and the West harbored strains of skepticism about the actions of the national government, and this may have made the rhetoric of free trade appealing. The politics of earlier years that linked trade to containment policy also likely helped cement support for free trade, given the robust anti-communism that existed in these regions. The South, in particular, had a deep ideological commitment to free trade relative to the North, which had long been more receptive to economic management by the government and was less committed to militaristic foreign policy. For southern Democrats, ideology and interest dovetailed to drive the region's continued support for free trade.

While the situation was only a shadow of what was to come, by the early

1970s a concentration of economic decline was noticeable in the industrial core economies of the northern and Pacific Coast states, the areas that had powered the country's economic growth for most of the previous century. The story of deindustrialization is by now quite familiar. Due to the costs associated with aging plants and equipment, a highly unionized labor force, growing competition from the rebuilt and reorganized economies of other industrialized countries, and diminishing energy resources, U.S. industrial manufacturing found itself increasingly disadvantaged in the world economy. The basic industries of the North which had defined the country's earlier economic strength—steel, rubber, textiles, and autos—suffered the most.[51]

In the face of escalating costs, larger and more flexible companies took advantage of developments in technology and transportation to move their production sites out of the country or to the less expensive regions of the South and West. Foreign production sites, with their tax advantages, access to restricted markets, lower wage rates, and fewer regulations, offered multinational corporations significant business advantages. Similarly, the "friendly business climate" regions of the South and West had histories of less government interference, more local government inducements, lower costs of living, cheaper energy prices, and non-unionized labor, and thus provided many of the same advantages. As businesses moved out of the states of the old industrial core, so did jobs and people.[52]

Between 1960 and 1970, growth in nonagricultural employment was highest in the South and lowest in the North.[53] With fewer new employment opportunities available, these plant closings and job losses hit northern workers and the labor unions that represented them especially hard. Although national unemployment in March 1973 stood at 5 percent, 35 major labor areas recorded unemployment above 6 percent and were defined as "experiencing substantial or persistent unemployment;" 34 of these 35 areas were in the North and Pacific Coast states.[54] This loss of jobs eroded union strength. Even when jobs did not disappear, the threat of a more mobile capital effectively silenced the demands of labor.

By 1973, the trends in regional industrial decline were well enough advanced that organized labor, for the first time in its history, shifted support away from free trade and instead advocated protection.[55] Although courted heavily by the administration, AFL-CIO president George Meany proved unshakable in his opposition to the trade bill, saying of the Nixon trade proposal that it "would open the door to further deterioration of America's position in the world economy and to the further export of American jobs."[56] Members of the Ways and Means Committee made further efforts to placate labor in their version of the bill, which included stronger adjustment assistance and import relief provisions. Labor was equally dissatisfied with this version, however, calling the committee's bill "worse than no bill at all."[57]

In light of the North's economic deterioration and with this signal from labor, which formed one of the Democrats' strongest bases of support, northern Democrats took up the fight for protection. Cognizant of their party's history of supporting free trade and the reversal they were contemplating, they urged fellow party members to recognize the profundity of the economic changes that were occurring and to rethink the value of trade liberalization. The case of Representative James Burke, a Democrat from Massachusetts, illustrates the transformation that occurred during the 1960s among many northern Democrats. In 1962, Burke voted across the board for free trade, but eleven years later he was the sponsor of a broad-based import quota bill (the Burke-Hartke bill) and a leading protectionist.

In a long speech on the floor, Burke described the changes in the world economy since passage of the 1962 Trade Expansion Act. Noting the growing barriers to export of America's manufactured goods posed by the European Common Market and other emerging regional trading blocs, the rejuvenation of other industrial economies, and the growing energy crisis, Burke stressed that conditions would only worsen and that this justified the need to break with the past.

> I rise today to urge defeat of the so-called Trade Reform Act of 1973. As I have said so many times over the past months, this bill would encourage the President to take almost any action he chooses to encourage manufactured imports and will, if passed, lead to the erosion of America's industries, America's skills and jobs, and further inflationary pressures from poorly managed trade policies. . . . When the trend seems to be steadily moving in one direction over an extended period of time, and against us at that, then it would appear that a reexamination of existing trade policies and practices is not only appropriate but essential for any nation whose prosperity is of concern to its leaders. In other words, there comes a time when sitting a crisis out, or riding out a storm, can make an already serious situation worse and rather than contributing to one's chances of survival can be a recipe for certain disaster.[58]

Burke, like many other northerners, equated the manufacturing decline of their region with the economic decline of the nation, which justified their demand that the country's long-standing liberal trade policy be "reexamined." But northern Democrats decried more than just the economic effects of liberalization. They now challenged the ideological underpinnings of free trade as well. Pennsylvania Representative John Dent voiced concerns that were particularly potent in the aging cities of the North and Pacific Coast states.

> Sixteen million on relief, 14 million drawing food stamps, 7,695,000 drawing unemployment compensation checks as of the first week July, 30 million on public so-called social security. Millions more on pensions—all nonproducers in our economy. . . . How come, if [the trade bill] is such a great, wonderful, public give away and peacemaker, we have had war every year since it passed in 1962, we have had unemployment growing week after week and have had a great deal of sacrifice we never had before?[59]

The bitterness of Dent's remarks reflects the deep divisions splitting the Democratic Party across economic and foreign policy and helps to explain the intensity of the newfound northern antagonism to free trade. Growing economic difficulties meant that more people would have to rely on social welfare and unemployment compensation programs, placing a particularly heavy burden on northern states, where (as Chapter 4 makes clear) such programs were among the country's largest and most expensive. As far as northern Democrats were concerned, if free trade meant more job loss and plant shutdowns, it also meant community abandonment, inner-city deterioration, more people on public assistance rolls, and greater strain on shrinking state revenues.

At the same time, northern Democrats were increasingly unwilling to support the idea that free trade was vital to American foreign policy goals, as Dent's comments also make clear. Part of the success of free trade in earlier decades had rested on its ideological centrality to containment policy; trading with allies helped secure their loyalties and bolstered their economies. By 1973, Vietnam had rent the consensus on containment, and northern Democrats were often the loudest detractors.[60] While President Nixon was trying to forge a new link between global economic trade and the peace of détente with the Soviet Union, Democrats in the North, representing districts that had been hurt by free trade and a growing new constituency of antiwar activists, were no longer willing to make any ideological justification for free trade. With their practical investment in free trade over and with an "unwinnable" and unpopular war making containment policy less attractive, northern Democrats were unwilling to support claims of a connection between free trade and foreign policy security goals.[61]

Wary of the protectionist label and the Smoot-Hawley legacy with which it was associated, northern Democrats adopted new language, referring to "fair trade," a position of being open to trade agreements but sensitive to the impact of changing times and conditions on small businesses and workers. Bella Abzug of New York argued for a "rethinking of what constitutes a free trade position,"[62] and Harold Donohue of Massachusetts claimed that while he had "never . . . been opposed to fair trade agreements legislation," he opposed this particular bill. In what would soon come to be the classic "fair trade" rhetoric of those wanting to limit trade liberalization, Donohue went on to explain,

> the expanded import programs embedded in this measure will unquestionably accelerate the disastrous decline and expiration of domestic industries, such as the textile, shoe, leather, machine tools, steel, electric appliances, and long list of others that are so vital to the sustained economy of my own home region and the entire Nation. . . . Those of us who have maintained a steadfast concern for our essential regional and national domestic industries and their employees ask only for a constructive measure that will actually provide fair and reasonable adjustments and considerations to these beleaguered American businesses and citizens in order that they may have an equal chance to compete in our domestic markets with excessive foreign imports and I emphasize that an equal chance is all that these good citizens want.[63]

Demanding that government roll back its trade policy now made sense in the increasingly disadvantaged North, and the rhetoric used fit northern Democrats' emphasis on equal opportunity and economic justice. Republicans and southern Democrats both found this case less compelling and continued to rally behind free trade. Northeastern Republicans had favored free trade since the height of Cold War internationalism, but by 1973, the new torchbearers for free trade were Republicans from the West and Pacific Coast states. In the 1962 trade battle, 85 percent of western Republicans had voted for protection; now, 80 percent voted for free trade. Similarly, Pacific Coast Republicans shifted from 70 percent support for protection to 95 percent support for free trade. With support for free trade coming from Republicans in all regions, the party was more uniform in its trade position in 1973 than it had been in earlier decades or than it would be in coming years. Far from signaling acquiescence to northern Republican policy dictates, the reversal on trade coming out of the West was indicative of the regional direction on which the party was hoping to build.

Despite rapidly diversifying economies, the West as a whole remained the country's premier agricultural region, and growers of crops such as wheat, soybeans, and corn were now increasingly dependent on their ability to export. Agricultural groups and their representatives were among the most vocal supporters of free trade in the 1973 debates, a shift in position that reflects changes in world agricultural trade in the late 1960s and early 1970s. In the latter half of the 1960s, American farmers had begun to suffer as a result of the European Economic Community's newly instituted Common Agricultural Policy (CAP), which provided a system of subsidies, tariffs, and price supports to aid European agriculture. The export of CAP-protected agricultural products from the U.S. declined by 40 percent in the last three years of the 1960s alone.[64] Additionally, international farm commodity prices leapt after 1971, to the benefit of American exporters.[65] Agriculture became a key proponent of the trade liberalization bill, particularly in the area of nontariff barriers, such as export subsidies and quotas, which was the focus of the 1973 bill.[66]

Republicans and southern Democrats argued in defense of free trade. Calling the trade bill of "vital importance to agriculture," Republican Wiley Mayne of Iowa stated emphatically, "American farmers must continue to have the opportunity to trade—to share in the growth of their traditional markets and to seek greater access to new markets."[67] Georgia Democrat Phillip Landrum concurred with Mayne, remarking, "I would say to the Members from my region of the country, which is concerned primarily with raw agricultural products and textiles, that it is imperative that we have this rule and have this bill." Landrum warned that without the legislation, the region's agriculture and industry would suffer employment losses and setbacks.[68]

Southern and western support for free trade did not rest only on pressure from agriculture. Much of the new manufacturing base of these regions was also invested in trade liberalization. Spurred by the infusion of defense dollars, companies producing high-technology electronics and other instruments, transport equipment, and the aerospace and chemical industries were in the forefront of new manufacturing development in the West and South. As states like Arizona, Texas, Florida, and North Carolina, along with Pacific Coast areas such as southern California, became centers of new economic growth, their representatives promoted free trade as a way to preserve and create jobs. Minnesota Republican Bill Frenzel argued that his state needed foreign trade opportunities not just to benefit Minnesota farmers but also to aid workers in the state's new growth areas of data processing and other scientific industries.[69]

The mix of agriculture and high-tech also accounts for Pacific Coast Republicans' new demand for free trade.[70] California had long possessed a diverse economy, and the predominantly Democratic representatives of older manufacturing areas voted, like northern Democrats, for protection, while representatives of the newly modernizing agribusiness and defense areas tended to favor free trade. (That both agriculture and new technology–based industries in California and throughout the West would be beneficiaries of liberalization is not surprising, because it was in these two areas that the United States still maintained comparative advantage in the 1970s.[71])

In some ways, the South's economic landscape mirrored California's. Despite economic developments and high rates of growth, a subset of industry, especially in the Southeast, still concentrated in traditional low-wage manufacturing sectors, such as lumber, apparel, and textiles. Indeed, one out of five manufacturing employees in the South in the 1970s worked in textiles.[72] Although imports heavily pressured industries such as textiles, comments like those of Representative Landrum make clear that even these areas of the South by and large supported the trade legislation. President Nixon, as Kennedy had done, explicitly solicited and aided the textile industry before Congress considered the bill, by securing a GATT restraint on manmade fibers, wool, and cotton textiles. Because this agreement depended on passage of the trade bill, textile interests, unlike the older manufacturing interests of the North, were vested in the bill's passage. Nixon's "southern strategy" brought them on board.[73]

Nixon's targeting of the South was part of a larger regional reorientation of the Republican Party. After Barry Goldwater's campaign in 1964, Republicans had recognized the South as an untapped electoral resource. More than just Republican presidential candidates fared well in the South. As Chapter 2 pointed out, congressional seats lost to Democrats in northern core states in the 1960s and 1970s were at least partially offset by Republican gains in the West and in the former Democratic stronghold of the South. Thus, real electoral incentives spurred Republicans to pursue policies favorable to the South—and bend potentially unfavorable ones to better fit the region's needs.

Trade policy fits this pattern. By 1973, Republicans had established their party as supportive of free trade. Cementing their position in opposition to the Democratic majority, now located in the older industrial areas of the North and Pacific Coast, Republicans demonstrated the compatibility of their agenda with that of southern Democrats, whether they hailed from new or old economy districts. If northerners were wresting control of the Democratic Party away from the South, Republicans were ready to profit.

By uniting southern Democrats with Republicans in the West and Pacific Coast to pass the Trade Reform Act, Nixon followed the path Kennedy had laid before him: a multiregional and bipartisan coalition in favor of free trade. While Kennedy sought to bind the fortunes of South and North with his trade proposal, Nixon sought to build a new Republican order in the Sun Belt: the rising, export-oriented regions of South and West. What allowed both a Democrat and a Republican to use free trade for the purpose of building very different party coalitions was the shifting of the regional economic order. The conservative coalition of Republicans and southern Democrats that passed the 1973 House legislation peaked in the early 1970s and gave the bill its bipartisan flavor, yet it was also part of the machinery that set in motion the political reorganization of the regions and parties. In subsequent years, as Republicans gained further control of the South and West, the conservative coalition would make fewer appearances. Instead, southern and western Republicans squared off against northern Democrats over the issue of trade, leading to greater levels of partisanship.

THE PARTISAN BATTLE: FAST-TRACK TRADE AUTHORITY IN 1998

In the twenty-five years following passage of the 1974 Trade Reform Act, both the economic environment and the political landscape continued to evolve. Changes in the parties' regional bases, only beginning to reveal themselves in the early 1970s, developed further, driven in part by the parties' responses to the economic restructuring of the 1970s and 1980s. By the latter half of the 1990s, the Republican Party had shed all vestiges of its traditional northeastern establishment image. Whereas the Rockefeller Republican had defined the party in earlier decades, Georgia's Newt Gingrich and Texas's Tom DeLay had become the new standard bearers, particularly so in the aftermath of the 1994 "Republican Revolution." Similarly, the Democratic Party was now associated primarily with the interests of the northern and Pacific Coast states, and the concerns of what had come to be called the "Rust Belt" defined the party's political commitments. As region and party became increasingly synonymous, party conflict intensified. For the dwindling numbers of northern Republicans and southern Democrats, the increasing partisanship meant that they were often in the crossfire between the demands of their party and the demands of their constituents.

These dynamics were revealed in the 1998 battle over the renewal of presidential trade negotiating authority, specifically what were dubbed "fast-track" provisions. First established in 1974, fast-track procedures ensure but limit Congress's role in the president's negotiation of nontariff barriers. They enable the president to engage in negotiations but require that Congress be consulted about the negotiations and that it vote on the final agreements within 90 days in a straight up-or-down vote. Because fast-track provisions limit the ability of Congress to make changes to the trade agreements once they are submitted by the president, however, the granting of fast-track authority vests the executive with greater trading power. Fast-track authority is temporary; it had been renewed several times before being reconsidered in 1998. When brought to the floor in September 1998, after two years of effort, fast-track trade authority was defeated by a vote of 243 to 180, a significant victory for protectionist forces. In a sign of the times, it was delivered to President Bill Clinton, a Democrat out of Arkansas, whose political success derived from his ability to position himself as a centrist between the two regional and party poles defining the country's politics.

Unlike the trade issues in 1962 and 1974, the fast-track vote was intensely partisan. The vote on the rule under which to consider the legislation was essentially a straight party vote. Every Republican voted for the closed rule, while 96 percent of Democrats voted against it. Because Republicans held the majority, the closed rule passed. On the implementing legislation, 68 percent of Republicans voted to renew authority (or, for free trade). Democrats were even more unified in their opposition as 85 percent voted to deny fast-track authority to President Clinton, their own party's leader.

The trade debate in 1998 split the regions as well as the parties. Significant regional differences existed even within the parties (see Table 3.3), and these differences show that regional division was primary. Although the parties by this point were geographically sorted, the regional differences observed are not simply an artifact of where the parties were located, because they hold even

TABLE 3.3. REPRESENTATIVES VOTING IN FAVOR

OF TRADE PROTECTION, 1998

	ALL REPRE- SENTATIVES	DEMOCRATS	REPUBLICANS
North	**120**	**91**	**28**
	(95.4)	(79.4)	(23.1)
Pacific Coast	33	25	8
	(36)	(28.2)	(9.5)
South	69	41	**28**
	(77.7)	(48.7)	(25)
West	18	12	6
	(30.9)	(12.8)	(12.4)

Source: Calculated from roll call data.

Notes: Number voting *against* fast track (HR 2621). Numbers are observed values of the vote. Numbers in parentheses are expected values, given the division of overall votes and regions. Numbers in **bold** signify groups in which the observed value is greater than the expected value (i.e., actual support for protection is higher than expected). Pearson's chi-square as follows: All representatives (30.126, p = .000); Democrats (22.607, p = .000); Republicans (7.154, p = .067).

within the parties. As the first column of the table makes clear, regardless of party, northern lawmakers were disproportionately disposed toward protection, while representatives of other regions, which were more competitive internationally, were more inclined toward free trade. In other words, more northern lawmakers supported protection than would be expected, given the overall number of northern representatives and the overall number of representatives voting for protection (there were 120 northern protectionist votes, relative to an expected 95.4 votes). Turning to the dynamics within the parties, while a majority of Democrats from each region voted against fast track, opposition was greatest in the North, the regional seat of protection. Similarly, the majority of Republicans in each region voted for fast track, yet support was greatest in the West, the new center of free trade.[74]

DIVERGENT REGIONS, POLARIZED PARTIES

By 1998, northern and Pacific Coast representatives made up 64 percent of House Democrats. During the economic dislocations of the 1970s and 1980s, they had built the party's protectionist reputation by demanding "fair trade" on behalf of failing industries and unemployed workers. In an effort to counteract Ronald Reagan's landslide reelection in 1984, Democrats had taken advantage of worsening trade deficits to drive home their message of retaliatory trade restrictions. Sounding uncharacteristically bellicose, they argued for the need to "get tough" with countries (namely Japan) whose policies were depicted as unfairly handicapping American manufactured products. Trade at this time was the "Democratic macho issue," according to Representative Tony Coelho of California, the Democratic campaign committee chair in the House.[75] In a particularly vivid demonstration of the partisan posture in 1988, Missouri Democrat Dick Gephardt offered an amendment to the Omnibus Trade Bill to establish import barriers against countries that failed to immediately reduce their bilateral trade surpluses with the United States. Nearly 80 percent of Democrats supported this amendment while only 10 percent of Republicans did so. The concept of fair trade, first introduced into debates in the 1970s, was now Democratic Party dogma, and despite the nationwide economic recovery of the 1990s, House Democrats remained staunch promoters of protective trade measures.

The electoral stakes involved in the fast-track debate of 1998 were particularly high for congressional Democrats as a result of the 1993 North American Free Trade Agreement (NAFTA). NAFTA had been a major and early victory for President Bill Clinton. As a leader of the "New Democrat" movement of political moderates, a movement largely based in the South and West, Clinton, a for-

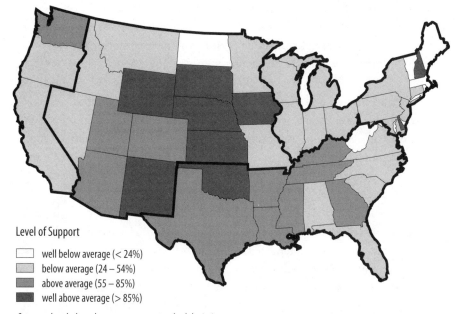

Level of Support

☐ well below average (< 24%)
☐ below average (24 – 54%)
☐ above average (55 – 85%)
■ well above average (> 85%)

Category breaks based on mean ± one standard deviation.

Figure 3.5
House Support for Free Trade, 1998

mer Arkansas governor, was well aware of his party's difficulties in his home region. He hoped as president to remold the Democratic Party image to revive its prospects nationwide, and his successful promotion of NAFTA was part of this strategy: by signaling Democratic friendliness to the business and financial interests promoting the bill, Clinton countered the protectionist image his party had developed since the 1970s. While NAFTA contained environmental and labor provisions, environmentalists and unions were generally disappointed by the legislation's weak enforcement mechanisms with regard to these issues.[76]

By 1998, congressional Democrats were being called to answer for Clinton's NAFTA. With the post-NAFTA dissatisfaction of environmentalists and labor spurring them forward, House Democrats, especially northerners, voiced their renewed support for trade restrictions. As the map of House support for free trade in 1998 (Figure 3.5) shows, northerners were unified in their resistance to fast-track provisions. In debates, they spoke most often of the need to save American jobs, claiming that liberalization would make it easier for multinational companies to move to cheaper production sites outside of the country and to outsource jobs. Indiana's Dan Visclosky attributed the loss of 72 American jobs per day to the implementation of NAFTA alone.[77] Citing layoffs in Ohio by Levi Strauss, Kodak, and Huffy, Representative Marcy Kaptur blamed fast-track procedures for worsening trade deficits and argued that the types of trade agreements made since 1974 were biased toward large business interests. "Our trade policy serves the needs of nominally American multinational corporations whose business visions and plans are global in scope and which maintain no national allegiance," Kaptur railed. "Our trade policy has failed America's small business families, America's working families, and America's consumers."[78]

These Democrats' rhetoric stands in stark contrast to that common in the 1960s, the heyday of late New Deal internationalism. No longer did it argue for the national interest but often returned to the classic division between big business and labor. To the extent that Democrats did invoke the national interest, it was to question the patriotism of multinational corporate leaders. While some Democrats, such as Rosa DeLauro of Connecticut, shunned the party's protectionist reputation, arguing that the dissension was over the means, not the ends, of free trade, others found it advantageous to embrace protectionist imagery and rhetoric that rang with economic populist overtones.[79] Arguing for the interests of Main Street over Wall Street, Illinois Democrat William Lipinski said,

> Free trade advocates want the American people to believe that those of us who oppose fast track are ignorant of the new international economy and are pursuing an "America-last" strategy. They think we are protectionists, as if it were some kind of dirty word. Well, if trying to protect American jobs, the American standard of living, and American working families makes me a protectionist, then I will gladly wear that label.[80]

For Democratic lawmakers in the old industrial economy regions of the North and Pacific Coast, where labor was still influential, supporting free trade and President Clinton had become a political liability.[81] Despite declining membership, unions in 1996 still covered 19 percent of all workers on average in the northern states and 20 percent in Pacific Coast states. In New York and Michigan, unions covered more than a quarter of workers. By comparison, only 13 percent of workers in the average state in the West and 10 percent in the South were affiliated with unions. Also indicative of regional union strength, 11 of the 14 southern states and 10 of the 15 states of the West were right-to-work states, while no such states existed in the North or Pacific Coast regions.[82] Union strength was regional and its opposition to fast-track authority was in abundant evidence. The AFL-CIO spent an estimated $1 million on advertising against the legislation.[83]

While Democrats sought to reassure labor with their trade stance, they also tried to appeal to environmentalists, who, in the 1990s, increasingly joined labor in opposing unrestricted free trade. Opposition to fast-track authority centered on the language of the legislation, which environmentalists argued was written to enable the exclusion of important environmental objectives.[84] For Democrats coming from areas that were more export dependent, such as those in the Pacific Coast states, environmental concerns generally, and the deleterious effects of NAFTA on the environment specifically, were often the reason cited for representatives' opposition to fast-track legislation. California Democrat Nancy Pelosi is a case in point. Saying that the people of San Francisco thrived on trade but that they also recognized the link between the economy and the environment, Pelosi lamented that the legislation did not give the president the needed authority to implement environmental controls; because of this, she said, she would have to vote against fast track.[85]

By making the concerns of environmentalists a central tenet of their trade stance, Democrats were attending to a new and growing constituency, also located largely in the North and Pacific Coast states, both of which host key national environmental advocacy organizations.[86] As important, Democratic voters were much greater supporters of regulating business to protect the environment than Republican constituents. Among Democrats, there was significant regional variation, with the greatest support for environmental regulations being concentrated in the North and Pacific Coast. Twenty-six percent of Democrats in these two regions strongly supported environmental regulations in 1996, while only 17 percent of Democrats in the South and 14 percent in the West indicated that they felt this way.[87]

Democrats' coupling of the concerns of labor and environmentalists proved a savvy electoral move, uniting very different types of constituents in the party's growth areas—traditional economic progressives and social (or "postmaterial") progressives. While the combination was ideologically justified by the party's commitment to government activism, labor and environmentalists have not always been happy bedfellows, and uniting the two represented the front line in the Democrats' battle to merge economically progressive with socially progressive constituents.

Across the aisle, Republicans promoted free trade and the need for new markets, such as those found in a post-NAFTA Mexico, as necessary prerequisites for business and agriculture to succeed in the global economy. Here, too,

Republican rhetoric served the interests of some more than others. Though Republicans from around the country voted for free trade, the strength of Republican free trade sentiment was in the West and Southwest, as the map in Figure 3.5 suggests. These states were somewhat or very much above the national average in their support for renewing presidential fast-track authority.

Western Republicans were the most unified of the four regional groups in favor of free trade, with fully 85 percent voting for renewal of fast-track procedures. In the West, economic development had accelerated and diversified with each postwar decade. By the 1990s, the economies of western states were among the most integrated of all states' into the global economy, and western producers depended on their ability to export, especially to markets in Asia and Latin America. Agriculture still characterizes many of the plains states, but capital investment, the relocation of firms, and high-technology employment has increasingly benefited states such as Arizona, Colorado, and Utah, as well as those along the Pacific Coast. In the Southwest, developments in petroleum and chemical industries have helped generate income and, to a lesser extent, employment growth.[88] By the mid-1990s, states in the West were also among the country's most dependent on service industries for income. Sixty percent of western states in 1996 derived more than twice as much of their gross state product from services and from the "FIRE" industries (finance, insurance, and real estate) than from manufacturing.[89] Energy, insurance, telecommunications, and transportation industries were big beneficiaries of NAFTA, and restrictions on access and exports were expected to ease further in coming years.[90]

By the time Congress was deciding on renewal of fast-track legislation in 1998, the West was the regional frontrunner in export growth. During the first six years of the 1990s, western states had seen an average increase of 125 percent in their exports. States in the South and Pacific Coast were next, with increases of 81 and 79 percent, respectively. Northern states saw the least growth, with exports increasing 72 percent.[91] The contrast between the West and the North elucidate when we look at trade balances in different sectors in the 1990s. Despite the country's overall trade deficit, key sectors in the western economy, such as advanced-technology products, agriculture, and services, still maintained large trade surpluses in 1996.[92] In agriculture, in 1996, for example, exports exceeded imports by $26.7 billion, and the farm products in which exports most surpassed imports were largely western: wheat, soybeans, corn, meat, and animal hides. In that same year in the area of manufactured goods—which still constitutes the bulk of trade—the value of imports exceeded exports by $176 billion. Much of this deficit, however, was concentrated in the fixed heavy manufacturing industries of the North: machinery, iron, steel, and automobiles.[93]

Representatives from throughout the West and Southwest—Minnesota, Iowa, Kansas, Texas—argued for fast-track procedures on behalf of both agribusiness and high-technology constituents. Of particular concern in the 1998 debates was the growing financial crisis in Asia, a major market for western agriculture, and the effects of 1996 legislation phasing out farm subsidies. Republican representatives urged all rural representatives to unite to pass fast-track legislation without delay, to stave off the potential repercussions of the crisis.[94] George Nethercutt, a Republican from Washington State, put it most simply, "If you support agriculture, vote for fast track."[95]

While much of the West and South were prospering, development of the southern economy had continued along two distinct tracks since the 1970s. As a result, the region overall was not quite as unified on trade as the North and West. While states like Texas continued to prosper, low-wage and older manufacturing areas in the Southeast began to experience the same decline that had beset the North. States such as South Carolina and North Carolina (outside of the Research Triangle) suffered from serious setbacks in industries long plagued by difficulties, such as apparel, textiles, and furniture. Southern representatives were therefore divided in their opinions on trade. Greater support for protection concentrated in the Southeast, an area that was also more Democratic than the Southwest (44% of House seats were held by Democrats in the Southeast as opposed to 24% in the Southwest).

THE PARTISAN EPILOGUE: TRADE IN THE 2000s

On the heels of congressional Democrats' rebuke of Clinton in 1998, President George W. Bush made renewing fast-track authority a priority after he assumed office in 2001. By reassuring potential trade partners that Congress would not alter the agreements negotiated with his administration, fast-track authority would allow the president to aggressively pursue new trade opportunities. Bush even renamed the legislation the Trade Promotion Authority.

Congressional debate over the bill was fierce, and the House passed an initial version in December 2001 by just one vote. True to partisan patterns of the 1980s and 1990s, 89 percent of the Republican members in the House voted to authorize fast-track authority while only 10 percent of Democrats did. On the conference bill, which contained increased concessions (including subsidized health coverage for affected workers and injured firms but lacked the labor and environmental standards demanded by Democrats), 88 percent of House Republicans voted in favor compared to just 12 percent of Democrats.

In addition to sustaining the partisanship of the 1990s, the 2002 trade bill generated the same pattern of geographic support as in recent decades. Support was greatest in the West, where 69 percent of representatives voted for the conference bill. The South followed closely, with 60 percent of the region's representatives endorsing fast-track authority. In contrast, neither the North nor the Pacific Coast regions gave majority support. Thirty-nine percent of northern lawmakers and 44 percent of representatives from the Pacific Coast voted to give the president fast-track trade authority. With labor and environmental groups again in opposition, few Democrats were willing to defect from the party line. Of the 25 Democrats who voted for free trade, only one was from the North, Representative Hill from Indiana. In contrast, 3 were from the far more sparsely populated (and less Democratic) West and 7 were from the Pacific Coast. More than half, 14, of the defecting Democrats were from the South. These Democrats, all with ties to business, were subjected to intensive lobbying and pressure from key administration officials before the vote. Of the 27 Republican House members who voted for protection, none were from the West and only two were from the Pacific Coast; 12 were from the North. And, reflecting the mixed impact of trade on the southern economy, 13 of the Republicans' protectionist votes came from the South. Many of these lawmakers represented textile districts, such as those in North Carolina (where 4 of 7 Republicans voted against the final bill), which anticipated losses as a result of the bill.[96]

By mid-decade, impending difficulties for Republicans on the issue of trade were increasingly apparent. The 2005 Central American Free Trade Act (CAFTA) was passed with essentially the same partisan and geographic divisions as the 2002 legislation, yet Republican leaders had greater difficulty generating party unity. In a rare visit to Congress, President Bush went to the Hill on the morning of House debate to urge support for his bill. Even then, Republican leaders were forced to keep the roll call vote open for an hour in order to cajole from their members the necessary votes. Conversely, Democrats increased their unity from 2002, with only 15 party members defecting to the free trade position, 8 of whom were from the South.[97]

The electoral consequences of these trade battles were apparent in the 2006 congressional elections, especially in the Midwest and South where lawmakers' positions on this issue led to tight races and upsets. In Ohio, the swing state that had brought victory to Bush in 2004, outspoken anti-trade Democrat Sherrod Brown successfully challenged Republican Senator Mike DeWine. In Michigan, incumbent Democratic Senator Debbie Stabenow was forced to run campaign ads touting her toughness on trade to defend her seat. And in the South, lawmakers' 2005 CAFTA votes, both for and against, were issues in a number of campaigns. In two of the day's closest elections, North Carolina House Republican Robin Hayes, a textile heir who cast the deciding vote in favor of CAFTA, defeated his challenger, a former textile worker, by a mere 329 votes, while Georgia Representative John Barrow, a Democrat, won by just 864 votes, after his opposition to CAFTA was made a campaign issue.[98]

As the number of plant closures and outsourced jobs has increased, voters in the 2000s have made it clear that they care about lawmakers' positions on trade. Yet, which position, free trade or protection, makes electoral sense still depends largely on the region from which the lawmaker hails. With the parties increasingly aligned along a regional axis, trade partisanship continues for now. But with older industry in the South in an increasingly perilous position, rising protectionist sentiment in the region is clearly a possibility; and in that case, a new bipartisan coalition favoring protection may develop. If it does not, Democrats' exploitation of the issue stands to help the party make inroads into the region.

REGIONAL CHANGE, ELECTORAL INCENTIVE, AND TRADE PARTISANSHIP

In the early 1960s, the New Deal Democratic regime still dominated national politics. On the basis of a strong manufacturing-based economy and with the threat of Soviet expansion, the party established a free trade agenda that was virtually unassailable. The economic benefits of trade were widely distributed, and it was a justifiable component of the party's national security message—making it a perfect vehicle for maintaining and strengthening the party's cross-regional coalition. Using trade policy for that purpose was necessary, too, because cracks in the North-South alliance were, by the early 1960s, beginning to surface on issues such as race. The regional incentives for free trade were strong enough not only to help the party fortify its coalition but to undercut the Republican opposition. Northern Republicans' support of free trade led to bipartisanship.

By the 1970s, with both economy and ideology in doubt, trade had lost its potency as a tool for uniting Democrats. As American postwar economic hegemony diminished, northern manufacturing suffered disproportionately. At the same time, the build-up of the country's defense capabilities played an important role in the development of the West and South and led to the greater integration of these regions into the international economy. With regional fortunes diverging, northern and southern Democrats also divided, and Republican electoral opportunity was found in this split. Northern and Pacific Coast Democrats took the party in a protectionist direction, cultivating labor, old industry, and environmentalists, and strengthening their regions' hold on the national party. Southerners, wooed by the Republican shift to liberalization and the party's accommodation of their region, found a new ally in the similarly changing West, and the usefulness of trade as a coalition-building tool was resurrected.

Both 1962 and 1973 were moments of bipartisanship, yet the first was predicated on the use of trade to bind a cross-regional coalition going into decline, and the second was given form by a cross-regional coalition just emerging. The bipartisanship of the old conservative coalition foretold a shift in the geography of the parties, and as this occurred, trade conflict that was both regional and partisan intensified.

Ideological divergence and changes in House operations played roles in the polarization of the parties over trade policy. Yet, the parties did not become more dogmatic in their beliefs about trade; they actually switched positions. They did so because of changing regional conditions and regional political identifications and the emergence of new political constraints and opportunities. Similarly, rule changes in the House in the 1970s which curbed the power of committee chairs clearly aided northern Democrats in the pursuit of their policy agenda by removing obstacles that had been placed by senior southern Democrats. But, the very desire for rule changes was a sign of the illness of the New Deal regime, and the policy agenda being thwarted was largely a northern one. Thus, while institutional factors contributed to the reorganization and subsequent intensification of party conflict, they were part and parcel of a regional strategy.

From the 1930s to the 1970s, trade policy changed from being a powerful tool in the New Deal Democratic arsenal to a liability for the party. It was not the biggest liability; by the 1960s, issues connected to race were a more significant danger for Democrats. Incorporating measures such as industry-specific protections and links to security issues, trade policy afforded Democrats and then Republicans the opportunity to negotiate the support necessary to keep a political coalition together even when economic interests proved insufficient to that task. Welfare policy functioned similarly for many years, helping the Democrats retain and even enhance power in the face of various re-gional interests. Yet, as issues of race created contention in the 1960s, the wel-fare compromises fashioned in the past became untenable. Linked to race and to state economies, welfare policy ultimately inflicted irreparable harm on the New Deal regime. Chapter 4 examines this downward spiral in detail.

CHAPTER 4

CHANGE COMES TO THE COTTON BELT

RACE, REGION, AND THE POLITICS OF WELFARE POLICY

IN 1996, the federal government terminated what had been the country's premier program of cash assistance to poor families, Aid to Families with Dependent Children (AFDC), the origins of which rested in the Social Security legislation of the New Deal. The 1996 welfare reform legislation did away with the entitlement status of AFDC, instituting time limits on payments to recipients and handing over control of the program to state governments, delivering the funding in the form of block grants. An initiative of House Republicans and one of the party's early triumphs after winning control of Congress in 1994, welfare reform signaled the crumbling of a major edifice of the New Deal Democratic regime. Not unexpectedly, the two-year battle over it was hard fought and intensely partisan.

The 1996 legislation capped thirty years of efforts by both parties to reform the country's welfare system, during which time there was increasing partisanship on the issue. Figure 4.1 shows changing levels of party difference on all social welfare issues in the postwar era.[1]

Partisanship over welfare policy reached its lowest point in the late 1960s before beginning to climb steadily. These trends on social welfare in general mirrored those in party battles over AFDC specifically. Congress often instituted changes to AFDC through amendments to general Social Security legislation,

Figure 4.1
Mean Difference between Parties on All Social Welfare Votes, 80th through 105th Congresses,
1947–1998
Source: Calculated from vote data provided by Keith Poole and Howard Rosenthal at voteview.com.

yet there also was a series of legislative efforts confined to public assistance, including welfare reform initiatives put forth by almost every administration
since Kennedy's. Figure 4.2 illustrates not only the trend in party conflict in
each of these successive efforts but also party position on welfare.[2]

Bipartisanship on the welfare expansion legislation of the early 1960s was
the product of strong support from Democrats and from roughly half of the Republican Party. In the late 1960s and early 1970s, bipartisanship was the result
of the parties' moving closer together on welfare; Democratic support for expansion dropped somewhat while Republican support increased. After these
episodes of bipartisanship, the partisan gulf again began to widen. Partisanship was fully restored by the late 1970s, lasting through the 1990s and beyond.
Unlike trade policy, on which party positions switched, general party positions
on welfare remained consistent. Throughout the postwar era, Democrats have
been the party more in favor of extending, expanding, and, by the 1970s, fed-

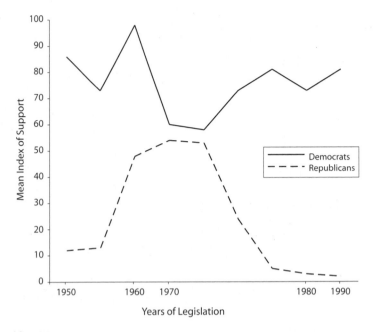

Figure 4.2
Mean Party Support for Welfare Expansion, 81st through 104th Congresses, 1949–1996
Source: Calculated from roll call data.
Note: Figure represents major welfare legislation, as described in note 2. The number of key welfare bills voted on each decade varied.

eralizing AFDC, while Republicans have attempted to restrict welfare and to minimize federal contributions to the program, which federal and state governments jointly administered and funded.

Given the stability of the parties' stances, it would be easy enough to dismiss the changes in welfare policy as the triumph of Republicans over Democrats, but these general party stances mask changes within the parties which, over the years, surfaced in congressional battles as regional differences. Regional cleavages within the parties were the most significant characteristic of the legislative coalitions on welfare in the early 1970s, and it was the alliance of northern Democrats with the Republican Party that created this period's bipartisanship. As with trade, the division between northern and southern Democrats on welfare contributed to the geographic shifts of the party bases, which stimulated the growing partisanship of the 1980s and 1990s. A sense of these geographic differences can be gleaned from Table 4.1 by examining changes in support for welfare programs by region over time.

Especially noteworthy is the plummet in southern support for welfare after the 1960s. All regions were favorably disposed toward expanding welfare in the early 1960s, as they were toward liberalizing trade. By the early 1970s, however, this issue, too, had become regionally divisive. Lawmakers from the North and Pacific Coast, representing states with rapidly growing welfare caseloads, continued their strong support for AFDC and focused on pushing program costs to the federal government, but support for the program dropped in the West and dropped precipitously in the South. By the late 1970s, a consensus was developing on some of the program's deficiencies, and it led to a decline in support for AFDC throughout the country, or, rather, to greater receptivity to reform initiatives. Still, no consensus existed on what that reform should look like, and the basic regional differences first evident in the early 1970s continued even through the 1996 legislation.

These shifts are evident in three episodes of welfare policy making which bear a striking similarity to the episodes of trade policy discussed in Chapter 3. The first case focuses on a welfare expansion initiative undertaken by President Kennedy in 1962, supported by members of both parties. Because of the massive

TABLE 4.1. LEVEL OF SUPPORT FOR WELFARE PROGRAMS BY REGION, 1962–1996

REGION	1962 (%)	1970 (%)	1988 (%)	1996 (%)	CHANGE FROM 1962 TO 1996 (− INDICATES LESS SUPPORT)
North	74	74	52	42	−32
New England	85	91	67	60	−25
Mid-Atlantic	80	73	50	44	−36
East North Central	64	70	49	35	−29
Pacific Coast	71	81	52	44	−27
South	91	24	37	35	−56
Southeast	90	24	37	34	−56
Southwest	92	24	38	37	−55
West	65	54	28	28	−37
West North Central	57	50	33	35	−22
Mountain	82	62	21	21	−61

Source: Calculated from roll call data.

Note: Based on mean index support score for pro-welfare position in the 87th, 91st, 100th, and 104th Congresses.

migration of African Americans from farms in the southern Cotton Belt to northern cities, the problem of urban poverty, especially among African Americans, was becoming increasingly visible. Representatives from both parties in the North strongly supported the welfare legislation, which was designed to combat unemployment among recipients by providing new monies for job training and social services. Most important to its passage, however, was that the 1962 Public Welfare Amendments married program expansion with greater state administrative flexibility, ensuring strong southern support. As described below, the legislation built a multifaceted patronage system for Democrats in the North while simultaneously enabling the southern planter elite to exercise paternalistic control over the benefits received by rural blacks and poor whites. By accommodating both regions, the bill helped hold together the New Deal coalition in an area of increasing weakness—racial politics. To make this patch effective, however, the regional incentives were made so strong that northern Republicans signed on as well. As with the 1962 trade initiative, the incentives for the North and South aligned to produce bipartisanship.

Ten years later President Nixon offered the Family Assistance Plan (FAP) to the country, an unprecedented effort to replace AFDC with a federally guaranteed, national minimum income. While the plan ultimately failed, it again received bipartisan support in the House. This time, however, the coalition that passed the legislation consisted largely of Democrats and Republicans from the North and Pacific Coast states. Lawmakers in these regions came from states with growing caseloads, dwindling resources, and escalating racial tensions in their cities, and they turned to FAP for federal assistance with all of these problems. While some of the most liberal northern Democrats resisted FAP as still insufficient for combating poverty, clear majorities in the North and Pacific Coast supported Nixon's proposal. In the South, however, the "Second Reconstruction" of race relations was well underway, and the region was hostile to any federal program that might accelerate this process, as FAP appeared to do. The intensity of southern opposition to Nixon's plan equaled supporters' fervor, establishing the poles in the welfare debate. The highly regional nature of this legislative contest demonstrates the extent to which welfare functioned as a wedge issue, one which Republican leaders deployed to break up the New Deal Democratic coalition.

The final case of welfare reform legislation, in 1995 and 1996, completes the story of regional and party division. Having successfully divided the Democratic Party in the 1970s, Republicans in subsequent decades built momentum to roll back the welfare state by drawing on support from their base in the South and increasingly in the West. New Deal Democrats had once forged a welfare package that accommodated the different demands of key northern and southern constituencies. Now, Republicans used their anti-welfare position to link new regional constituencies in the South and West. Welfare reform in the 1990s enabled the Republican Party to appeal simultaneously to religious conservatives and to business. The social regulatory aspects of the bill appealed to the religious right, a constituency geographically concentrated in the South and, to a lesser extent, in the West, while the bill's spending limits and the shift to state-managed block grants appealed to the party's business constituency. One of the elements that contributed to the business friendly climate of the South and West was the prominence of local "pro-growth" business and political elites who were committed to limiting government spending on many domestic programs. Republicans' rhetoric of reform, which stressed limited government and local control, thus had particular resonance in these regions.

With the historic North-South compromise on race and welfare broken, Democrats in the 1990s solidified their defense of federal responsibility for the program. Welfare growth had for decades been concentrated in states like New York, California, and Illinois. That growth, combined with past efforts by the party to meet the needs of their urban constituency with social welfare spending, had created an infrastructure that many in these regions were vested in maintaining. From the 1970s onward, as economic growth continued to slow, welfare caseloads expanded, and fiscal crises developed, northern and Pacific Coast states sought to expand (or at least maintain) federal involvement as a way to share the costs of their welfare infrastructure with other regions. And while the tremendous economic growth of the mid-1990s made reform more palatable than in the past, states in these two regions were still the least supportive of the 1996 reform legislation.

THE 1962 PUBLIC WELFARE AMENDMENTS

The changes to welfare proposed by President Kennedy in 1962 mark a turning point in the history of United States welfare policy. Between passage of the landmark Social Security Act of 1935 and the Public Welfare Amendments of 1962, the country's public assistance programs went through minor revisions, typically incremental expansions in eligibility, benefits, or federal participation. One scholar referred to the first thirty years of welfare policy making as the "era of normalcy." Another described welfare as an issue legislated "with few partisan overtones," while yet another described the period as one in which political controversy was limited to how best to expand the program.[3] By the time Congress was considering the 1962 legislation, however, AFDC (then ADC) had become the largest of the public assistance programs, and welfare was beginning to be cast as a problem in need of a solution. This would initiate more than thirty years of efforts at welfare reform.

Kennedy's proposal called for a shift in the goals and emphases of welfare. While the original goal of ADC had been to enable, indeed encourage, women who had been widowed (and, to a lesser extent, those who had been deserted) to stay at home to raise their children, the goal of the 1962 legislation was to facilitate the move of public assistance recipients, growing numbers of whom were divorced or had never been married, off welfare and into work. Correspondingly, the Kennedy proposal placed a new emphasis on family unemployment and a new priority on providing services—prevention, rehabilitation, and job training—to welfare recipients and potential recipients. While demanding more immediate resources, this type of service intervention, the president argued, would prepare individuals for economic independence and thus ultimately lead to decreases in welfare dependency.[4]

Financial support came from a number of measures, including a proposed increase in the federal reimbursement (from 50% to 75%) for state expenditures on services to recipients and potential recipients of public assistance. The plan authorized federal funds for training welfare personnel, and federal money was allocated for community work and recipient training programs. Relative to what had existed, this was a veritable give-away to service providers. Kennedy's proposal also included the continuation of welfare payments to children in two-parent families whose poverty was the result of parental unemployment (as opposed to desertion, disability, or death), a provision enacted for the first time on a temporary basis in 1961. By adding new services, extending benefits for the children of the unemployed, and authorizing increases in the federal financial responsibility for the program, Kennedy's request amounted to a significant enlargement of the ADC program.[5]

The new focus on preventive and rehabilitative services would become fully entrenched in American social policy under President Lyndon Johnson. The vast complex of his Great Society programs, established in the following years, continued and expanded upon the idea that poverty was in large part a social problem that could be eradicated with a full commitment of government resources. This approach, accompanied by the tremendous increase during the 1960s in the number of recipients, set the stage for the debates and conflicts that dominated welfare politics in later decades.

In 1962, however, welfare had not yet become a flash point for partisan politics, and, despite acknowledgment that his proposed amendments would initiate "far-reaching changes" in the welfare program, Kennedy's proposal received little opposition in Congress. As a Capitol Hill observer remarked, "little noticed in the 87th Congress amidst the controversy surrounding many key administration proposals has been the quiet, uncontroversial progress of HR 10606, the public welfare amendments of 1962. Yet HR 10606 is not an old and familiar proposal, but one designed by the Kennedy Administration to give new direction to federal welfare programs."[6]

Limited Congressional Conflict

The welfare bill traveled through Congress with remarkable ease. Sent to the House in February of 1962, the bill was brought to the floor from the Ways and Means Committee under a closed rule, with debate limited to two hours. The only controversy the bill faced surfaced in an attempt to recommit the bill to the committee with instructions to strike a committee amendment. The committee's amendment raised the federal contribution to adult assistance programs (a secondary aspect of the legislation) above what had been requested by the president, at an estimated additional cost of $140 million. Republicans protested the committee's amendment on the grounds that it was fiscally irresponsible and that the president himself had not requested the increase. In a noteworthy display of double speak, Wilbur Mills, the Democratic Chair of Ways and Means, countered that, "if the administration is against the amendment, they have not told me so in terms that they have asked me to see that it was defeated."[7] While generating some partisan controversy, the motion was defeated by a fairly wide margin of 155 to 232.

Following the vote on the motion to recommit, the House overwhelmingly supported HR 10606, passing the measure by a lopsided vote of 319 to 69. All but four Democrats supported the final bill, ensuring passage. Correspondingly, while Republicans cast 94 percent of the votes against final passage, a solid majority of the Republican Party (59 percent) voted in favor of the welfare amendments. After the legislation's smooth progress through the Senate and bicameral conference, President Kennedy signed into law the Public Welfare Amendments.

As with the 1962 Trade Expansion Act, support for the welfare legislation reflected President Kennedy's ability to rope together the New Deal Democratic coalition. The bill included key benefits to both North and South to ensure the broad Democratic support necessary for final passage. To a greater extent than with trade, however, welfare required the party leaders' careful compromise.

Trade, and foreign policy more generally, was still a unifying issue, a talisman of sorts around which Democrats could rally in the early 1960s. Welfare, on the other hand, was increasingly being linked in the public mind to black poverty. As a result, the issue pressed upon what was fast becoming an insurmountable regional fissure in the Democratic coalition: the politics of civil rights for African Americans. With the country still in the early stages of the civil rights conflict, however, the 1962 legislation reflected a final moment of unity on the issue of welfare.

Forging Cross-Regional Support for Welfare Expansion

Kennedy's welfare proposal received support from representatives in both parties and from all regions of the country. Support for the public welfare amendments from all of the states averaged 78 percent, and, as the map in Figure 4.3 shows, support was above 56 percent in all but six states. This reflects not only the strength of Democratic support throughout the country but also the moderate degree of support provided by Republicans in each region of the country; only among western and Pacific Coast Republicans was the average level of support less than 50 percent.[8] As with his trade policy, Kennedy was able to rely on the strength of the New Deal Democratic coalition, as well as the support of a large number of primarily northern Republicans to pass welfare reform.

Much of the basis for northern support of the 1962 welfare changes can be found in a 1961 report of the Ad Hoc Committee on Public Welfare which served as the blueprint for Kennedy's proposal. Organized by the Department of Health, Education, and Welfare (HEW), the committee was headed by Sanford Solender, the executive vice president of the National Jewish Welfare Board. Wayne Vasey, the dean of the Graduate School of Social Work at Rutgers University, served as the committee's chief consultant. The committee cited three recent social and economic trends in making their recommendations. First, people were relocating, from region to region and from farm to city, and were having a difficult time adjusting to their new communities. Second, industries were decentralizing and shifting from one section of the country to another, leading to disruptions in local economies. Third, technological changes in agriculture and industry were increasing layoffs and creating demand for new work skills. As HEW Secretary Abraham Ribicoff said in testimony before the Ways and Means Committee, the country was up against a "new kind of poverty," which the administration's proposal was designed to combat.[9]

Much of this "new poverty" was linked to the massive relocation of rural southern blacks that was then underway. Between 1940 and 1970, 5 million

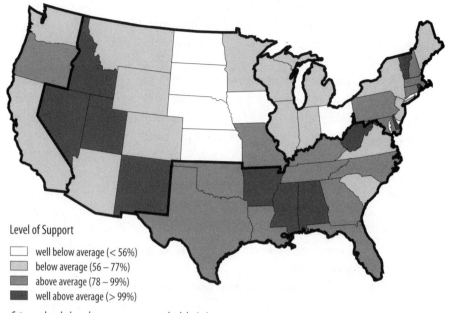

Level of Support

☐ well below average (< 56%)
▢ below average (56 – 77%)
▨ above average (78 – 99%)
■ well above average (> 99%)

Category breaks based on mean ± one standard deviation.

Figure 4.3
House Support for Welfare, 1962

African Americans moved from the South to the North, in what has been called one of the largest and most rapid internal migrations in world history.[10] Changes in federal agricultural policies and increased mechanization of cotton farming—especially the introduction of the mechanical cotton harvester in the South—displaced large numbers of primarily black tenant farmers. In the face of a paucity of alternative employment options and low wages in the ones that existed, an exodus of African Americans from the Cotton Belt resulted.[11] While many moved from the farms to southern cities, the migrants' primary destination was the large industrialized urban centers of the North.[12]

Despite northward migration, by the 1960s employment difficulties plagued African Americans. While earlier waves of urban immigrants had found employment in the unionized and high-paying industrial sector, these opportunities did not exist to the same degree for migrating blacks. As a result, rates of unemployment and underemployment among African Americans were significantly higher than those of whites.[13] In 1962, for example, the unemployment rate for whites nationwide was 4.9 percent while for blacks it was 10.9.[14]

Between 1960 and 1964, manufacturing employment rose by 3 percent nationally, but it dropped in the country's major industrial cities, New York, Chicago, Los Angeles, Detroit, and Philadelphia, where blacks were increasingly concentrated.[15]

Because they comprised a disproportionate share of the country's poor, African Americans were becoming disproportionately represented on the welfare rolls. The number of African American children and families receiving ADC had grown significantly in the 1940s and 1950s, despite the features of the program that accommodated southern interests in limiting black participation. While African Americans accounted for just 13 percent of the ADC rolls in 1937, by 1961 the number of black children on the rolls had grown to nearly equal the number of white children on ADC.[16] The increase during these decades was due, in all likelihood, to the migration of blacks out of the South, which had the country's most restrictive eligibility rules, to states outside of the region which had fewer restrictions.[17]

With a growing influx of poor migrants and the loss of many working- and middle-class residents to the suburbs, northern and Pacific Coast cities stood to gain much from the type of increased federal assistance promised in the 1962 welfare legislation. In 1961, AFDC-UP, a program that provided benefits to families with an unemployed father in the home, was initiated on a temporary basis, and the vast majority of the states that chose to implement the program were in the North and Pacific Coast.[18] By extending this coverage to families of unemployed parents and by placing new emphasis on the provision of vocational education, training, and social services, the 1962 welfare proposal provided federal resources of particular benefit to urban areas with high concentrations of unemployed and poor families, many of which were headed by individuals lacking manufacturing skills. Because training featured prominently in the 1962 legislation and because ADC generally targeted those whose occupational histories had excluded them from the coverage of unemployment insurance programs (such as agricultural workers), this aid and the new emphasis work were neither racially nor geographically neutral.[19]

The welfare legislation's new focus on moving individuals into the mainstream of work and economic self-sufficiency also helped legitimize the program at a time when economic prosperity prevailed.[20] The welfare amendments were seen as a way to integrate and provide opportunity to migrating blacks—a purpose that appealed to liberals—in a way they would also mitigate the effects of social change in the North, which appealed to conservatives.[21]

TABLE 4.2. ANALYSIS OF STATE SUPPORT FOR EXPANDING
PUBLIC ASSISTANCE, 1962

	b (se)
Constant	0.141* (0.081)
Size of ADC program	9.040** (4.201)
Democratic	0.725*** (0.101)
South	−0.176** (0.085)
West	−0.179*** (0.069)
Pacific Coast	−0.158 (0.121)

Sources: Welfare and Democratic (ICPSR); size of ADC program (calculated from data in U.S.
Health, Education, and Welfare's *1961 Annual Report* and state population data in *1961 Statistical
Abstract*).
OLS analysis: *Adj. R²*: .68; *N*: 48
$*p \leq .10; **p \leq .05; ***p \leq .01$
For more details about the OLS analysis, see note 22.

With such all-purpose appeal, the proposal was both compatible with Kennedy's pro-business stance and endorsed by labor.

States with larger Democratic contingents in the House and those with more people on welfare were especially supportive of Kennedy's proposal (see Table 4.2[22]), "Especially supportive" best fits states in the solidly Democratic South, where the party still held a large majority of the states' seats. Although other regions had growing ADC caseloads, the South still had the highest rates of dependency. In the average state in the South, 2.2 percent of the population was on ADC, as compared to 1.5 percent in the West, 1.5 percent in the North, and 1.7 percent in the Pacific Coast. Size of caseload had a large effect on legislative support for welfare programs: a 1 percent increase in the percentage of people on welfare resulted in a 9 percent increase in welfare support, all else being equal. These results also indicate where Kennedy found backing for his proposal within the Republican Party. Greatest Republican support came from the northern states, particularly in the New England and Mid-Atlantic regions, that had both urban and rural poverty as well as welfare dependency—states such as Massachusetts and Pennsylvania.

Once the strong effects of Democratic Party presence and the amount of a state's welfare dependency are held constant, region had a small independent effect on state support for welfare expansion. Relative to the North, the South, along with the West, was then slightly less supportive of welfare. These regional variables likely reflect the cultural predispositions that prevailed in their states. It is not surprising that the North was culturally more inclined toward welfare. States in that region had long traditions of supporting government activism to manage economic life and redress social inequities. In contrast, the South and West were both historically skeptical, though in slightly different ways, of strengthening the central government.

Given the racial politics of the early 1960s, the overwhelmingly strong Democratic support for expanding welfare is at first surprising. But a consideration of the policy's political calculus helps explain the broad support. In arguing for the amendments, northern Democrats emphasized that the new measures were imperative because of the changing socioeconomic landscape. Explaining that "the traditional arguments of earlier years did not seem persuasive," Massachusetts Representative James Burke applauded the bill's expansion of federal resources to aid families in poverty because of the head-of-household's unemployment (as opposed to death, disability, or desertion) and to provide job training and children's services.[23] Eugene Keogh of New York concurred, arguing that the program had to be made more flexible to accommodate modern social conditions. By addressing unemployment and by recognizing the day care needs of the growing number of working mothers, this bill, he suggested, provided an efficient and realistic federal response to current trends.[24]

More than just addressing modern conditions and needs generally, the 1962 welfare amendments were instrumental in the Democratic Party's northern coalition-building efforts.[25] Because of growing racial and ethnic diversity in the national population, the party directed its regional efforts at accommodating a multiracial coalition, often targeting specific group interests. As Steve Erie has argued, machines in many of the large northern cities used welfare, along with other material benefits, to court the African American vote.[26] Frances Fox Piven and Richard Cloward suggest that for many urban political leaders, increasing welfare was a more readily feasible way to placate politicized blacks than meeting other civil rights demands, such as school integration or fair employment laws.[27]

Political machines, such as Mayor Daley's organization in Chicago, urged their congressional representatives to push for greater federal resources for ADC as a way to appease black demands while relieving the burden on city treasuries and white taxpayers.[28] At the same time, the emerging social service sector was quickly becoming a primary employer of urban blacks, allowing machines to channel African Americans into employment without threatening the traditional sources of city jobs for whites (fire and police departments, for example).[29] Providing further evidence for the relationship between urban machines and the political use of welfare, Robert Lieberman has demonstrated that cities with a higher degree of machine organization, in addition to paying higher benefit levels to welfare recipients, extended the greatest coverage to African Americans. Because cities with strong political machines were stingiest in their overall coverage, Lieberman concludes that the machines used the provision of benefits selectively to court black constituents.[30]

The welfare amendments' social services component and the provision of additional federal funds for training social workers helped build a different Democratic clientele, as well, one that was largely middle class, increasingly multiracial, and that had an intellectual base in northern universities. The 1961 report on which the administration's proposal was based grew out of a committee guided by northern social welfare scholars and practitioners. Elizabeth Wickenden, a well-known advocate for children and family services from the New York School of Social Work and a veteran New Dealer, heralded the legislation as a "major landmark" when she testified in support of it before the Ways and Means Committee.[31] Representatives of the National Association of Social Workers and the American Public Welfare Association also spoke out in favor of the proposal.[32] As the number of public and not-for-profit social service providers grew in the 1950s and the 1960s, these organizations and their employees became Democratic constituents with an investment in maintaining and expanding the welfare state.[33]

The biggest champions of the increase in federal support for social services were northern Democrats. New York Democrat William Ryan, for example, stressed the importance of providing federal funds to train and increase the number of personnel in state and local welfare agencies. Strengthening the ranks of local welfare personnel was necessary because of the (also necessary) increase in federal emphasis on rehabilitative services. With these services, he argued, recipients would "be afforded, as they should be, an opportunity to become productive individuals, able to support and care for themselves."[34] Northern Democrats promoted the federally funded training and services components of the welfare bill as ways to respond to the growing problem of urban, particularly black, unemployment without burdening state and local tax resources. The resultant funneling of funds, services, and employment opportunities into cities also helped Democratic efforts to build new urban constituencies.

Northern Democrats engaged in this type of party building at the risk of alienating southern Democrats. The potential boon of wooing migrating blacks to the Democratic coalition with the promise of forward movement on civil rights was tempered by the increasingly real possibility of losing white southern voters. Following President Truman's 1940s endorsement of civil rights and welfare measures, southern Democrats (including most notably the Dixiecrats) signaled their discontent with the national party and their willingness to withdraw future support in both electoral and legislative arenas.

In his 1960 presidential campaign, Kennedy had pledged action on civil rights and poverty related issues, and the support provided by northern cities proved to be crucial to his slim victory over Richard Nixon.[35] While carrying most southern states in 1960, Kennedy lost Florida, Tennessee, Kentucky, and Virginia; Republicans were beginning to establish their foothold in the South. Once in office, President Kennedy backed away from his campaign promises on civil rights, opting instead to promote more moderate proposals, in an attempt to maintain the support of southern Democrats.[36] Despite this, southern support for the national party continued to erode as members from the region blocked much of what they considered to be the president's liberal northern agenda. As one House member described in response to a *U.S. News and World Report* survey of congressional attitudes at the time, "It's just hell being a Southern Conservative Democrat with a left-wing Democrat as President."[37]

Given the well-known friction between Kennedy and southern Democrats, especially about issues of race, it at first appears surprising that southerners in Congress turned out in such numbers to support the welfare proposal. Not only did they provide the bulk of support for the bill, it was a southerner, Wilbur Mills, who successfully shepherded the bill through the House. Southern support becomes easier to understand in view of several key elements of the legislation, as well as the timing of the bill.

One reason for southern support of welfare in 1962 was the decision made in the Ways and Means Committee to increase the amount of federal funds for adult assistance programs, both proportionally and in total, above that which the administration had proposed. Until the late 1950s, when ADC surpassed it, Old Age Assistance (OAA) was the largest public assistance program (and it remained by far the largest of the adult assistance programs). Southern states had a disproportionate share of individuals who relied on this program, with an average rate of dependency that was half again as much as the average state in any of the other three regions and more than three times the amount in the North.[38] This is both because of the decades-long exclusion of farm operators and agricultural workers from participating in Social Security (thus forcing older individuals to rely on OAA) and because, once included in Social Security, these workers still earned so little as to warrant their continued reliance on OAA. At the same time, the exodus of young male workers from the South was statistically aging the remaining population, simultaneously reducing tax revenue and increasing welfare burdens.[39] Because of the large numbers served and because federal matching funds were tied to state income levels (poorer states receiving more funds), states in the South received the greatest amount of federal dollars for the program. Although the South spent the least amount of money per recipient, the average state in the region received 80 percent more in per capita federal grant money than in the rest of the country.

With the committee amendment calling for an increase in the federal match of roughly $4 per recipient, states in the South stood to gain a windfall in federal resources. Moreover, the windfall was unfettered, as Republicans pointed out in floor debate: no language in the bill specified that the money be used to increase the dollar amount of benefits actually received by recipients. Thus, states could use the money to further reduce their share of welfare expenses if they so desired. In explaining Republican opposition, John Byrnes of Wisconsin charged that this particular increase in federal monies was in essence a boondoggle, inserted into the legislation at the last moment by committee Democrats to benefit state governments without any assurances that the money would go to recipients.[40]

Republicans attacked the proposal as an unbudgeted measure and one that would lead to greater deficits and greater federal involvement in welfare. By targeting their opposition to this aspect of the bill, Republicans may have been attempting to eliminate a provision of the welfare legislation that was particularly appealing to southerners, thus ultimately splintering Democratic support for the welfare amendments, although it is not entirely clear that this would have happened. Even if the increase in funds for adult assistance sweetened the pot, southerners had a history of compromising with northern Democrats on family welfare legislation, and this bill was no exception. If northerners got federal dollars for services and training, southerners got the increased local discretion and flexibility that they had demanded since the Social Security Act in

1935, as their price for signing on to welfare expansion.[41] Wilbur Mills made it clear that even with more federal funds, this bill promised to enhance local control.

> In other parts of the bill everyone will admit we are giving the States greater discretion, greater control over the operation of the programs in some respects than they ever had in the case of abuses, getting people off the rolls that are not in the opinion of the State entitled to be there. . . . So the bill does give this latitude to the States in cases of abuse, and it can be a relaxation of Federal intervention in the program.[42]

Mills repeatedly returned to the issue of state and local discretion, reflecting the concern of southerners that they be allowed to administer their relief programs with maximum freedom in the designations of eligibility and benefit levels. The welfare proposal, as amended in committee, gave states a greater degree of flexibility in that it allowed them more discretion in reducing "abuses" of the program and in taking steps deemed to be "in the best interest of the child," including substituting services or vouchers for direct payments, without losing federal matching funds. In these respects, the timing of the measure was especially important. During the 1950s a number of southern states had toughened their eligibility rules and regulations in response to growing caseloads.[43] "Suitable home" decrees and other restrictive actions, including a notorious decision in Louisiana to cut 22,500 children from the rolls because of their illegitimacy, were directed primarily at African American families. Though these state laws provoked political controversy at the national level, the federal government could do little, short of rescinding federal funds.[44] Because the amended legislation ensured that states had considerable latitude to determine and punish "abuses" and to determine what was in the "best interest of the child" without sacrificing federal dollars, it gave tacit approval to state actions. While welfare advocates protested that the provision would invite discrimination, many state and local governments, as well as the powerful southern-based American Farm Bureau Federation, supported the measure.[45]

Yet, given that southerners regularly opposed civil rights legislation and that the issue of welfare was increasingly being connected to black poverty, the reason for southern support for welfare programs is still not fully explained. As the map in Figure 4.3 shows, the South was the region with the highest support for welfare, with all but two states above average (78% to 99%) or well above average (100%) in their support of the legislation. What explains this degree of support? Why should southern Democrats support legislation with loopholes when they certainly had the power to simply derail the legislation wholesale?

The explanation lies, at least in part, with timing. Lee Alston and Joseph Ferrie argue that local control over welfare benefits had long been instrumental to the maintenance of a system of paternalism in the South. Since the end of the Civil War, the provision of certain benefits (including, for example, access to medical care and protection from violence) had been one of the mechanisms through which white planter elites had maintained control over black and poor white agricultural workers.[46] Because cotton remained the least mechanized agricultural product in the United States until the 1960s, the demand for plentiful, steady, and cheap labor was higher in the South than, for example, in the agriculturally rich West, and a system of paternalism evolved after the abolition of slavery as the most inexpensive way to retain a steady and loyal labor supply.[47]

The development of a national welfare system in the 1930s threatened to provide a substitute for, and thus undercut the value of, the benefits of paternalism to workers. For this reason, southern congressional representatives were vested with the responsibility of ensuring that social welfare programs were either limited or under local control. Local control was important for many reasons, among them that benefits could be made to function in tandem with the seasonal needs of agricultural production. As Jill Quadagno writes in describing southern welfare provision in these years, "Welfare officials supported field hands at federal expense during the winter and cut them off the rolls in the spring and summer."[48] In short, by voting for expanded welfare with greater local control, southern representatives were able to supply key constituents with discretionary resources.

With the mechanization of cotton, the need for paternalism declined, both because mechanization decreased the overall demand for labor and because, with greater unemployment, farm owners could more easily elicit high productivity rates from those working for them.[49] In 1962, however, when Congress was considering this welfare legislation, mechanization was still unfolding. In 1960, just 42 percent of upland cotton was harvested mechanically; by 1965, this proportion had grown to 82 percent, and by 1969 it had reached nearly 100 percent.[50] But, even as late as 1970, congressional hearings described the provision of welfare in the South as one in which "recipients are made to serve as maids or to do day yard work in white homes to keep their checks. During the cotton-picking season, no one is accepted on welfare because plantations need cheap labor to do cotton-picking behind the cotton-picking machines."[51]

In 1962, as civil rights agitation gained momentum, southern members of Congress represented a region in the early stages of a transformation of social,

economic, and political relations. The watershed years of the civil rights movement and of southern economic modernization were still ahead. Considered in
this light, southern support for the welfare bill, legislation that expanded resources but also expanded local control, makes sense. The system of paternalism had not yet fully eroded—neither the perceived economic need for cheap labor nor the cultural association, the "southern way of life," that accompanied
it. At the same time, the threat posed by the civil rights movement was credible and imminent, which in all likelihood exacerbated the need to exercise control over who received welfare benefits and under what conditions.

DIVIDED COUNTRY, DIVIDED PARTY: RACE AND ECONOMY IN THE EARLY 1970s

Despite claims that the services and training provided by the 1962 Public Welfare Amendments would lead to a reduction in welfare dependency, the re-
mainder of the decade witnessed a rapidly expanding AFDC program. Between
1962 and 1970, the number of families receiving AFDC jumped from 932,000 to
2,552,000, a nearly 200 percent increase in less than a decade. In these same
eight years, payments to the program increased from just under $1.4 billion to
over $4.8 billion.[52]

Expansion of the welfare rolls in the 1960s was not uniform throughout the
country. Thirty-nine percent of the national AFDC caseload increase in the
1960s came in the Northeast, followed by 26 percent increase in the West (including the Pacific Coast states), 18 percent in the South, and 17 percent in the
North Central states.[53] A full 60 percent of the increase occurred in major urban
counties outside of the South.[54] Thus, the "welfare explosion" of the 1960s was
largely a phenomenon of the big industrial cities of the North and Pacific Coast.

This dramatic increase helped bring attention to the persistence of poverty,
particularly African American poverty, in an era of overall economic prosperity.
As the civil rights movement gained momentum and as African Americans
gained electoral visibility, President Johnson initiated a patchwork of War on
Poverty and Great Society programs that generated new levels of federal involvement in fighting poverty, much of which was targeted at urban centers.[55]
These developments, among others, laid the groundwork for growing racial
tensions and urban unrest, and they helped to precipitate widespread calls for
new welfare reform, a task to which President Nixon set himself upon entering
office in 1969.[56]

Nixon proposed the Family Assistance Plan (FAP) in August of 1969, and the
House Ways and Means Committee reported it with only slight modifications
as HR 16311 in the spring of 1970. Though passed in the House, the legislation

was eventually defeated in the Senate. The proposal was complicated, but, in essence, it would have replaced AFDC with a program centered on what was popularly referred to as a guaranteed annual income. An idea first voiced inside the Johnson administration, the proposal's key provisions included establishing a national payment floor, which amounted to $1,600 for a family of four with no earned income, paid for by the federal government. Benefits would also be extended to the "working poor." For the first time, families making up to $3,920 annually would be eligible to receive benefits while still retaining earnings. Food stamps and medical assistance were linked to payments. The proposal also established a set of work and training requirements for adult recipients and included provisions for day care, financed largely by the federal government.[57] By including working families, some estimated, the program would extend coverage to an additional 15 million recipients at minimum at an initial cost of at least $4.4 billion dollars (on top of existing federal outlays for assistance).[58]

President Nixon cloaked the expansive and costly elements of the proposal in conservative rhetoric. In an approach similar to Kennedy's eight years earlier, Nixon argued that the emphasis on work incentives and family stability would help eradicate dependency in the long run. The proposal required work or training of almost all adult recipients (with some key exceptions). Because the proposal allowed parents to retain some of their wages while also receiving benefits, families would not have to choose between employment and welfare, a flaw of the AFDC program that critics claimed provided a disincentive to work. Further, AFDC prohibited payments to families with working fathers present in the household and, in many states, to households with nonworking fathers present (i.e., those states that did not have the AFDC-UP program). Under FAP, providing benefits to all families, including those with employment income, was a way to encourage families to stay together.[59]

When FAP was brought before the full House, average support among Democrats stood at 60 percent, while among Republicans, the average was 54 percent.[60] Like Kennedy's bill eight years earlier, a majority of both parties endorsed Nixon's FAP. However, this bipartisan coalition consisted primarily of Democrats and Republicans from the North and Pacific Coast states; southern Democrats joined southern and western Republicans in opposition to the president's proposal. Regional cleavages were of paramount importance in determining support for the bill to federalize welfare.[61]

Support for FAP, for establishing a greatly federalized program of uniform benefits for nonworking and working-poor families, varied considerably by region. At the two poles of the debate were northern and Pacific Coast representatives, who provided strong support for the measure, and southerners, who were adamant in their resistance. These regional divisions transcended party affiliation. Notably, Pacific Coast Democrats and northern Democrats occupied the extreme opposite end of the welfare debate from southern Democrats (88, 87, and 22 percent, respectively). The New Deal Democratic coalition on welfare, one that had for years combined program expansion with local administration and control of resources, was now defunct.

The Northern Push for Federal Take-Over

The debates in 1970 over FAP, a plan that came down significantly on the side of increased federal intervention in the states' welfare programs, showed just how tenuous the cross-regional New Deal Democratic coalition had been. As the map of support for FAP in Figure 4.4 makes clear, the North and South were now firmly on opposite sides of the debate. While the states of the North were, by and large, above average or well above average in their support of FAP, states in the South were, by and large, below to well below average in their support, a dramatic change from just ten years prior.

Casting their arguments in terms of regional disparities, northern Democrats now called for an end to local control over welfare. After decades of supporting a welfare system premised upon states' rights, lawmakers from the North and Pacific Coast now pushed for the transfer of welfare responsibility from the states to the federal government as the only way to ensure an equalization of the nation's welfare burden. These advocates of FAP saw three related problems with the existing welfare system. First, northern states, which had the nation's highest per capita income levels, had historically received the least reimbursement for welfare expenditures from the federal government and thus bore a disproportionate share of the burden of welfare costs. Second, this burden was now increasing because of the explosive growth in the number of welfare recipients, a growth concentrated in their cities. And third, representatives attributed much of this growth to the migration of poor southerners to their cities, a phenomenon they said was driven in part by the extreme disparities in the benefit levels offered by states in their regions compared to those in the South.[62]

For lawmakers from the North and Pacific Coast, federalizing welfare was a way to alleviate regional inequities, stanch the flow of regional migration, and redistribute the costs of the program around the country. Complaints about

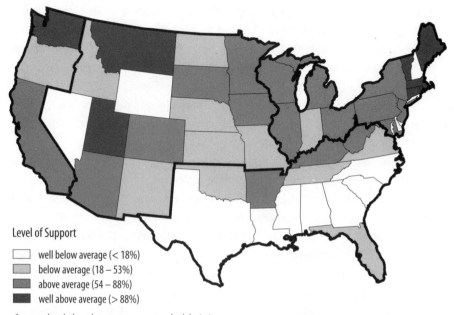

Level of Support

- ☐ well below average (< 18%)
- ◻ below average (18 – 53%)
- ▨ above average (54 – 88%)
- ■ well above average (> 88%)

Category breaks based on mean ± one standard deviation.

Figure 4.4
House Support for Welfare, 1970

the burden on cities became routine during floor debate. As New York Democrat John Murphy said:

> Over the years, the large urban areas of America have borne the brunt of the national problem without having the national resources needed to provide effective and productive welfare assistance. Our cities can no longer be expected to shoulder this burden alone. . . . only under the Federal plan will the welfare system fill the needs of those who it is intended to serve, and distribute the burden evenly throughout the Nation. . . . National standardization will stop the drift of poor into the already intolerable ghettos of the cities, and give hope to those who subsist on welfare.[63]

The regional and racial implications of Murphy's argument are clear. The states with low benefit levels were concentrated in the South, while states with higher benefit levels were in the urban North and Pacific Coast. The average monthly payment per family in the North was twice the payment level in the South, and the Pacific Coast's monthly payment was almost twice the South's.[64] Representative Richard Ottinger, another New York Democrat, pointed to the effect of regional disparities in payment levels more bluntly. "[I]t encourages the poor to flock to overcrowded cities where welfare payments are higher," he noted. "When a family of four receives $44 a month in Mississippi and could be eligible for $264 a month in New Jersey, who could resist the impulse to emigrate?"[65]

In making arguments about regional disparities in payment levels, northerners typically failed to mention that part of the reason they had higher benefit levels was because their states also had higher costs of living, higher income levels, and larger tax bases—realities that might have lessened the moral force of their argument. The other reason for downplaying this aspect of regional difference was perhaps related to the increasingly worrisome (and also racially charged) fiscal environment of states in their regions.

By 1970, suburbanization was siphoning off much of the taxpayer base of northern cities. Business closings and relocations to the South and West as well as to other countries were accelerating and further eroding cities' revenue sources.[66] This tax drain was particularly troubling given the growth in social welfare expenditures during the previous decade. As Michigan Democrat Martha Griffiths explained:

> At the present time, one of the heaviest burdens that rests upon your State or your city has been placed there by the Federal Government—and it is the burden of welfare. This is the thing that is destroying most of America's cities. As that tax burden on property becomes heavier and heavier to pay these welfare costs, more and more people move out of the city and more businesses move out. If there were no other reason for voting for this bill, the proper reason for voting for it is that welfare should not rest upon the property in cities or in States, but it should be paid for by the Federal Government out of the General Treasury of the United States.[67]

Growing welfare expenditures imposed fiscal constraints, reducing state and local governments' flexibility in other areas, such as economic development, education, and law enforcement—areas that served a broader business and middle-class constituency. To the extent that the federal government would assume welfare costs, cities and states could concentrate their resources on wooing back the businesses and citizens departing for the suburbs and other regions.[68] Noting that his state stood to gain $200 million in the first year of FAP alone, California Democrat Corman praised the proposed increase in federal responsibility for welfare costs along similar lines:

> [C]ertainly the most important part of this bill, as far as the State of California is concerned, is that a substantial increase in the share of welfare costs will be borne by the

Federal Government. . . . It would then be possible for the State government to assume the balance of California's welfare costs, thereby completely relieving the counties in the State of this financial burden. Such a step would permit welfare costs to be shifted to the broader state and Federal tax base, leaving the local tax base free to bear the cost of education and other municipal requirements.[69]

Though addressing the concerns of multiple constituencies, northern and Pacific Coast lawmakers most immediately were answering the demands for fiscal relief from state and local officials, particularly those from the large industrialized states that bore the heaviest financial burden of welfare. FAP appeared attractive because, unlike federal aid for welfare programs in the past, large northern states now stood to gain a windfall in federal funds. Nearly 70 percent of the FAP funds were to be divided between California and five large states in the Northeast.[70] Governors and county officials from the large industrialized states threw their support behind FAP.[71] The executive director of the National Association of Counties, for example, called it a "do or die" moment for welfare reform because of the desperate need for fiscal relief at the county level in many states.[72]

Several representatives from these regions made it clear that they would vote for FAP, yet they also said that the bill did not go far enough to fully federalize the costs of the program. Calling FAP a "monumental breakthrough" and a "vital and historic step," Democrat Ogden Reid of New York nonetheless urged that the federal government assume all program costs within five years, and he noted that this plan was receiving support from key New York Republicans.[73]

While much of this argument expressed a desire for regional parity and fiscal relief, another issue was also in play: alleviating the racial tensions then wreaking urban havoc. In the latter half of the 1960s, with the explosion of the civil rights movements and the political mobilization of African Americans, racial politics within cities were combusting. In the first nine months of 1967 alone, there were 164 race riots, and that was before the murder of Martin Luther King.[74] For Democrats and Republicans alike, demonstrating a commitment to resolving the "urban crisis" was a political imperative. Business leaders, among others, had become increasingly jittery about the urban unrest, since it meant that production processes and markets were more likely to be disrupted. Just as businesses pressured foreign governments to create stable business environments, they pressured the U.S. government to do the same in the nation's cities. Welfare policy was a tool that many believed could be used to help quell the strife.

Politicians understood this. Future Democratic senator Daniel Patrick

Moynihan, then working as an urban affairs advisor to the Nixon White House, would go on to write that a large welfare class was "the normal and manageable cost of doing urban business. It is in ways a political subsidy, as irrational perhaps as those paid to owners of oil wells, wheat fields, or aerospace companies."[75] Since 1967, leaders in the business community had been working with policy makers to increase the provision of welfare, including extending assistance to the working poor, as one way to resolve the turmoil in the inner cities.[76] FAP was designed to function in this way, by allowing women with children to stay home while "channel[ing] poor men, particularly black men, into the low-wage sector of the economy."[77]

Northern and Pacific Coast lawmakers linked urban unrest directly to regional disparities in benefit levels. Comparing AFDC benefits in Mississippi and New York, Representative Boland, a Massachusetts Democrat, explained the situation for the rural poor:

> They are virtually streaming into our Northern cities in a futile search for a better way of life. Their hopes, of course, are dashed at once. They exchange a country shack for a ghetto slum, a diet of dried rice and beans for one of packaged rice and canned beans. The migration from the countryside to the city has helped turn our inner cities into teeming slums. It has helped breed the crime, the dope addiction, the street rebellions now making headlines throughout the United States.[78]

By making the case that regional differences in benefit levels were contributing to the turmoil, lawmakers like Boland made a compelling case for FAP—one that businesses, especially those with operations in the nation's large industrial cities, could support. And providing this support were leaders of some of the country's largest firms, particularly in the capital-intensive industries of the North. The National Association of Manufacturers, for example, favored FAP and lobbied for passage of the bill.[79] In addition, a veritable Who's Who of executives from the country's largest corporations signed a statement of the Urban Coalition Action Council, a social action group that was precursor to Common Cause, urging passage of FAP as a first step toward "a sound and more equitable welfare system."[80]

With mayors, governors, key business constituencies, and labor leaders standing firm behind FAP, all but the most liberal northern Democrats in the House, who were dissatisfied with the amount of the benefit, endorsed Nixon's plan.[81] Northern Republicans, too, voiced their support of FAP, citing in particular the extent to which their business constituencies favored the legislation. Illinois Republican John Anderson, for example, reminded party members of the range of business organizations that had expressed support for FAP. In addition to the groups like the National Association of Manufacturers, he noted the support of the New England Council and the National Federation of Independent Businesses.[82]

Anderson and other Republicans also focused on FAP's work incentives as key selling points, defending the program as different from earlier plans presented by Democratic administrations. Anderson described the work incentives and training requirements as "the real heart of this welfare reform proposal," a part of the proposal's strategy for keeping fathers at home with their families and preserving the family as "the very basic unit of American society."[83] Similarly, the ranking Republican on the Ways and Means Committee, John Byrnes of Wisconsin, defended FAP against the charge that it was nothing more than a guaranteed income program.[84] Under FAP, he argued, "society's assistance will be conditioned on the head of family doing everything to help himself and his family that he is capable of doing. He must take training; get a job; and go to work."[85]

Focusing their rhetoric not just on work but also on family allowed Republicans to appeal to social conservatives while addressing business worries about social unrest. The 1965 Moynihan report had linked crime to welfare dependence and both of these to the instability of black families. By focusing on the potential of FAP to both preserve families and require work, Republican lawmakers were promising a solution that would move young black men off the streets and into the home and workplace—in the words of Representative Byrnes, a solution that would "enable them to become self-sufficient participants in the American economic system."[86] Ironically foreshadowing a marriage that would characterize later efforts to eliminate the federal role in welfare, Republican lawmakers linked the social conservatives' goals of strengthening the traditional family with the business goals of creating a stable and profitable business environment in this promotion of an expanded national welfare program.

Southern Resistance

While northern and Pacific Coast Democrats were FAP's strongest proponents, southern Democrats were its biggest detractors, as the map in Figure 4.4 suggests. In the nearly ten years that had passed since the 1962 amendments, the South's political economy had transformed, prompting a sharp decline in the willingness of the region's representatives to continue supporting welfare expansion.

By 1970, modernization of the region's commercial agricultural industry was virtually complete. In addition to mechanical cotton pickers, farmers routinely used chemical weed killers, a combination that eliminated the vast majority of the jobs once performed by sharecroppers and later by day laborers.[87] In the 1960s alone, the farm population in the South dropped by roughly 50 percent, and by 1970 farmers represented less than 7 percent of the region's entire population.[88] Without the need for cheap and steady labor, southern agriculturalists no longer placed a premium on the paternalistic system, and the need to control the provision of alternative sources of benefits, such as government assistance, declined.[89]

Southerners still remained interested in local control of their states' economic and social relations, though. While the need to guard local prerogative for the purpose of maintaining a paternalistic hold over farm labor supply had diminished, a different problem now existed: despite decades of out-migration, the South suffered from an excess supply of workers without the skills for jobs off the farm. The jobs being created in the rapidly industrializing South of the early 1970s were largely unattainable for displaced agricultural workers. Many of the new defense-related industries moving into the region brought with them their own highly educated, typically white, labor force; industries such as aerospace, electronics, and chemicals offered little in the way of opportunity for the region's poor and less-educated blacks and whites.[90] With farm employment gone, employment in traditional low-wage manufacturing industries such as textiles declining, and much of the new growth concentrated in only certain industries and geographical areas, the region's poor, rural blacks in particular, were being bypassed by the economic growth.[91] As author Gilbert Fite writes, "The South's problem was not how to develop a progressive and productive agriculture but what to do with surplus farmers who had no place in the rapidly changing rural economy."[92]

By the late 1960s, in the context of the civil rights movement and the growing militancy of the northern Black Power movement, the problem of unemployment among black workers had become acute. The passage of the Civil Rights Act, the Voting Rights Act, and other significant 1960s legislation aimed at redressing southern racial inequalities ensured that change in the region's social and political order, beyond what was already underway, was imminent. The responses of southern white elites to this "Second Reconstruction" varied but included a number of efforts to slow down and minimize the impact of these changes in their region.[93]

These responses included efforts to encourage further out-migration by black southerners. Some argue that mechanization itself was adopted with such speed in reaction to the civil rights movement. As Fite writes, "One black farmer in Alabama declared in 1967 that 'them white folks got a lot more interested in machinery after the civil rights bill was passed.'"[94] While separating the economic from the social incentives of mechanization may not be fully possible, little doubt remains that mechanization eradicated the need for the paternalistic system and that civil rights made the enforcement of traditional hierarchical relationships between the races costly. As economists Lee Alston and Joseph Ferrie have written, encouraging out-migration was, in effect, a way to dissipate the effects of civil rights gains by African Americans.[95] One journalist writing in 1985 described the stance of southern politicians on out-migration thus:

> New York's welfare system was the most generous, and in the years when southern farms and plantations were mechanizing, the agricultural workers displaced by machines were frequently given a bus ticket, a token amount of cash, and the address of the welfare office in New York. New York's one-time glamour mayor, John Lindsay, was a congressman in those years, and his southern colleagues would clap him on the back and say, "John, we're sending 'em right up to you."[96]

In this context, FAP was disastrous to many southern elites. By nationalizing benefit levels, FAP would remove one of the supposed incentives for out-migration, the higher benefit levels of the North. Additionally, not only would the incentive disappear, but because the cost of living in the southern states was so much lower than in the rest of the country, the FAP benefit would have its greatest purchasing power in the South, disproportionately benefiting poor southerners. It could possibly even serve as an incentive for the poor in high-income states to migrate back to the less expensive South—particularly if it was a South with a new set of legal civil rights protections.

While urban lawmakers in the North and Pacific Coast used the rhetoric of "burden" and "the need for relief" to make their arguments, southern representatives focused on the idea of a "guaranteed national income," arguing that FAP was the "dream of every Socialist" and would "wreck our incentive system of production." Lawmakers used anticommunist language to indict FAP for its standardized benefit levels and for federal interference in local determinations of benefit levels and eligibility. As Democrat Joe Waggonner of Louisiana declared, "What's wrong with a guaranteed national income? Nothing, if you believe in socialism. Everything, if, like me, you believe in democracy and the free enterprise system."[97] More than just invoking longstanding southern opposition to centralized power, anticommunist rhetoric at the time was used more generally in the South, to stir white fears that black civil rights mobilization was organized and sponsored by communists.[98] Using the anticommunist frame to discredit the welfare legislation thus intensified the racial and civil rights dimensions of the debate. Representing rural Virginia, Democrat Watkins Abbitt complained that FAP's national standard "undercuts the established patterns of welfare systems in many states."[99] Quoting from the *National Review*, Louisianan Waggonner explained that the uniform national benefit wouldn't hurt states like California or New York but would devastate the South. Relative to incomes in the Deep South, such a high benefit would "tempt a third or more of the population to quit their jobs and climb aboard the welfare wagon, or to draw supplemental handouts. This could put a tremendous strain on precisely the state budgets that could least afford it. A uniform minimum national welfare handout, in a nation with divergencies of up to 138 per cent in median earned family incomes among the states, would create far more serious problems than any it might solve."[100] Few southerners responded directly to the complaints of northerners that the disparity in benefit rates was inducing rural-to-urban migration, an omission perhaps telling in its silence. Rather, their comments focused on the disruptive effects of FAP on the region's economy and, in effect, its class and social relations.

The FAP benefit, which was higher than the existing AFDC benefit in most southern states, would provide nonworking welfare recipients with more money. In addition, because of the preponderance of low-wage employment in the region, far more individuals in the South would qualify for benefits as working poor than in other regions.[101] According to HEW estimates, FAP would increase the number receiving benefits by up to 50 percent in high-benefit states in the North, while in states in the South, the increase would likely be as much as 400 percent.[102] In Mississippi, an estimated 40 percent of the population would qualify for FAP.[103] Thus, while the greatest numbers of AFDC recipients resided in the North and Pacific Coast, the greatest number of FAP recipients would reside in the South. FAP, with its uniform benefit levels, would place a relatively greater amount of money in the hands of many more poor in the South than in any other region.

The identity of the beneficiaries of FAP was not lost on southern Democrats. One of the bill's few advocates in the South, Wilbur Mills, a sponsor of the bill, made his pitch directly to his southern colleagues.[104]

> I want to talk to my Southern friends. . . . Who are the working poor? What are they like? Over 50 percent of the working poor families covered under the bill live in the South; only

12 percent live in the Northeast. A high proportion of such families live in rural areas and on small farms. Seventy percent of them are white; 30 percent are nonwhite. . . . My friends from the South, I would urge you above anybody else in this House to be for this legislation. It will do more . . . for the Southern states than any proposition I have ever had the privilege of supporting or being for on the floor of the House. Think of it: 50 percent of the total number of these poor working families are in our several Southern states.[105]

Given the civil rights unrest in the South, dampening the out-migration of African Americans and dramatically increasing the income of poor southerners, which would disproportionately benefit black southerners, was equivalent to the federal government's proposing to underwrite internal dissent. By facilitating the economic liberation of poor black southerners, FAP would help make the political rights achieved by African Americans all the more effective. As Moynihan wrote in reflecting on southern opposition to the bill, "Family Assistance was income redistribution, and by any previous standards it was massive. It was a necessary and massive threat to an established political order that already knew itself to be half-disestablished. For southern politicians, there was nothing at all subtle about FAP."[106]

In their arguments about welfare, northerners and southerners were both responding to the myriad changes of the 1960s, yet the implications of these changes—different for the two regions—were becoming a source of friction. The result was the polarization of the regions in their support for FAP that was evident in the map in Figure 4.4. These regional differences are also captured in Table 4.3, which shows that state support for FAP reflected the influence of the key economic and social variables previously described.[107]

Unlike in 1962, a state's party affiliation played no significant role in determining support for FAP. But the size of a state's AFDC burden—that is, the amount of money spent on AFDC relative to the overall revenue within the state—was a highly significant indicator of support. The higher its welfare burden, the more likely a state was to want to federalize some of the costs with FAP; a 1 percent increase in the burden led to a more than 12 percent increase in support for FAP, all else being equal. Spending, on average, 4 percent of total revenue on AFDC, states in both the North and Pacific Coast had greater welfare burdens than states in the South (which spent on average 2 percent) and West (2 percent). The northern and Pacific Coast industrialized states had started with higher expenditures and experienced the greatest increase in costs as a result of expanding rolls.

Also significant and influential was the size of a state's black population,

TABLE 4.3. ANALYSIS OF STATE SUPPORT FOR THE FAMILY
ASSISTANCE PLAN, 1970

	b (se)
Constant	0.272** (0.106)
Size of welfare (AFDC) burden	12.244** (3.160)
African American population	−2.073** (0.478)
Democratic	0.203 (0.136)

Sources: Support for welfare expansion and Democratic (ICPSR); African American population
(*1972 County and City Data Book*); and welfare burden (calculated from data in *1969 US Statistical Abstract*).
OLS analysis: *Adj. R²:* .47; *N:* 48
*$p \leq .05$; **$p \leq .01$
For more details about the OLS analysis, see note 107.

which directly aligned with southern concerns about FAP's impact on civil rights.[108] An inverse relationship existed between the size of a state's African American population and its support for FAP. Increasing the proportion of a state's population that was African American by 1 percent results in a 2 percent decrease in FAP support, all else being equal. Despite outward migration, states in the South—those least supportive of FAP—still had, proportionally, by far the highest black populations in the country. The average state in the South was 19 percent African American, relative to 7 percent in the average northern state, 3 percent in the Pacific Coast states, and 2 percent in western states.

Once these key social and economic factors are controlled, the variables for the regions had no independent effect on state support for welfare support (and thus were dropped from the model). This suggests that there was no significant regional cultural stance that influenced states' attitudes toward the welfare bill independent of the key demographic and economic factors. Though somewhat surprising given the strong positions on welfare taken in every region (with the exception of the West), it is likely that the large effects on welfare support in 1970 of welfare burden and size of African American population, variables that varied substantially by region, sufficiently dampened any independent regional effect.

Welfare as a Wedge Issue

Like the 1962 amendments, FAP generated bipartisan support in the House; yet, unlike the the earlier bill, FAP's bipartisan support came from a split in both parties—a reflection of the regional divide between North and South over the issues of race and welfare. By the mid-1960s, Republicans were using race as a wedge to drive apart the Democratic coalition.[109] Welfare policy, in which race was the pervasive but largely unspoken issue, was deployed in this way, rending Democrats along regional lines in an area where the party had long maintained a working consensus.

In 1970, where a representative from North or South stood on federalization of welfare depended on whether his or her region was plagued more by burgeoning AFDC costs or by the disintegration of traditional race-based political economic hierarchies. The issue of welfare also forged greater policy similarities between northern and Pacific Coast Democrats. Lawmakers in both regions knew that their states stood to gain from federalizing welfare.

Because these were the defining features of the welfare debate, representatives from the West remained largely silent on FAP. Westerners did not face the dramatic increase in numbers and costs with which northern and Pacific Coast states were grappling. Throughout most of the 1960s, the costs associated with AFDC grew in states in the West by an average of $9.2 million, small as compared to an average of $81.6 million in the North and $152.5 million in the Pacific Coast (they grew by $15.4 million in the South).[110] With high growth centered in states like New York, Illinois, New Jersey, and California, the North's average welfare expenditure increased by 186 percent during the 1960s and Pacific Coast's by 142 percent. By comparison, increases in the South and West were 86 percent and 100 percent, respectively. Neither were states in the West facing the realignment of social and political relations that states in the North and particularly the South were experiencing. Western states had relatively small black populations and thus less profoundly felt the effects of the civil rights movement. Western states were undergoing economic development and diversification but, lacking the history of the South, the region's economic changes did not hold the same portent for the political establishment.

With the stakes not nearly so high as in the other regions, the response of western lawmakers to FAP proved unremarkable. Few contributed to the House debates, and in their voting behavior westerners remained in the middle of the road. Average support among the region's representatives for federalizing welfare stood at just over 50 percent, slightly higher among Democrats (62 percent) and slightly lower among Republicans (48 percent). This translates into a predictable pattern on the map of congressional support for FAP: seven western states were above or well above average in their support for FAP and eight were below or well below average.

One of the conundrums of the Family Assistance Plan is why a Republican president, one with a (virtually) self-proclaimed southern strategy, would promote legislation that would be anathema in the South. The answer in all likelihood is that Nixon was never fully invested in passing the legislation. He introduced the idea for the program in a televised speech to the nation on August 8, 1969, and he submitted the program to Congress several times; but after his initial investment in the proposal, he spent no additional political capital ensuring its passage.[111] And yet, Nixon was aware that significant politicking would be needed to get the legislation passed. Just prior to his speech, congressional liaison Bryce Harlow outlined some concerns in a memorandum to Nixon advisor John Ehrlichman: "If it is the President's object to loft this program without regard to (1) Republican resentment or (2) likelihood of Congressional approval, I of course understand and readily acquiesce. . . . If however he desires to enact the FSS [FAP] rather than merely propose it, then I consider the present plans inadequate."[112] An entry from the diary of H. R. Haldeman, Nixon's chief of staff in July of 1970, makes the president's intentions with regard to FAP clear: "About Family Assistance Plan, [president] wants to be sure it's killed by Democrats and that we make a big play for it, but don't let it pass, can't afford it."[113]

In the aftermath of Nixon's August speech, domestic affairs aide Kenneth R. Cole, Jr., circulated a White House document analyzing press reactions to the welfare proposal, sending it to key administration officials and strategists along with a note saying, "The President thought you would find it [this] interesting." The document excerpted responses of thirty-one editorial writers and twenty columnists in the nation's major newspapers and news magazines to characterize the general reaction of the papers and to highlight specific concerns raised. The editorial responses were organized according to region, and they were introduced with the note that "regional considerations are . . . paramount in the editorial assessments." While the northern papers, including those from the Midwest, were described as predominantly in favor of the plan, the analysis noted that there was "a division of opinion" among southern papers, based on ideology. Among all of the editorials, four of the five that were described as being firmly opposed to the president's plan were southern papers.[114]

In perhaps the most revealing remark, a statement in the analysis read:

"The Atlanta Journal acknowledges that under the plan the South would stand to benefit more than some of the industrialized northern states, and quite candidly admits to favoring the plan nonetheless."[115] The phrasing, "candidly admits" and "nonetheless," is interesting, because it indicates that the endorsement was unexpected, even though, from a purely rational perspective, one would expect a positive reaction to the offering of greater benefits. It only makes sense when one adopts the political perspective and understanding that the Nixon administration anticipated opposition from the South because the plan provided federal dollars to low-income black southerners.

Thus, not only did the Nixon administration anticipate opposition to the proposal, they knew what region in the country it would come from—all well in advance of Congress's consideration of the proposal. Nixon knew it would take significant work to get the legislation passed, and this work was not done. In all likelihood, the president's primary intent with FAP was to make a public relations splash, one that would inoculate him from criticisms by the left that he cared neither about the nation's poor nor about the crises in the nation's cities at a time when both were high-profile issues. By promoting a federally provided national minimum income, Nixon went beyond what any Democratic president had done and effectively silenced most liberal critics.

Yet, in part because of its very audaciousness, the proposal invited opposition and defeat (that the defeat took as long as it did is what is perhaps most remarkable), and thus the risk of truly alienating the South was fairly minimal. This was particularly so given the relationship that Nixon had established with southern political leaders. During the 1968 presidential campaign, Nixon had won the support of Strom Thurmond and other reactionary southerners with promises to curtail the progress of civil rights. Nixon's subsequent Supreme Court nominations and his efforts to undermine fair housing legislation, weaken federal civil rights offices, and slow school desegregation indicate that he was mindful of the bargain that he had struck. One of the implied promises at the time was a "southern veto" of administration policies affecting the South.[116] Whether or not FAP received this so-called southern veto, the Nixon administration knew that North and South would divide over the proposal before it was launched, and this split, on an issue linked to both race and economy, had clear electoral benefits.

The president simultaneously outflanked the northern Democratic opposition and administered a devastating blow along the regional axis of the New Deal Democratic coalition. While the 1962 welfare amendments, in the New Deal tradition, had nurtured two distinct Democratic constituencies, the FAP proposal exploited their differences in a way that harmed the party. Seen in this light, FAP, the welfare program that never was, was a political success.

RISING PARTISANSHIP AND ENDURING REGIONAL DIVIDES

Following the failure of FAP in the early 1970s, Presidents Carter and Reagan each undertook efforts to reform AFDC. Reagan's popularity and his repeated denunciations of "welfare cheats" and "welfare queens" convinced many that AFDC would not survive the decade, and by the end of his first term, analysts of American politics were debating the future of the welfare state with a seriousness indicative of the monumental sea change toward conservatism that had begun in the 1970s. Some observers, noting the sustenance of the program and the continuity of many of the basic elements of social welfare provision, argued that the welfare state was robust, institutionalized by the strength of the New Deal ideology and a vested constituency of private interests. Others, pointing to cutbacks in Great Society programs, the disarray within the ranks of the Democratic Party, and the success of Reagan's ideological appeal, were less optimistic.[117] What none could have predicted, though, was that the eventual termination of AFDC in 1996 would take place with the approval of a Democratic president, Bill Clinton.

The welfare reform efforts that followed FAP and culminated in passage of the Personal Responsibility and Work Opportunity Reconciliation Act in 1996, the legislation that eliminated AFDC, increasingly divided the two parties, as Figure 4.2 made clear. But, at bottom, welfare is an issue with profound regional stakes, and welfare politics have more often been politically rational than they have made policy sense or been ideologically consistent. This explains how a Republican president could promote an expansive welfare program and a Democratic president could sign the termination of a longstanding welfare program.

The success of the postwar welfare state depended on the ability of New Deal Democratic presidents to unite northern political and economic desires for program expansion with southern political and economic desires for local discretion. As long as these incentives motivated both regions, there was little opposition to the program and the political coalition of the Democratic Party thrived. Kennedy's welfare initiative exemplifies this New Deal tradition, even as it began to shift the policy emphasis to accommodate emerging northern needs. Ultimately, however, this shift set in motion the demise of the New Deal coalition and inaugurated the era of the "welfare problem." With the strengthening of the civil rights movement and the linkage of welfare to black poverty, the cross-regional balance could no longer be sustained. To capitalize on the imbalance, President Nixon offered a welfare proposal the most enduring feature of which was the strength of its impress upon the regional cleavage in the Democratic Party. At the intersection of race and economics, the debate over welfare in the early 1970s aligned along a regional axis more than anything else, in part because the issue was made resonant with historic regional social and cultural conflicts. While welfare wedged apart the cross-regional coalition of the New Deal Democratic Party and set the stage for the geographic restructuring of the Republican Party, it also forged a bond between northern and Pacific Coast Democrats that has lasted until the present.

Just as the Democratic Party had once drawn strength from its ability to offer different enticements to different constituencies under the umbrella of one policy position, Republican strength has grown through its ability to do the same. Republicans adopted a position on welfare that allowed them to simultaneously cultivate the two different constituencies of fiscally conservative business and socially conservative religious groups. Not only did both groups support welfare reform in the 1980s and 1990s, both have been influential forces in the South and West. That the dissolution of AFDC occurred just after Republicans recaptured control of the House in 1994 is hardly surprising, especially given that, for the first time in history, a majority of the Republican Party's House seats were held by southerners and westerners.

From the perspective of this new regional realignment, the dissolution of the welfare state owes more to successful Republican strategy than to Democratic fragmentation. Disarray among Democrats was a factor, but that division was the result at least in part of earlier Republican strategy and the political choices made by Democratic leaders. Moreover, as the following pages show, the Democratic Party in Congress was unified in opposition to the 1996 welfare reform. Yet, by that point, the Republican Party had successfully entrenched a welfare counteroffensive in their new political base in the South and West. The success of this Republican effort is evident in the fact that President Clinton, a Democrat holding a position with a national constituency, had felt it necessary to make "ending welfare as we know it" a campaign promise in order to win national office and then felt politically obliged to honor this pledge.

Welfare became a regionally divisive issue for both parties beginning with the 1970s debate over FAP, and these regional divisions continued until AFDC ended. Regional divisions fed party divisions, and because the two parties were increasingly in different regions, party conflict escalated. Regional divisions were sustained within the parties, though, even as the parties became more unified in opposition to each other.[118] Southern and western Republicans could not automatically count on support for limiting welfare from party members in other regions, nor could northern and Pacific Coast Democrats always find full support for expanding welfare from Democrats in other regions.

Ending "Welfare as We Know It"

The contours of these regional and partisan battles are evident in House Republicans' protracted but successful effort to pass legislation to end the federal guarantee of AFDC in 1995–96. When signed into law in August of 1996, the Personal Responsibility and Work Opportunity Reconciliation Act terminated AFDC as a federal entitlement program, replacing it with the block-grant program, Temporary Assistance to Needy Families. The new program requires that recipients be moved off welfare within two years and limits recipients to a lifetime total of five years of cash assistance. Federal expenditures were reduced in several ways, including through the elimination of benefits for legal immigrants and through cuts to the food stamp program. Finally, by using block grants, the federal government devolved a significant amount of responsibility, giving the states greater freedom in the design, implementation, and financing of their programs than ever before. The size of a state's AFDC grant in the years before the passage of the legislation determined the size of the block grant, in most cases.[119]

The legislation was the product of intense wrangling between Democratic president Bill Clinton and House Republicans. As a "New Democrat" and a cofounder of the centrist, largely southern, Democratic Leadership Council, Clinton had promised to "end welfare as we know it" during his 1992 presidential campaign. This helped neutralize the Republicans' customary use of welfare as a wedge issue during the campaign. Once Republicans assumed control of the House in 1994 and drew up the Contract with America, however, the issues of welfare and Clinton's campaign promise were again theirs to exploit. Between the first introduction of their bill in 1995, a draconian measure by any account, and Clinton's signing of the bill in 1996, the House voted on some aspect of welfare legislation more than thirty times. The president vetoed two bills before a slightly compromised bill, put in motion by the National Governors' Association and acceptable to the president, passed and he signed it into law.

The intensely partisan nature of the debate over this legislation is evident from the index of support for welfare (or opposition to the reform). Using this index, mean Democratic support for preserving AFDC was 81 percent while

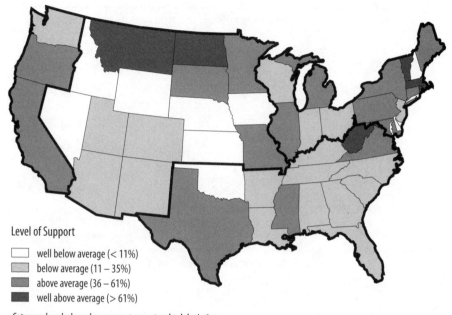

Level of Support

☐ well below average (< 11%)
▨ below average (11 – 35%)
▨ above average (36 – 61%)
■ well above average (> 61%)

Category breaks based on mean ± one standard deviation.

Figure 4.5
House Support for Welfare, 1995–1996

mean Republican support was just 2 percent.[120] Party was by far the most decisive factor in voting on welfare reform this time.

Given the strength of party divisions, it is surprising that welfare nonetheless divided the regions and that these divisions were sustained even within the
parties.[121] While all regions generally supported welfare reform, southerners
and westerners were the most in favor of reform, and Pacific Coast and northern lawmakers were the least supportive.[122] The map of congressional support
for preserving AFDC in Figure 4.5 shows these general regional differences.
Above average support for AFDC was concentrated among states in the North,
especially in New England and the Mid-Atlantic, as well as in the Pacific Coast
and among the northernmost states of the West. Conversely, most states in the
West and South were below average in their support of AFDC; it was lawmakers in these regions, especially the West, that were most in favor of eliminating the program.

Table 4.4 further elaborates the regional dimensions of party position on

TABLE 4.4. STRENGTH OF REGIONAL SUPPORT FOR THE PARTY POSITION, 1995–1996

	DEMOCRAT	REPUBLICAN
Mean pro-welfare index score	81	02
(sd)	(18)	(05)
N	199	234
Percentage of Regional Party within 1 sd of Party Mean*		
North	85	90
Pacific Coast	85	94
South	66	86
West	75	100

Source: Calculated from roll call data.

*For Democrats, figure is the percentage that has index scores above 63 percent. Technically, 1 sd away from the mean would be from .63 to .99, so those who voted every time (100%) for welfare maintenance would be excluded. Since the concern is with outliers who act less like their party and are closer on the continuum to the Republican position, this exclusion is not a problem. For Republicans, figure is the percentage with scores below 7 percent.

the 1996 welfare reform legislation, showing the degree of cohesion within each regional party for the party's mean position on welfare. Northern and Pacific Coast Democrats were the most committed to the party's position of maintaining AFDC; 85 percent of party members in these regions were within one standard deviation of the Democratic mean. Among southern Democrats, this number was just 66 percent, and among western Democrats, just 75 percent. In other words, there was greater defection from the party's position of supporting AFDC among southern and western Democrats. Support for constricting the federal role and eliminating the program had historically been strongest in the South, but it now shifted to the West. Western Republicans were the strongest proponents of ending welfare (100 percent being within one standard deviation of the party mean), followed by Pacific Coast and then northern Republicans.[123]

Selling Reform in the South and West

By 1995, welfare reform was a popular initiative with the public, and members of both parties were under pressure to revise the existing program of family assistance. The debate rested on the nature of the reform. While Republicans emphasized strict spending limits, assignment of power to the states, and work requirements, Democrats pressed for a continued federal role and the provision of services, training, and jobs. There was strong intraparty unity in support of the parties' respective positions, and a high degree of partisanship was generated. Even so, the party positions were consistent with different regional histories, and it is from this that the parties drew sustenance for their positions.

Republican rhetoric about limited spending and increased local control appealed to the party's nationwide business constituency. In the debates over reform, party members claimed that the cost savings associated with their plan were essential to balancing the budget, which, as a step toward stimulating business investment, was a priority.[124] They attacked the system of AFDC as a colossal waste of taxpayer money that was uselessly driving up the deficit. Drawing on an argument first made by Robert Rector of the Heritage Foundation that placed total expenditures on all means-tested programs for the prior thirty years at $5.4 trillion dollars, Republicans argued that the Democratic welfare program had done little more than build a bureaucratic empire.[125] Republican Porter Goss of Florida made it clear which party was the party of efficiency and thrift and which was the party of governmental waste:

> In the early 1970s the United States declared a war on poverty. That was the cry, and despite the best intentions and $5 trillion of taxpayer funds, we just about have to say that we lost the war, that it is time to surrender and do something different. . . . The Republican welfare reform bill . . . consolidates programs to minimize bureaucracy, fraud, and hopefully gets rid of some of the waste we have got, in order to ensure that our finite resources, and they are increasingly finite, reach those who truly need help.[126]

During the national economic restructuring that began in the 1970s, with profit levels stagnating and with increasing competition from abroad, business had abandoned its support for social welfare programs. Many of the groups that had been key supporters of FAP in the early 1970s, such as the National Association of Manufacturers and the National Federation of Independent Businesses, now regularly joined forces with newer organizations such as the Business Roundtable and a host of corporate political action committees to press for rollbacks in social welfare spending.[127] These efforts to eliminate social spending were part of a larger agenda to renegotiate the postwar social welfare compact that included, most prominently, cutting the costs of labor and governmental regulation. The comments made by Goss and others made clear that the old Democratic regime, with its welfare state, had been the problem and that Republicans were the solution.

Republican rhetoric had particular resonance in the South and West. In the broad assault on the welfare state, the bargaining power of business had been enhanced by its increasingly multinational status and its ability to move capital out of the country. Business leverage had also been strengthened, however, by its ability to move within the country, fostering competition among states. The postwar economic growth of both the South and the West was premised on the ability of states in these regions to lure firms with their "business-friendly" climates. Republican strength has grown in these areas concomitantly because the party has promoted measures consistent with the economic development plans of state and local pro-growth political coalitions.

These state and local efforts to lure business southward became particularly successful after the urban unrest in the North in the 1960s. In addition to the attractiveness of areas with less political strife, business was drawn to the South and West because of their histories of non-unionized labor, lower costs of living, lower wage structures, cheaper energy prices, tax breaks, and commitment to minimal government encumbrances, particularly in the area of social welfare spending.[128] As economist Mancur Olson put it, "One of the classical public policy recommendations for a state is to induce the in-migration of profitable businesses by tax breaks and to encourage the out-migration of unemployables by low levels of public assistance to the least fortunate."[129]

State per capita spending on programs and services has historically varied widely between the regions, and even in the 1990s, the highest levels of spending occurred in the states of the North and Pacific Coast, while states in the South and West tended to spend the least.[130] These differences are particularly apparent in spending on AFDC. In 1996, the average amount of money spent by states in the North on AFDC, when adjusted for the number of people living below the poverty line in the state, was $790 per person, and in the Pacific Coast, it was $834. By comparison, in the West, the average spent was just $391, and in the South, $247.[131]

Welfare spending, including AFDC and the range of War on Poverty programs initiated in the 1960s, had been targeted largely at the urban centers of the North, areas then and now represented by Democrats. By contrasting the new Republican program with the Johnson legacy, as Representative Goss and others repeatedly did, Republicans invoked, at least implicitly, old regional divides and suggested that it was time to move away from a system calibrated to the needs of northern cities. This message also contained racial overtones, although it never explicitly referred to race. Ronald Reagan and the "New Right" had cemented the vision of a bloated, bureaucratized national government spending taxpayer money on black "welfare queens," when justifying cuts in these "wasteful" programs. By the time Republicans took over Congress in 1994, this had become a party mantra.[132]

Devolution of authority was a second pillar of the Republican welfare reform plan, which lawmakers justified as a step that would result in more efficient and innovative programs for the poor. The welfare issue was "ground zero" in the fight over the role of the federal government.[133] Sounding much like the southern Democrats of an earlier era, Republican Mac Collins from Georgia defended the local discretion provided by the measure: "The Republican plan will remove the one-size-fits-all entitlement system. This measure will transfer the management authority from the bureaucratic Federal level to the States. Local authorities will finally have the ability to design a welfare program that best meets the needs of the poor in their region."[134]

By providing states with the flexibility of block grants, the bill would free states from the modest obligations that the federal government had previously imposed. Critics feared that this would lead to a "race to the bottom," in which states would compete with each other to lower benefits and channel savings to more profitable policy endeavors.[135] Advocates for the poor were clear about the intent behind the rhetoric of block grants. As the director of the Washington bureau of the NAACP explained, "We saw this as a throwback to the issue of states' rights, and our history tells us enough about that. It's negative and frightening."[136] An attorney for the Center for Law and Social Policy, a liberal think tank, bluntly stated, "The states have no obligations to the poor under the program"; then he quipped, "The governors settled for more federal funds and fewer state responsibilities."[137]

The desire for greater state control was not isolated to the South and West, but the Republican theme was particularly attractive in these regions. John Mollenkopf argues that the political culture in southwestern cities, which had been dominated by business-backed pro-growth political coalitions since the 1970s, intersected with conservative forces at the federal level and with private enterprise to promote economic development.[138] Mollenkopf and others note that, while local pro-growth politicians have long sought federal resources for development expenses like the construction of roads and other infrastructure, they have traditionally avoided federal dollars that redistributed wealth among socioeconomic classes and that required local social welfare commitments.[139]

For both South and West, the federal government's investment in AFDC meant that their tax dollars had been subsidizing a program the infrastructure of which had long ago become concentrated in the cities of the Democratic coasts. Lacking the South's plantation history and lacking the North's history of urban politics and development, the West had never invested in the AFDC program to the same extent as the other regions, and by the late 1960s the South had begun withdrawing its commitment to the program. Just as important, both regions had historically harbored suspicions of programs imposed by a northern-dominated federal government. Devolution of control would free state and local political leaders of the federal strictures that had accompanied AFDC and allow considerable latitude in the use of federal funds. Describing the success of the Contract with America in the South, Bill Gustafson, chair of the Cobb County, Georgia, Republican Party, said, "We want big government off our backs. What happened in 1994 has been coming for a long, long time, building up over the last 40 or 50 years."[140]

Focusing on devolution of control over welfare spending enabled Republicans to satisfy another clientele, one based largely in the South but increasingly in the West as well: conservative Christians. By 1995, evangelical Christians accounted for one-third of the Republican Party, and half of all evangelicals lived in the South.[141] The West, too, has experienced a rise in evangelicalism, brought in part by migrating southerners; tellingly, Oral Roberts established his headquarters in the southwestern city of Tulsa, Oklahoma.[142] Evangelicals were important as a grassroots base, but their affiliated organizations, most notably the Christian Coalition, offered an anchor for Republican social conservatism. Larry Sabato, who studies political parties, has called the Christian Coalition "the Republican Party's No. 1 interest group" for its ability to influence the party's social policy.[143]

Groups like the Christian Coalition became interested in welfare reform in the early 1990s, both as an avenue for voicing concerns about "family values" and illegitimacy and as a way to incorporate new social issues, beyond their traditional ones of abortion and school prayer. Consistent with their concerns about the sanctity of the American family, these groups promoted measures designed to limit out-of-wedlock births, such as the imposition of family caps on welfare benefits and the denial of benefits to the children of unmarried teenage mothers.[144] Early versions of the Republican reform plan mandated measures such as these, to appeal to the religious right. This overture was particularly important because there had been little else of special appeal to these groups in the Republican's Contract with America. As Gary Bauer, head of the Family Research Council, said, welfare was "one of the few areas that the party leadership could signal to us that we were of interest to them for something more than votes every two years."[145] In response to strong opposition from Democrats and moderate members of their own party, Republicans eventually removed the family cap mandates and the denial of benefits to teenage mothers from the legislation, instead giving states greater discretion to decide whether to impose these measures.

Devolution of control, allowing states flexibility, thus became a way for Republicans to unite social and economic conservatives under the welfare reform banner. By handing authority back to the states, local leaders were freer to decide what sort of antipoverty measures would work for their constituents and how much money would be directed to the effort. More important, by joining social and economic conservatives, Republicans' welfare reform proposal played to the sentiments of two key constituencies in their growth regions, the South and West.

For Republican Party leaders, the welfare reform legislation had another regional purpose. Republicans had long understood that the welfare state infrastructure of nonprofit organizations, state and local government agencies, and professional educational programs amounted to, in essence, taxpayer financing of a key Democratic constituency. Welfare programs drew on national resources for what was largely a party-specific and regionally concentrated constituency. Newt Gingrich and other Republican leaders hoped that in ending the federal entitlement they could use welfare reform to "defund" and thus disable this component of the Democratic coalition.[146] Because undermining this infrastructure would have its largest impact in the big Democratic cities of the North and Pacific Coast, passage of welfare reform would result in the execution of a significant reversal of regional political fortunes.

Defending the Federal Entitlement in the North and Pacific Coast

The GOP bill granted the same privileges of devolution to all states, of course. And while the North and Pacific Coast states lacked the conservative Christian base of the South and West, some of the same economic incentives were at play. Here too, for example, political leaders at the state level had begun to seek ways to reduce AFDC expenditures and shift revenue to other policy areas, in part to entice business back to the area. New York Governor Pataki, for example, called for a 26.5 percent reduction in benefit levels to compensate for tax cuts and breaks provided to individuals and businesses just before the welfare reform legislation.[147]

Yet, welfare programs had become an integral and extensive part of the local public infrastructure in northern and Pacific Coast states to a far greater degree than in the South or West. This was particularly true in the regions' aging industrial cities, which had most benefited from federal welfare dollars. Devolution of administrative control and the end of the federal entitlement would mean that the responsibility for funding and maintaining this infrastructure would fall squarely on local political leaders, and in the North and Pacific Coast that change was not especially welcome.

As the debate over welfare reform unfolded, the loudest detractors of devolution and block grants included associations representing local administrators such as the U.S. Conference of Mayors, the National Association of Counties, and the National League of Cities. They were joined by advocacy and research groups based largely in New York and Washington, D.C. Groups such as the Children's Defense Fund and the Urban Institute had emerged from the civil rights and antipoverty activism of earlier decades and now had well established links both to Democratic constituencies and to party elites. Leaders of these groups and associations complained that the effect of devolution and the cuts in federal funds would be not only to increase poverty and associated problems but also to force local governments and nonprofit organizations to find the solutions without the federal assistance they had had since the inception of the welfare system.[148]

Democrats in the North and Pacific Coast argued that their regions had long borne undue responsibility for welfare and that reform would increase this burden. Using the same regional examples that had been used during the previous thirty years of debate, Representative William Coyne from Pennsylvania explained.

> The bill before us today will end the Federal guarantee of economic assistance for families in need. This means that individual States will determine who will be eligible for assistance and how to provide for these families with limited Federal dollars. Under this system, if you are poor and happen to live in New York, you may be eligible to receive welfare assistance, while if you are poor and happen to live in Mississippi, you may not be eligible to receive any assistance at all. This is hardly an equitable means of distributing Federal dollars.[149]

The imprint Presidents Kennedy and Johnson had left on welfare emphasized the federal government's commitment to providing services and training along with cash assistance to poor people. Ideologically, this framed poverty as a problem of unequal opportunity, making it therefore a responsibility of government—state and, specifically, federal government. Politically, this strategy had operated on several fronts. It built a Democratic base among non-white, particularly black, Americans, who made up a disproportionate, though not majority, share of the beneficiaries of antipoverty programs, as well as among the cadres of welfare workers who had become part of the institutionalized welfare state. Also, to the extent that public relief functioned as a method of social control for non-mobile industries, the federal government aided businesses by freeing them of some of the costs of the capitalist enterprise. This, of course, was particularly beneficial in the 1960s and early 1970s, when mounting social unrest was driving up the cost of doing business in America's leading industrial cities.

By the early 1990s, however, deindustrialization and recession had increased the costs of maintaining the welfare infrastructure in the North and Pacific Coast states. Lawmakers from those regions had pressed throughout the 1970s and 1980s for increased federal responsibility for the programs, as a way to pass off some of the fiscal burden to other regions. By fixing the amount of federal money available to the states, the 1996 reform threatened to severely limit any such burden sharing. Despite the economic recovery of the mid-1990s, if the need for assistance should increase, as it had in the past, more generous federal resources would prove essential. Maxine Waters, a Democrat from California, laid out a scenario in which globalization would lead to job loss and the need for assistance: "This bill gets rid of all the entitlements. . . . [A] mother and father worked hard for the last twenty years and all of a sudden they are downsized on the job, . . . the job exported somewhere to a Third World country for cheap labor."[150] Waters's concern was that, with the entitlement program gone, a family in this situation might not get any support because "Money has run out."

Waters's argument addressed more than just economic necessity; it was about political imperative as well. Because of the strong investment that northern and Pacific Coast states had made in the welfare state, literally and ideologically, local political leaders, particularly urban leaders, had the most to lose as the result of any future problems with the new system. Saddled with fuller responsibility for a welfare infrastructure that had traditionally provided jobs, helpful programs, and federal mandates, these local leaders would now have to make tough calls about resource priorities and handle the political fallout of the decisions they would make.

In making their stand against the Republican plan, Democrats focused on a broader problem that had been endemic to the cities in the North and Pacific Coast after 1970: lack of desirable jobs for unskilled and semi-skilled workers. Since that time, lawmakers, especially in the North, had argued that the shortage of private sector jobs in their region was a critical problem that any welfare reform initiative would have to address. Groups such as the Northeast-Midwest Economic Advancement Coalition urged solutions that focused on making public- and private-sector jobs available to recipients, and opposed plans that simply required recipients to work.[151] A natural outgrowth of the loss of employment opportunities that had accompanied decades of plant closures and business relocations, the demand for job creation was still popular among Democrats. Representative Donald Payne of New Jersey contended that Republicans were missing the point of what drove welfare dependency.

> Because we are not addressing the root causes, the lack of adequate jobs, the underlying conditions of the problem will continue to exist. An experiment conducted in my home state of New Jersey and also in Illinois found that 80 percent of welfare recipients who found jobs were able to break the cycle of poverty. It was very simple. They were able to work their way out. Yet, only 2 percent of those that had to depend on the system were able to break the cycle of poverty. The answer is jobs. We had 100 jobs available in the city of Newark. Fourteen hundred people started to get in line at 6 a.m. for those 100 jobs. It was not even 100. They said possibly up to 100, but maybe 50. Fourteen hundred people went and waited for hours and hours to apply for the jobs. So the answer is certainly there.[152]

Arguments such as this sought both to remind listeners of which regions had experienced the most acute job loss and to recast the image of the needy from the "welfare cheat" of conservative rhetoric to the industrious job seeker left unemployed by regional economic trends. Democrats from the North combined their demand for job creation with a request for more services and training to help accommodate sector shifts in employment. All of this, they argued, the federal government should insure. Claiming that the Republican bill would throw low-income people into the streets, Detroit Democrat Cardiss Collins elaborated on Payne's themes.

> There are very few low-skill, entry-level jobs nowadays that pay a living wage, but instead of improving our job training program or increasing the minimum wage, or providing affordable child care or creating jobs or offering a possibile alternative to poverty, this bill, which is a hatchet act, punishes Americans for being poor. . . . It just wipes out the critical entitlement status of most of our current systems and replaces them with State block grants and Federal funds with no strings attached.[153]

Democratic rhetoric, rather than praising the flexibility of devolution and the possibility of innovative state solutions, focused on the federal abandonment of poor families. Devolution, Democrats, particularly urban Democrats, argued, did not guarantee that state governments would continue to invest in welfare at earlier levels. The welfare infrastructure had developed in past decades as the result of a political and economic investment by the Democratic Party in the cities. Those decades also witnessed ever-greater levels of racial and economic segregation between cities and their surrounding suburbs. If the federal entitlement was dropped, state governments, responsive to their suburban constituencies, might also choose to pass off the responsibility to local communities.

With the burden of the nation's welfare program still carried by the cities of the North and Pacific Coast, Democrats from these areas were intent on maintaining some level of federal involvement and aid. Conceding the need for reform, they argued that the Republican plan was more interested in cost savings than in putting people to work. In an economic climate that, despite overall prosperity, was characterized by layoffs, stagnating wages, and a growing income gap—particularly pronounced in the major industrial cities—Democrats charged, those most likely to pay the price for the Republican plan were the families and children dependent on AFDC. A price, as the lawmakers knew all too well, would also be paid by the states and the cities of the North and Pacific Coast.

DEPENDING ON WELFARE: REGIONAL STRATEGIES
AND THE POLITICS OF REFORM

The wholesale shift within the United States from a New Deal discourse of equality and government activism to a conservative discourse of individual responsibility and local government control underscores the importance of ideology in American party politics. The dominant New Deal ideology rationalized welfare expansion and set the boundaries of legitimate opposition just as conservative ideology legitimized welfare contraction and established new boundaries for the opposition. But, knowing the parties' ideological debates is insufficient for understanding why the parties came into conflict when they did and how policy changed as a result. After all, it was a Republican president, Richard Nixon, who promoted what is arguably one of the most progressive welfare reform proposals the country has seen, and it was Bill Clinton, a Democratic president intent on making his party more nationally competitive, who allowed AFDC to end. Amidst regional divisions, both presidents acted on national political logic as much as for ideological reasons.

Understanding welfare policy and the battles around it requires reference to specific and multifaceted regional developments and their effects on party coalitions. And, as with trade, this necessitates knowledge of the changing economic conditions of the regions. The mechanization of cotton is an essential factor in the decline in southern support for welfare. Deindustrialization and urban fiscal crises are critical aspects of sustained northern support for welfare federalization. Yet, regional economic changes alone do not explain welfare politics. Party conflict was also inflected by regional efforts to manage changing demographic realities. Race relations shaped, and were in turn shaped by, changing material conditions. The effect of the civil rights movement on the South and the impact of racial tensions and white flight in the North are as central to welfare partisanship as are economic conditions. Historic regional attitudes about the role of the national government in managing economic change and in negotiating social relations also play their role. The North has long looked favorably upon using government to direct economic life, a position consistent with the region's support for national welfare. In contrast, the South has long used government to manage social relations, and the region's position on welfare policy has reflected this.

Both parties pitched their positions on welfare to key regional constituents, but this required artful policy combinations to manage potential conflicts within their respective coalitions. National program expansion with local control allowed Democrats to placate industrial centers and the planter elite society simultaneously. Republicans combined national program reduction with greater social regulation to forge common cause between business elites and religious conservatives. When they did so, Republicans united one of their traditional constituencies, business, with a new one, social conservatives, a constituency that, as the next chapter demonstrates, would prove increasingly important to the party's regional success.

CHAPTER 5

THE POLITICAL RESURRECTION OF THE BIBLE BELT

RELIGION, MODERNIZATION, AND THE INTENSIFICATION OF ABORTION POLITICS

THE U.S. SUPREME COURT'S 1973 decision in *Roe v. Wade*, establishing a woman's constitutional right to have an abortion, brought the issue of abortion into the national political arena. The landmark decision also launched one of the most controversial political battles of the last thirty years. Related legislative proposals in Congress began immediately. The Court handed down the decision in January; representatives cast their first vote to restrict abortion-related funding and services that spring. In the ensuing months and years, the issue galvanized voters, energized pro-life and pro-choice interest groups, began and ended the careers of individual politicians, and divided the political parties.[1] Not since civil rights has an issue provoked the level of conflict, moral outrage, and political violence that has accompanied the debate over abortion. It has become the defining issue of the culture wars of the late twentieth and early twenty-first centuries.

Much of the conflict has taken place literally "in the streets"—at abortion clinics and between interest groups—yet the major political parties have also become combatants in the debate. By the early 1980s, between 80 and 100 percent of all abortion-related votes in the House were being cast along party lines. By the early 1990s, the average difference between the parties' positions was regularly more than 50 percentage points. This level of partisan conflict was not

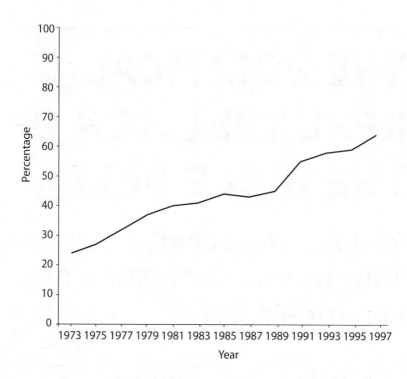

Figure 5.1
Mean Difference between Parties on All Abortion Votes, 93rd through 105th Congresses, 1973–1998
Source: Calculated from vote data provided by Keith Poole and Howard Rosenthal at voteview.com.

present at the outset of voting on abortion. As Figure 5.1 shows, party differences rose gradually.[2]

Given the vitriol of the abortion debate and the uncompromising nature of the issues involved, it is surprising that the growth in party differences occurred so slowly. Figure 5.2 illustrates average party positions over time. Both parties were originally largely resistant to abortion rights. The average Democrat was only slightly more pro-choice than the average Republican at the outset of voting on abortion. But, while the Republican Party has remained steadily opposed to abortion, the Democratic position has gradually shifted to greater support for abortion rights. Party differences emerged only as the Democratic Party became more consistently pro-choice.[3]

In the immediate aftermath of the Court's decision, Republicans and Democrats worked together in an attempt to limit abortions. Much like the cases of welfare and trade, though, Democrats were divided geographically on abortion

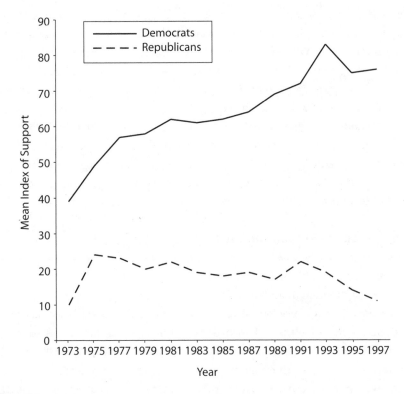

Figure 5.2
Mean Party Support for Abortion Rights, 93rd through 105th Congresses, 1973–1998
Source: Calculated from roll call data.

rights. Republicans, too, were divided geographically, although to a much lesser extent. As the geographic centers of the parties shifted and weakened the intraparty divisions, partisanship increased. By the end of the 1980s, a 50-point gap separated the two party positions. Partisanship had become the norm.

Both sides in the abortion debate, pro-life and pro-choice, claim fundamental rights as the basis for their position: the right of the fetus or life of the unborn versus the right of a woman to privacy and reproductive freedom. Although the positions are seemingly so irreconcilable that the contest has been called "the clash of absolutes,"[4] neither national party entered the fray with the ideological clarity and unity one would expect concerning an issue cast in terms of such stark alternatives. They started instead from regional positions. Pacific Coast and northern lawmakers on the whole were more supportive of the pro-choice position than southern and western lawmakers. Over the course of three decades, the Democratic Party shifted from moderate opposition to ardent support of abortion rights as the regions favoring this position became dominant within the party. While Republicans have been more uniform in their opposition to abortion rights, the southern and western delegations have provided the staunchest opposition, but the party has achieved greater national unity on policy in the areas of welfare and trade.[5]

To understand how abortion came to be the lightning rod for the parties, the issue must be examined in the context of the unfolding regional realignment of the parties. Introduced in the midst of the regional shake-up of the parties, the abortion issue fueled regional divisions among Democrats and provided Republicans with a useful new tool for geographic consolidation.

REGIONALISM AND ABORTION OVER TIME

Relative to trade and welfare, abortion is new to regional politics. Trade has prompted geographic division since the beginning of the republic, and welfare was managed throughout much of the twentieth century through a tenuous interregional compromise, one always ready to break apart. In contrast, abortion entered national politics when many thought regional differences on their way to extinction, chased away by industrialization of the historically agricultural regions and by achievement of civil rights in the South. And, while trade and welfare had strong political economy components, abortion more clearly reflects differences in moral valuation. In the national consumer society of the 1970s, there was no ready reason to expect a geographic pattern to such fundamental ideas about life. Yet, just as with trade and welfare, regional divisions in abortion voting have been apparent throughout the three decades of legislative activity on the issue (see Figure 5.3).

As a whole, Pacific Coast lawmakers have consistently supported abortion rights. Northern lawmakers have followed them statistically, with their region's pro-choice support rising steadily over time. While northern lawmakers were at first generally opposed to abortion rights, by 1993, they were nearly as supportive as Pacific Coast representatives. Southern and western representatives, on the whole, have been the least supportive and the most likely to favor greater restrictions on access to abortion. Neither region ever produced a pro-choice index score above 50 percent.

Within these general regional patterns, however, there exists some sustained subregional variation, especially in the heavily populated territory of the North. This subregional variation is important, because it helps explain the issue's appeal for the Republican Party in the party's efforts to build a national majority. Table 5.1 makes these subregional divisions clearer.[6]

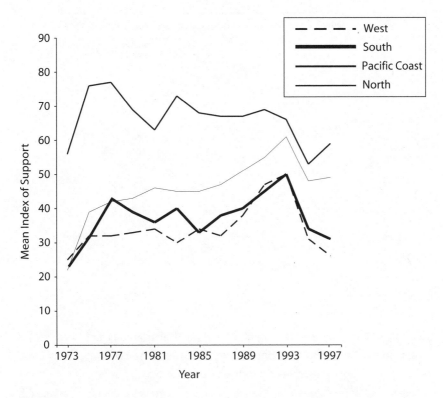

Figure 5.3
Mean Regional Support for Abortion Rights, 93rd through 105th Congresses, 1973–1998
Source: Calculated from roll call data.

Representatives from the East North Central subregion, hailing from Midwestern states such as Ohio and Indiana, have voted more like representatives from the South and West. This anomaly in the North reflects the extent to which the issue of abortion energizes the Bible Belt, and thus cuts across the geographic territory of the North. Because East North Central states, the southernmost of which are considered part of the Bible Belt, are included in the North, the region's aggregate index scores are lower and closer to those of the South and West than they otherwise would be. Lawmakers in the rest of the North, including the Mid-Atlantic and New England states, became more like Pacific Coast representatives over time.

These regional (and subregional) divisions are sustained even within the parties, indicating the primacy of geography for lawmakers' abortion positions. Within the Democratic Party, lawmakers from the Pacific Coast and the North provided the strongest support for abortion rights from the early 1980s to

TABLE 5.1. LEVEL OF SUPPORT FOR ABORTION RIGHTS BY REGION, 1975–1996

REGION	1975–76 (%)	1987–88 (%)	1993–94 (%)	1995–96 (%)
North	39	47	61	48
New England	50	61	93	82
Mid-Atlantic	45	52	60	54
East North Central	29	39	51	31
Pacific Coast	76	67	66	53
South	32	38	50	34
Southeast	35	40	52	34
Southwest	24	33	48	33
West	32	32	50	31
West North Central	30	33	49	35
Mountain	37	31	51	27

Source: Calculated from roll call data.

Note: Based on mean index support score for pro-choice position in the 94th, 100th, 103rd, and 104th Congresses.

the 1990s. But, as with the general regional pattern, among northern Democrats, lawmakers from New England and the Mid-Atlantic were markedly more supportive of abortion rights than those from East North Central states. When considering these subregional breakdowns, it is largely Democratic lawmakers on the country's two coasts—in the Pacific Coast, New England, and Mid-Atlantic states—that have driven support for abortion, and party pro-choice uniformity developed only as time passed.

Among Republicans, regional divisions have remained pronounced, although on a smaller scale overall than those of the Democrats. As with Democrats, northern and Pacific Coast Republicans have been more supportive of abortion rights than Republicans from the West and South. Some similar subregional variations exist as well. New England and Mid-Atlantic Republicans are, on average, more pro-choice than most other Republicans. In contrast, southern Republicans, in both the Southwest and the Southeast, have been the strongest proponents of restricting abortion.

On abortion, in an even more exaggerated manner than on welfare and trade, positions found most commonly in the politically ascendant regions of the parties became the general party positions. The question is, Why? Why did Pacific Coast and northeastern lawmakers propel the Democrats toward the party's pro-choice stance? Conversely, how did southern Republicans become the anchor for their party's pro-life position?

The rest of the chapter focuses on two specific abortion battles. The 1976 voting on the Hyde Amendment, stipulating when federal funds could be used for an abortion, largely reinforced the existing regional cleavage among Democrats. The rhetoric of the debate framed the issue as a choice between tradition and modernization, and the regions responded differently to those options. In areas with long histories of economic development, like the Pacific Coast and Northeast, the changes driving the demand for abortion rights and gender equality were welcomed. In areas newly experiencing economic development and widespread change, such as the historically rural South and West, tradition and social stability were prized. The general result was a further fracturing of Democrats and a fueling of conservative bipartisanship as large numbers of southern and midwestern (i.e., East North Central) Democrats joined with Republicans to champion values that generally hold abortion to be unacceptable. The debate helped establish the importance of the Bible Belt, especially the religious conservatives in the South, to the Republican Party, and abortion became a new tool with which Republicans could target the region. East North Central Democrats were a second, important source of bipartisan support for restricting abortion. And because of this, the issue also revealed its potential usefulness to Republicans for leeching states away from what had become an increasingly Democratic North. This was an important development, because in the 1970s lawmakers from East North Central states were standing solidly with other northerners on issues to do with trade and welfare.

In the 1990s, the geographic alignments in the abortion debate hardened and partisanship on the issue was high. But with the Republican Party's broad and multifaceted success in the South and West, abortion had become a potential liability. The party's pro-life stance had only limited appeal to "New Economy" voters in the South and West, who were attached to the party for its free-market policies but were not especially socially conservative. Additionally, the violent tactics of some of the fringe pro-life groups tainted the efforts of the party to cast their position as moderate.

The party concentrated its efforts on the "partial-birth" ban. Repeatedly in the mid to late 1990s Congress passed legislation banning a particular type of abortion procedure used in later-term abortions, only to have it vetoed by President Clinton.[7] By shifting the focus on the abortion issue, Republicans successfully recast the debate so that claims for the rights of the unborn took on new significance; whereas in earlier decades limiting abortion had been perceived as limiting women's rights, it now was presented as a moderate measure to protect the rights of the unborn against the excesses of modern medical technology. In making this shift, the Republican Party not only circumvented the political pitfalls that had come to be associated with abortion; they reanimated the issue's geographic divisions. While this helped solidify the regional realignment of the parties, it also kept the East North Central states in play for both parties.

INTRODUCING THE ISSUE: MODERNIZATION, RESISTANCE, AND THE HYDE AMENDMENT

Since 1974, the year after the *Roe v. Wade* decision, each Congress has considered legislation to restrict Medicaid funding for abortions. In 1976, the House passed the Hyde Amendment, named after its sponsor, Representative Henry Hyde, and the Hyde Amendment has been passed annually since then as an amendment to the appropriations bill for the Department of Health, Education, and Welfare (the precursor to Health and Human Services).[8] The language that the House settled on in 1976, after much controversy, prohibited use of federal funds to pay for abortion unless carrying the fetus to term would endanger the life of the mother. Despite being in effect since 1976, the amendment has regularly stirred debate over the extent of the restrictions, which have been alternately relaxed and tightened around the circumstances of rape, incest, or whether the long-term health of the mother is in jeopardy.

When the House debated the amendment in 1976, members of both parties spoke out on both sides of the issue. In the midst of a presidential election, both presidential candidates hedged their positions. Despite the ambiguous message this diversity of opinion conveyed about the positions of the parties, when it came time to vote, House Republicans provided broad support for the funding ban. On the closest House vote on the Hyde Amendment, 73 percent of voting Republicans favored the funding ban along with 45 percent of Democrats. A Democratic split on the issue produced the bipartisanship behind the amendment's passage.[9]

Taking into consideration all of the votes cast on the House floor on the Hyde Amendment, the voting index for the 94th Congress confirms that Democrats, as a whole, were more pro-choice than were Republicans. The mean index of support for abortion rights among Democrats was 49 percent, while for Republicans the mean was 24 percent. Data on the median and the distribution of index scores is more revealing. The median index position for Republicans was 0 percent, while for Democrats, who were distributed at either end of the spectrum of index scores, the median position was 50 percent.[10]

Among Democrats, southerners and Pacific Coast lawmakers occupied the two poles of the debate. With a mean index score of 91 percent, Pacific Coast Democrats were the only major regional group that was more pro-choice than pro-life. They were joined in their pro-choice support by Mid-Atlantic Democrats, hailing from states like New Jersey and New York, who had a mean index score of 51 percent. The region least inclined toward abortion rights among Democrats was the South, where Democrats had a regional mean of 32 percent. The South's Democrats were joined by East North Central Democrats, who had a mean index of 39 percent. Republicans almost everywhere were more opposed to keeping abortion legal than were Democrats. The one noteworthy exception was in New England, where Republican lawmakers had a mean index score of 59 percent in support of choice, putting them on par with pro-choice Democrats in the Pacific Coast and the Mid-Atlantic subregion. Among Republicans, southerners and westerners anchored their party's pro-life position, with average abortion rights scores below 20 percent. Regional splits on abortion in the 1970s drove divisions in the parties, producing a bipartisan alignment of southern and East North Central Democrats with Republicans and making passage of the Hyde Amendment possible.[11]

The geography of support for the Hyde Amendment is evident in the map in Figure 5.4. Opposition to abortion rights reigned in the interior of the country. Eleven of the 15 states in the West were below the national average in their support for abortion rights, with 7 of those well below the national average. Similarly, 9 of the 14 southern states were below average in supporting abortion rights. In the East North Central states, which occupy the interior corner of the North, 4 of the 5 states were below average in their support of choice.

In contrast to the opposition to abortion rights that dominated the middle of the country, the greatest pro-choice support is evident on the coasts. The Pacific Coast was the only region strongly favorable to abortion rights in the mid-1970s, with all three states well above the national average in their support. Above average support for Medicaid funding of abortions also prevailed on the East Coast, with the exceptions of Pennsylvania, Massachusetts, and Rhode Island. States in the northern third of the South, with the exception of Kentucky, were also above average in support of abortion rights, an outcome seemingly at odds with their location in the Bible Belt.[12]

The general regional divisions over abortion make greater sense given the social disruptions of the 1960s and early 1970s and their geographic implications. The protest activities of the civil rights, feminist, gay liberation, and antiwar movements were centered largely on college campuses and in major cities. Nonetheless, television broadcasted those groups' demands for social

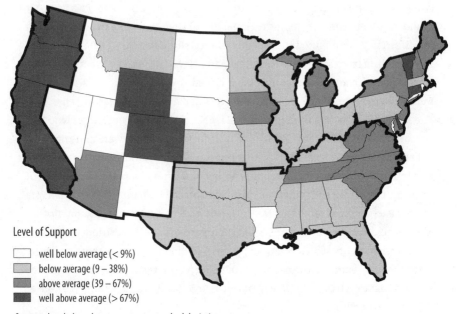

Level of Support

☐ well below average (< 9%)
▨ below average (9 – 38%)
▨ above average (39 – 67%)
■ well above average (> 67%)

Category breaks based on mean ± one standard deviation.

Figure 5.4
House Support for Abortion Rights, 1976

change to the entire nation, bringing pictures of political unrest and social order disruptions into living rooms everywhere. Republican leaders claimed that
the protest activity was undermining established law and order, and they argued that protestors, including students and intellectuals, were recklessly fostering violence to achieve their ends. Vice President Agnew, a chief spokesper-
son for the Nixon administration on these issues, warned Americans in a series
of speeches that young people were disregarding the "lessons of the past" to the
great peril of the nation.[13] Such statements by such a prominent official fostered the emergence of new cultural divisions—pitting young against old, progressive against conservative, modern against traditional, city and campus
against small town and suburb. To a not insignificant degree, this approach
also pit region against region.

The issue of abortion instantly added fuel to this incendiary mix. In 1976,
lawmakers considering the Hyde Amendment were already confronting mobilized campaigners on both sides of the issue. The effect that this had on their
voting calculus can be seen in analysis of state support for abortion rights.[14]

As suggested by the earlier discussion of party support for abortion, states

TABLE 5.2. ANALYSIS OF STATE SUPPORT FOR ABORTION RIGHTS, 1976

	b (se)
Constant	−0.592 (0.363)
Conservative Christian population	−1.104*** (0.256)
Catholic representatives	−0.701*** (0.137)
Women in labor force	1.667* (0.921)
College education	5.113*** (1.592)
Democratic	0.242** (0.111)
South	−0.051 (.099)
West	−0.206*** (0.076)
Pacific Coast	0.014 (0.128)

Sources: Abortion rights and Democratic (ICPSR); Catholic (*Almanac of American Politics, 1976; Congressional Staff Directory, 1975*); conservative Christian (*Churches and Church Membership in the United States 1971*); women in labor force (*1970 Census of Population*); college education (*1976 Statistical Abstract*).

OLS analysis: *Adj. R²: .63; N:* 48

*$p \le .10$; **$p \le .05$; ***$p \le .01$

For more information on the OLS analysis, see note 14.

with a larger Democratic delegation to Congress were more likely to support abortion rights (that is, to oppose the Hyde Amendment). Yet, once party is controlled, variation in state support for abortion rights was associated with differences between the states on key socioeconomic and religious factors. States in which a higher proportion of the population over age 25 had at least four years of college education were more likely to support keeping abortion legal, as were states with more women in the labor force (though the latter is at the edge of conventional significance, with $p = .08$). Conversely, states with larger numbers of conservative Christians and those with more Catholic representatives tended to be less supportive of abortion rights.

These factors varied significantly by region. As Table 5.3 shows, the aver-

TABLE 5.3. REGIONAL VARIATION IN FACTORS INFLUENCING ABORTION RIGHTS SUPPORT, 1976

	U.S. (%)	NORTH (%)	PACIFIC COAST (%)	SOUTH (%)	WEST (%)	ETA SQUARED (%)
Abortion rights support	39	47	79	31	28	22
	(27)	(28)	(4)	(19)	(32)	
Conservative Christian	15	4	8	26	18	42
	(11)	(4)	(2)	(8)	(18)	
Catholic representatives	24	42	11	8	23	26
	(26)	(31)	(10)	(12)	(30)	
Women in labor force	41	43	41	39	41	16
	(3)	(2)	(1)	(5)	(3)	
College educated	11	11	13	9	11	34
	(2)	(2)	(1)	(2)	(2)	
Democratic	64	55	83	78	57	12
	(32)	(31)	(18)	(17)	(42)	

Notes: Numbers in this chart represent average of state percentages within each region for each of the variables. Standard deviations are in parentheses. All have F statistics with $p \leq .05$, with the exception of percent Democratic.

age state in the North had more women in the labor force than elsewhere in the country, while Pacific Coast states had more college educated citizens than states in other regions. On average, the southern states had the largest proportion of conservative Christians, as well as the least number of women in the labor force and the smallest percentage of college educated individuals. The West followed the South in percentage of conservative Christians and was second to the North in the number of Catholic representatives, and these factors help to explain the region's resistance to abortion rights. Even once these factors are controlled, though, the West, as a region, was still significantly less supportive of abortion rights, suggesting that political culture, separate from demographic factors, had an effect on regional attitudes toward abortion. Given that the Hyde Amendment concerned abortion *and* federal government spending, the West's response may reflect a traditional morality rooted in the region's agrarianism as well as antipathy toward activist government, both of which transcend specific religious commitments.

Postwar technological advances and the growth of a prosperous consumer society caused an increasing number and greater variety of women to enter the labor force. Between 1950 and 1970, women's labor force participation doubled; and by 1970, 49.6 percent of women over the age of 16 were working.[15] More women were also becoming better educated. In 1950, one-quarter of all bachelor's degrees were awarded to women; twenty years later, this proportion had reached 43 percent.[16] At the same time, the make-up of the traditional family was changing. Childbearing rates fell from a high of 26.6 per 1,000 persons in 1947 to just 14.8 per 1,000 in 1973, the year of the *Roe* decision. Lower birthrates freed women to work outside the home.[17] And divorce rates more than doubled, from 9.2 per 1,000 marriages in 1960 to 21.1 per 1,000 in 1976, furthering women's need to work.[18]

The association between high percentages of working women and support for abortion rights is consistent with sociologist Kristin Luker's profile of pro-choice activists.[19] The overwhelming majority of activists that Luker interviewed worked outside the home. As she explains, when women began entering the workforce in significant numbers (especially middle- and upper-income women who had previously stayed home) and, perhaps more importantly, embracing that role as a substantial one in their lives, the discriminatory practices and gender segregation that they found on the job became problematic.

> Women found themselves segregated in what were now seen as relatively unattractive jobs or denied opportunities for rewards or advancement *because they were mothers or potential mothers.* When they began to compare themselves to men who had roughly similar "human capital" advantages, they found they were paying a very high price for being women.[20]

The importance of labor force participation extends beyond just the economic rationale that links reproductive rights and women's workforce opportunities. It reverberates in the larger social context within which notions of gender role and identity were being challenged and shaped. Much of this was happening on college campuses and among the growing college-educated professional class that had emerged as a significant political force shaping debate at the time.[21] As Table 5.2 indicated, the percent of a state's population with four or more years of higher education was a significant indicator of abortion rights support in 1976. All else being equal, a 1 percent increase in the size of this population led to a 5 percent increase in pro-choice support. This helps explain the regional poles of the abortion debate at the time, both generally and within the Democratic Party: Pacific Coast states had, on average, the highest proportion of college educated persons, while the South had the lowest.

The combination of education and women's labor force participation helps explain much of the cultural and political attractiveness of the pro-choice position. While married women's participation in the labor force rose in the 1960s and 1970s, the increase was concentrated among the wives of more educated men. As social trendsetters, these "upper-class" women established the social desirability of work outside the home, and they were responsible for the simultaneous status degradation of the homemaker. According to Jane Mansbridge, "As the paid labor force offered urban, educated women attractive options, the more rural, less-educated women found that the world judged the traditional job of homemaking less attractive."[22] As work became not simply more necessary in the postwar economy but also associated with greater social status, controlling reproduction became more important. For those women not entering the labor force at this time and staying, instead, in traditional homemaker roles, elevating the importance of motherhood and "keeping the home" became high priorities.[23]

The pro-choice constituency that emerged at this time was, more than simply being employed outside the home, also typically urban, educated, often affluent, and politically organized. As Susan Hansen notes, "Working women are more likely to be aware of public policies affecting their interests and are usually in a better position to mobilize on their own behalf than women who are homemakers, students, or retired."[24] This growing new constituency saw a woman's right to an abortion as an integral aspect of her ability to define herself independently of the actions of others, in keeping with a woman's ability to gain an education and earn her own wages. This social identity was being nurtured and defined to a large degree on campuses and in feminist organizations in the urban centers of the North and Pacific Coast.

That support for abortion rights and feminism was greatest in the Northeast and Pacific Coast is in keeping with scholarly analyses of where "postmaterialism" flourishes. For Ronald Inglehart, postmaterial values and concerns arise in advanced industrial societies in which the public has been more or less freed from the economic insecurities that plague poorer nations.[25] In the late 1960s and early 1970s, this developmental path comported far more with the historical experience of the industrial core regions in the North and Pacific Coast than with the South and West. The North and Pacific Coast regions had industrialized to a greater degree far earlier than the other regions, and, because of the strength of the labor movement in previous decades, economic security was more widely spread in these regions. By the 1970s, they were transitioning to the postindustrial age. After decades of affluence, with the children of factory workers now attending college, these regions were ripe for the flourishing of postmaterial concerns, including ones about equal access to the work and educational opportunities that the accumulation of material wealth had generated.[26]

With feminists mobilizing on campuses and in cities, Democrats from the

Pacific Coast and from the Mid-Atlantic and New England subregions of the North began arguing on behalf of this constituency to their colleagues in Congress. New York's Bella Abzug, for example, put the issue of women's rights bluntly during a floor debate.

> We have the right of privacy. The Supreme Court has said that it exists under the first, the second, the fourth, the fifth, the ninth, and the fourteenth amendments. It says that this issue is not a political issue, that this issue is not an issue which bishops or rabbis or anybody but the individual herself should decide. Herself, not himself, either. Herself. It is a right of the individual herself to decide what to do about her body, not him, not the bishop, not the rabbi, not the Congressmen.[27]

While Abzug reiterated that *Roe* granted women independence from traditional religious and patriarchal practices, many lawmakers opposed to the Hyde Amendment focused instead on the discriminatory effects of restricted Medicaid funding, the target of the amendment. Ban supporters had made it clear that the vote in Congress was a referendum on abortion, but by focusing on discrimination against poor women, those opposed to the ban could circumvent the conflicted moral terrain of abortion and instead use the rhetoric about equality that a growing portion of their regional constituency had already embraced. While the New Deal Party had been built on compromise to accommodate the different political economies and social structures of North and South, by the mid-1970s, the national Democratic Party was identified with a commitment to fighting racial and other types of discrimination.[28] Keeping the focus on discrimination and inequality aided northern Democrats in their attempts to appeal to both economically and socially progressive audiences while sidestepping the religious controversy surrounding the issue.

While feminists lauded the *Roe* decision, many religious citizens saw the Supreme Court's action as a harbinger of the decay of the family, of religious commitment, and of American moral life more generally. As Luker has described, *Roe* was a wake-up call for those whose moral commitments led them to believe that abortion was the taking of human life. One pro-life activist likened the decision to "a bolt out of the blue," and it instantly mobilized pro-life forces on a scope not before seen.[29] Institutionally, they were organized initially by the U.S. Catholic Conference, which funded the National Committee for a Human Life Amendment and, in 1975, adopted the "Pastoral Plan for Pro-Life Activities," which outlined the pro-life actions that Catholic agencies were encouraged to support.

The Catholic Church's antiabortion stance made the issue potentially divisive for the Democratic Party, especially in the North. While social progressives were concentrated in the region, the states with the largest Catholic populations and the greatest numbers of Catholic representatives were also in the North. And representatives, Democrats and Republicans alike, were reminded of the electoral consequences of their votes on abortion at every turn. The church had a congressional liaison, Mark Gallagher, who made his "unofficial home" the office of Representative Henry Hyde. A news report at the time described Gallagher's influence on representatives debating the Hyde Amendment: "Every time the Senate conferees make a compromise offer, Mr. Gallagher quietly walks to the conference table to tell a staff aide to the 11 House conferees whether the proposal is acceptable to the bishops. His recommendations invariably are followed."[30]

Although lay Catholics were divided on abortion, the church's position was unequivocal, and Catholic representatives were particularly responsive to the opinion of the church on abortion: in the regression analysis, the percentage of a state's representatives who were Catholic is negatively related to state support for abortion availability. Strongly Catholic districts thus undermined the northern tendency to support abortion rights, demonstrating the cross-pressures facing the region as a whole, especially in the early years of the debate.

Catholic constituents were an important influence on the antiabortion stance of some, largely northern, lawmakers. Abortion also rejuvenated another religious audience: evangelical and fundamentalist Christians, who were concentrated largely in the South and had removed themselves from politics after the Scopes trial on the teaching of evolution fifty years earlier. It was this group, already growing in numbers and institutional clout by the early to mid-1970s, that pushed the South and the Republican Party toward a pro-life stance.[31]

The size of a state's conservative Christian population is inversely related to the degree to which it is pro-choice. All else being held constant, a 1 percent increase in this population results in a roughly 1.4 percent decrease in mean state support for abortion rights. And, as is clear from Table 5.3, in 1976, conservative Christians, the majority of whom are Southern Baptists, were concentrated in the South and the West. Republicans already eyeing the electoral prospects of these regions, saw fertile soil.

With the exception of a small number of states, the South and West favored the Hyde Amendment.[32] Lawmakers supporting the amendment from these regions, such as Texas Republican Ron Paul, argued that it was necessary because the taxpayer dollars of "citizens with devout religious beliefs against abortion" should not be used to finance abortions.[33] And this group of citizens would grow; white evangelicals, the principal target audience of the Christian right, in the 1990s accounted for roughly one-quarter of the adult population in the U.S.[34] Already, in 1976, Southern Baptist membership alone numbered 12.5 million, and at their annual convention in Norfolk that year, members passed a resolution announcing their opposition to abortion.[35] Support for the Hyde Amendment also came from representatives in the West, particularly in states such as Idaho, Nevada, and Utah, which had a sizeable Mormon population, where abortion was often referred to as a "Mormon issue."[36]

In the mid-1970s, abortion was a mobilizing issue for the emerging political force of the Christian right, a movement spearheaded by charismatic and entrepreneurial leaders, such as Freedom Council founder Pat Robertson and Moral Majority founder Jerry Falwell, and based in a network of loosely linked conservative Christian churches and organizations. Through churches, talk radio shows, and television networks, leaders mobilized millions of previously inactive citizens around an effort to restore "traditional" values they described as consistent with biblical precepts to a country they felt was being undone by the advance of secular liberalism.[37] This outreach was highly successful. Estimates now suggest that at least two million people have become registered voters as a result of the political organizing of the religious right.[38]

Conservative Christians were an important new voter group for Republicans. Early surveys showed that supporters of the religious right tended to be residents of rural areas and were typically less-educated, white, fundamentalist Christians living in the South and in some of the midwestern states.[39] This bloc included people, low-income and rural citizens among them, who were not only typically less likely to vote but also had historically been considered likely Democratic supporters because of their economic status. Their mobilization by the religious right was thus a significant electoral development for Republicans. When combined with the intensity with which these citizens hold their political and religious beliefs, the mobilization of the religious right has given the conservative Christian movement significant political clout, particularly among officials elected in its growth regions of the South and West. And, while the Christian right has organized around a number of "morality" issues, including pornography, homosexuality, and school prayer, abortion is "perhaps the most important issue unifying religious right groups."[40]

Just as women's labor force participation was nestled in a larger web of meaning that informed pro-choice opinion, especially on the coasts, the rise of religious conservatism was also embedded in a larger cultural context that fed abortion antipathy. At one general level, the demographic variables of women's labor force participation and religious conservatism convey the difference in experiences and opinions between highly educated, urban, professional, and secular populations in the Northeast and Pacific Coast and low- to middle-income, highly religious populations living in rural and suburban areas largely in the South and West. Yet, in their regional contexts, these variables speak to larger cultural phenomena that have animated geographic differences.

Northern and Pacific Coast urbanization and industrialization, and the myriad social changes that attended these processes, began well over a century ago. The South and West, in contrast, began to industrialize in earnest only after World War II, and in ways that, because of their later timing, were different from the experiences of the North and Pacific Coast.[41] In just a few decades, these regions were transformed from sites of rural agrarianism into ones at the forefront of modern economic development, geographically diffused industrialization, and suburban metropolitan growth.[42]

The growth and shifts in job opportunities along with large-scale population movements altered the social landscape of these southern and western states, often within one or two generations. In the midst of this socially disruptive time, the potential implications of social change were magnified by media displays of the cultural and social progressivism on the coasts. One author writing of the rise of "Baptist Republicanism" in the early postwar decades writes,

> Interstate highways, jet airplanes, business conglomerates, economic expansion, television, radio, the wide distribution of blockbuster motion pictures, and national magazines would carry the national culture into the South. Suddenly the SBC [Southern Baptist Convention] longed for the good ol' days and found itself in the midst of a "reclaiming" movement of its own, similar to that of northern fundamentalists a generation or more earlier.[43]

As the South confronted the "national culture," regional wariness increased in such a way as to amplify the chasm between pro-choice and pro-life values, but this was less the result of the periphery regions' resisting national (i.e., northern or Hollywood) culture than it was a unique integration of modern change with existing patterns and traditions. The convergence of these two social worlds, modern and traditional, is perhaps most evident in the growing metropolitan suburbs of the South and West. Regional life was transformed from predominantly rural and centered in small towns to being defined by sprawling metropolises, suburban subdivisions, and population mobility. These new suburbs drew educated, middle-income, professional transplants out of surrounding small towns and other regions. Eminently modern, these new suburbs typically lacked the sense of history and community found in the small towns or in the older established cities of other regions. Into this void came the conservative churches and conservative political organizations. Not only did these institutions provide community, but by championing a return to society's "organic order" and by elevating "traditional values," they provided an anchor against the instability and disruption of the rapid change churning through these regions.[44] On the other hand, they did this using the processes and media of modernity, in ways that integrated modern change with traditional views. Thus, for example, an advertisement for Atlanta's Peachtree Baptist Church used the slogan "Being Born Again Means Being Plugged Into a New Power Source."[45]

Ambivalence about the process of economic development resulted in a fusing of economic modernization with traditional values. In the South and West, this was fueled politically by traditional populist rhetoric, which now transferred the blame for change from Wall Street to the northern cultural elite who dominated the Democratic Party. Conservative religious and political leaders in the South and West declared that the breakdown of traditional values was not due to economic change but to the partnership of northern intellectuals and liberal political elites who had run the national government since the 1930s. The culprits accused in Agnew's anti-liberal and anti-intellectual speeches, they asserted, were behind the confrontational demands for liberal change. And it was elites in previous decades who had steered the government away from traditional functions, like defense, toward taxpayer-funded social experimentation. Taking advantage of the history of South-North animosities, southern lawmakers tapped a potent mixture of change, anxiety, and populism and used the issue of abortion—and federal funding of abortion—as prime evidence of a liberal government gone astray.[46]

Most representatives who supported the Hyde Amendment in 1976 made only passing, if any, explicit reference to religion in their public comments. More typically, their rhetoric hinted at populist versus elite social conflict and contained a thinly veiled disparagement of the ongoing social changes of the time, including the efforts of feminists to redefine women's roles. For example, the amendment's author, Henry Hyde, a Republican (and a Catholic) from Illinois, argued, "[T]here are those among us who believe it is to the everlasting shame of this country that in 1973 approximately 800,000 legal abortions were performed in this country—and so far it is safe to assume that this year over a million human lives will be destroyed *because they are inconvenient to someone.*"[47]

Anti-abortion legislators often invoked the language of "convenience" in House debates. Convenience bespeaks luxury, which belongs to those who have the means to afford it. The regular use of the term is evocative of populist railing against the excesses of elites. While feminists argued that reproductive control was an essential precondition to women's equality and their social and economic independence, their opponents responded that abortion was an extravagance sought by women unwilling to accept their biologically ordained (or God-given) responsibilities. Beyond this, the image of destroying lives at the whim of convenience suggested a creeping amorality aided by the worst sort of modern technological excess. In his comments, Hyde contrasted the organic process of mothering with the vacuity of modern life.

> I think in the final analysis, you must determine whether or not the unborn person is human. If you think it is animal or vegetable then, of course, it is disposable like an empty beer can to be crushed and thrown out with the rest of the trash. . . . Once conception has occurred a new and unique genetic package has been created, not a potential human being, but a human being with potential. For 9 months the mother provides nourishment and shelter, and birth is no substantial change, it is merely a change of address.[48]

The naturalness of the link between mother and child, as Hyde and others described it, elevates traditional social orders, in which women's primary responsibility is bearing and raising children. By contrast, the idea of abortion was embedded in images of immoral behavior (alcohol consumption) and modern waste (the disposable beer can). In the framework of the dangers to tradition that modernity represented, abortion signified that the care and nourishment found in traditional social relationships could be replaced by carelessness, permissiveness, and self-gratification. The message resonated with the emerging religious right, centered in communities helping each other negotiate the fast track from tradition to modernity.

Some abortion opponents made the link between abortion and cultural degeneracy even more explicitly. John McCollister, a Republican from Nebraska, claimed,

> Since [*Roe v. Wade*], we have seen a weakening in the basic values of life. The weakening of these values, of course, cannot be solely attributed to the abortion decision. In fact, there is a much greater, underlying problem. Amid our material affluence, we are experiencing a deterioration of those personal values held by our people that made us great. Broken

homes, deserted families, empty churches, and lines at X-rated movies are signs of the times. Consequently, we've seen over the past ten years, mushrooming illegitimate births and abortions. Should the unborn child be the scapegoat of our declining morality?[49]

In interpretations such as this, abortion was a discrete evil made worse because it was both cause and consequence of the broader breakdown of traditional values and practices that accompanied economic modernization and affluence. Holding firm against abortion rights became part of the way to maintain traditional values in the face of inevitable and generally beneficial economic and technological advancement. Texas Republican Ron Paul, an obstetrician/gynecologist by training, echoed these sentiments. He recalled from his days in medicine that "young people came to my office asking for an abortion as if it were requesting an aspirin for a headache. . . . This lack of concern for human life is an ominous sign of a decaying culture. We as a Congress must not contribute to this decay."[50]

The comments of Paul, McCollister, Hyde, and others suggest the cautionary sentiment emerging in response to the changing social and economic conditions of the 1960s and 1970s. These representatives called on their colleagues to counteract or shepherd change by actively upholding social tradition. Lawmakers from around the country voiced this sentiment, but it was especially potent in the South and West, where change was happening most quickly. By juxtaposing modern changes against the values of a traditional religious order within the context of a singularly focused issue like abortion, representatives gave expression to regional anxieties and helped cultivate a new regional force, the growing Christian right.

MANAGING INTERNAL DIVISIONS BY SHIFTING THE FRAME OF DEBATE

Republican Party promotion of social conservatism integrated economic change with social stability, offering a type of security different from that of the New Deal regime. While the New Deal had emphasized policies providing broad-based economic security to quell fears about capitalist development, the Republican solution focused instead on the security of social stability, policies aimed at preserving social relations and upholding traditional beliefs, to quiet citizens' anxieties about the uncertainties of modernizing economic change. By the 1990s, this position had helped the party solidify its electoral domination of the South and West, where change was happening fastest. The 1994 Republican takeover of Congress brought forty new pro-life representatives to

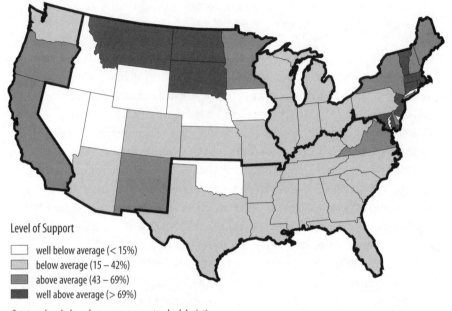

Figure 5.5
House Support for Abortion Rights, 1995–1996

Capitol Hill and pushed the center of geographical gravity in the GOP even further toward these pro-life regions.[51]

Once in office, the new Republican majority sought to curtail abortion
rights. The geography of this effort is evident in Figure 5.5, which shows state
support for abortion rights on all abortion-related votes cast in the 104th Congress (1995–1996). As in 1976, opposition to abortion rights in the 1990s was centered in the interior of the country and extending to the southeast, while support for abortion rights prevailed in the Northeast and Pacific Coast. Among the
states of the South, every state but Virginia was below or well below the national average of abortion rights support. Joining the South were all five East
North Central states, the midwestern portion of the North. Ten of the 15 western states also were below average in abortion rights support, with 6 of the 10
well below average, having scores of less than 15 percent.[52] Conversely, above
average support for abortion rights characterized the Pacific Coast region, as
well as the North generally. Ten of the 16 northern states were above average in
their pro-choice support, with 6 of the 10 well above average (scores above 69

percent). Among New England and Mid-Atlantic states, only Pennsylvania joined with the East North Central states in opposing abortion rights.

Calling for a limit on abortion rights helped Republicans win in the South, West, and midwestern corner of the North. One of the dangers of the abortion issue for Republicans in the 1990s, though, was that while it had earlier served as a useful tool for expanding the party coalition and securing power, the extreme views and violent methods used by some pro-life activists had alienated much of the general public.[53] As a result, abortion was not included in the national agenda outlined in the 1994 Contract with America authored by congressional Republicans, and party leaders kept the issue off the table in the first several months of Republican rule in Congress.[54] But by mid-1995, the social conservatives whom the party had courted in earlier decades and who had been instrumental in Republican electoral success were demanding action, and the leadership responded.[55] Welfare had been used by the Democratic Party through the 1960s to bridge divergent coalition interests, and Republicans found a way to use abortion policy similarly. By introducing legislation to ban what pro-life representatives called "partial-birth" abortions, the Republican Party satisfied the religious right without losing the appearance of moderation and thus maintained their more centrist supporters as well. In doing so, they also redefined the abortion debate.

Proponents of the legislation, which was first acted on in the summer of 1995, sought to ban a medical procedure called an "intact dilation and evacuation," one method used to abort late-term (after twenty weeks) fetuses. Supporters of the bill focused on the details of the procedure and used visual aids and graphic rhetoric to make their point. An example of this can be found even in the language of the proposed legislation, which described the procedure as one "in which the person performing the abortion partially vaginally delivers a living fetus before killing the fetus and completing the delivery."[56]

Only 1.3 percent of the 1.3 million abortions being performed annually were late term (statistics on the frequency of the procedure vary), so the ban applied to a very small number of abortions. But, in criminalizing a particular type of abortion procedure, Republicans were able to move the debate away from women's rights and into the more politically sterile, and thus more easily defensible, terrain of medical practice. Critics of the bill charged that Republicans were using the legislation to chip away at Roe, one procedure at a time. Yet, by using language that highlighted the potential viability of the fetus ("partial birth") and that equated medical procedures with taking a life ("killing the fetus"), Republicans reframed the issue to put the rights of the unborn on a plane in the American ethos equal to if not greater than the rights of women. This helped insure that even those moderately in favor of abortion rights were not alienated by the Republican proposal.[57] Frances Kissling, president of Catholics for a Free Choice, said, "There is no abortion procedure when described that is aesthetically comforting, whether at 6 weeks or 32 weeks. This is exactly the kind of abortion issue that people don't want to think about. They want women to be able to have this option in such extreme and terrible circumstances, but they know it's not pretty. It has to happen, but it shouldn't be in the newspaper."[58] Republicans made sure it was in the newspapers.

In their rhetorical reframing of the issue, Republicans struck a politically critical balance reminiscent of the old New Deal cross-regional balances on race-related issues. With the partial-birth legislation, Republicans satisfied social conservatives in their party that they were committed to ending abortion yet framed the issue in a way that would make it relatively innocuous to other elements of their expanding coalition—a step necessary not just to reach across the regional divide of the parties but also to manage the increasingly complex social realities of the South and West. After several generations of modernization and interregional migration, the South and West had become home both to traditional cultural politics and to moderate political sentiments. The partial-birth abortion ban represented the newest example of a political party navigating traditional cultural beliefs with changing demographic and economic realities.

REJUVENATING AND SOLIDIFYING REGIONAL COALITION BASES

Republican Senator Larry Craig from Idaho has said that abortion and other social issues are defining, "bright-light issues . . . that show the difference between the two parties."[59] Over the decades, abortion had become a touchstone issue for the parties, one that allowed them to signal their commitment to social change or to social tradition; it distilled the worldviews of their constituencies. These signals were clearly in evidence in the 104th Congress. On abortion generally, the mean Democratic abortion rights support index position was 75 percent while the mean position for Republicans was 14 percent. The difference was similar in the voting just on the partial-birth ban legislation. The average Democrat voted for abortion rights 67 percent of the time on the partial-birth ban, while the average Republican voted this way only 8 percent of the time.[60]

While now clearly generating partisan division, abortion in the mid-1990s

TABLE 5.4. MEAN SUPPORT FOR ABORTION RIGHTS ON PARTIAL-BIRTH ABORTION BAN
LEGISLATION, BY REGION AND PARTY, 1995–1996

REGION	ALL REPRESENTATIVES (%)	DEMOCRATS (%)	REPUBLICANS (%)
North	40	64	16
	(45)	(44)	(33)
Pacific Coast	46	95	6
	(49)	(17)	(21)
South	27	60	1
	(42)	(46)	(3)
West	24	55	6
	(38)	(45)	(18)
F statistic*	4.92	5.55	6.87
(p)	.002	.001	.000
N	426	192	233

Source: Calculated from roll call data.

Note: Based on mean index score of legislative support for the pro-choice position on partial-birth abortion ban legislation.
Scale is 1 to 100.

Standard deviation in parentheses.

*ANOVA results

reflected the same basic regional divisions it had in the 1970s, as a comparison
of the maps in Figures 5.4 and 5.5 shows. In the partial-birth ban by itself, support for abortion rights weakened throughout the nation, yet the same basic regional patterns held (see Table 5.4). And, demonstrating the potency of geography in abortion opinion, these basic divisions hold even once the geography
of the parties is controlled.

Regional differences on the partial-birth ban legislation reflect the regional
strengths of the parties in the mid-1990s. As Chapter 2 showed, in 1995 Democrats were disproportionately based in the North and Pacific Coast while Republicans were concentrated in the West and South. But the regional differences
tend to hold even within the parties. Pacific Coast Democrats were the most consistently pro-choice of all representatives and of all Democrats, followed by
northern Democrats, and these groups constituted the majority of the party. Republicans from the South were the most heavily pro-life of all representatives
and of all Republicans, followed by Republicans from the West and Pacific Coast.
Nor was this voting pattern simply reflective of the personal convictions of representatives. The pattern held among the public in each region as well. In the
early 1990s, support for a woman's right to have an abortion under any circum-

stance was, on average, 43 percent in Pacific Coast states and 37 percent in the North as compared to 30 percent in the West and 22 percent in the South.[61]

By this time, the parties were using abortion less to build new regional constituencies, as they had in the 1970s, and more to solidify those constituencies. Mobilization and countermobilization on both sides of the issue had escalated throughout the 1980s and 1990s, and their regional bases helped realign the geography of the parties. But, just as Democrats had once struggled to keep race from upending their coalition, Republicans now needed to manage abortion. Legislation banning partial-birth abortions was the tool.

The regression results in Table 5.5 show that the factors at work in the geography of abortion in the mid-1990s were similar to those of the 1970s.[62] In the 1970s, women's labor force participation gave a sense of practical gender activism and was correlated with support for abortion rights. For the 1990s, this social activism can be measured more directly using interest group membership.[63] The National Abortion Rights Action League (NARAL) is arguably the most prominent pro-choice interest group, and the more NARAL members in a state, the more likely the state's House delegation is to support abortion rights, both in general and on the specific issue of the partial-birth ban.

TABLE 5.5. ANALYSIS OF STATE SUPPORT FOR ABORTION RIGHTS, 1995–1996

	MODEL 1: OVERALL INDEX	MODEL 2: PARTIAL-BIRTH BAN INDEX
	b (se)	b (se)
Constant	0.080 (0.073)	−0.071 (0.059)
Conservative Christian population	−0.382* (0.176)	−0.099 (0.143)
Size of NARAL membership	0.162** (0.037)	0.188** (0.030)
Democratic	0.519** (0.071)	0.448** (0.057)
OLS analysis		
Adj. R^2	.73	.76
N	48	48

$*p \leq .05; **p \leq .01$

Sources: Pro-choice index and Democratic (ICPSR); conservative Christian population (Churches and Church Membership in the United States 1990); NARAL membership (Meier and McFarlane, 2002). For more information on the OLS analysis, see note 62.

Despite the growth and industrialization of the South and West, gender activism in the 1990s still had not penetrated these regions to the degree it had in the North and Pacific Coast. On average, there were 2 NARAL members per 1,000 in the Pacific Coast states and 1.6 members per 1,000 in states in the North in 1990; but the averages are only .80 NARAL members per 1,000 in the West and .49 per 1,000 in the South. Demographically, the NARAL membership was predominantly white, female, urban, well educated, and professionally employed.[64] Members were likely to have had an abortion or to know someone who had.[65]

It was to this audience that Pacific Coast and northern Democrats spoke when they voiced their support for choice and demanded the defeat of the partial-birth ban legislation. In language that echoed Bella Abzug's feminist speech thirty years earlier, New York Democrat Louise Slaughter waxed sarcastic:

> There is another underlying piece here, and that is that women do not have the right to choose. Maybe they are not smart enough, we cannot let them decide what is the best thing in the world for them to do. Some men have to sit around and decide what is best, usually deciding in legislatures all over the country and this Congress what . . . is appropriate for them. . . . [A woman] should not be considered [a] second-class citizen . . . that needs a big brother to tell her what is permissible and what is not.[66]

In the twenty years since the issue was first opened to national debate, Democrats had become more unified in their promotion of abortion rights and still framed the issue as one of gender equality. This made political sense, especially for lawmakers from districts with large numbers of highly educated, professional citizens—the Pacific Coast and Northeast, places where NARAL flourished. Yet, at the same time, wary of the backlash that their position could generate outside of their socially progressive base, pro-choice advocates and representatives were careful to emphasize women's desire to be mothers. Calling the partial-birth ban "antiwoman, extremist, unwise legislation," New York Democrat Carolyn Maloney nonetheless couched her criticism of ban supporters in terms of what they were doing to harm mothers. She castigated the ban's proponents for prioritizing the "doomed fetus" over "the life of a woman and *her ability to have children in the future*."[67] By arguing for the compatibility of abortion with motherhood, such comments attempted to neutralize pro-life rhetoric that still cast abortion as part of the modern turn toward convenience and away from traditional responsibilities. It offered, in a sense, a new interpretation of how modernity and tradition could coexist, one that emphasized the ability of doctors and women to make rational choices that valued both.

Many pro-choice lawmakers embraced this strategy. Many, if not most, recipients of late-term abortions are young, low-income, poorly educated women who abort for nonmedical reasons; yet pro-choice supporters used mature, concerned mothers as the lynchpin of their argument that women needed to be able to have late-term abortions because of fetal deformities or severe maternal health risks.[68] These women, many of them married, many with children, were called to testify in congressional hearings; their stories were retold in floor arguments, and they were present when President Clinton eventually vetoed the bill. By focusing on just one type of late-term abortion recipient—the distraught yet responsible mother—Democrats attempted to undermine the implicit argument being made by pro-life supporters and Republican leaders that the state was offering encouragement to women who were simply uninterested in motherhood. Kate Michelman, president of NARAL, explained, "The anti-choice community has done a very good job at painting a picture of a woman who has an abortion as frivolous, irresponsible, one who engages in sex without responsibility."[69] Michelman and other abortion rights advocates attempted to counter this image by focusing on how the procedure, and modern technology, could be used to aid mothers.

Democrats complained that Republicans were using the partial-birth legislation simply to curry favor with the religious right. Nita Lowey, Democrat of New York, lamented, "This entire debate is a pay-off to the Christian Coalition and an exercise in election year political theatre."[70] The "theatre" in fact was part of a more general Republican strategy that harked back to Agnew's attacks on his era's protestors and intellectuals. As Chapter 2 described, Republican strategists had long made clear the electoral value of directing populism at social issues. In the 1990s, Republican Party leader Newt Gingrich understood that, by assailing the "counterculture," Republicans could tap into class and cultural resentments and undermine Democrats.[71] Because abortion had come on the national scene as part of a broader set of concerns about a decaying national culture, it was still useful for this purpose. Put on the defensive, abortion rights advocates and their Democratic supporters attempted to assuage fears about changing social identities by focusing on the compatibility of abortion with responsible parenthood.

As was clear from the results for model 1 in Table 5.5, opposition to abortion rights still had strong appeal to conservative Christians. And the states with the greatest numbers of them were still concentrated in the South and in the West. The South led the country in the size of the conservative Christian population, with a state average of 29 percent. The average state in the West had

19 percent, while the Pacific Coast and North had just 9 and 4 percent, respectively. It is interesting, though, that the conservative Christian variable is not significant in the model of support for the partial-birth ban legislation, which indicates the appeal of that legislation beyond just the religious right and suggests the success of the Republicans' new strategy.

While Republicans had reframed the partial-birth ban legislation to be broadly appealing, they also intended it to energize the social conservatives in the party's base. Republican Party leaders and pro-life advocates expected that their message about the legislation, and about Democratic "extremism," would galvanize the Bible Belt areas of the South and Midwest where Christian conservatism was strong.[72] Christian Coalition leader Ralph Reed predicted that the issue of the partial-birth ban would mobilize "millions of evangelical and Roman Catholic voters who will go to the polls in record numbers" if the legislation was defeated.[73] Having achieved a long sought-after takeover of Congress, largely through the capture of seats in the South and West, Republicans anticipated that the partial-birth ban would be an instrumental issue in promoting and expanding their national electoral success.

Descriptions of the procedure used in the debate over the legislation depicted both women seeking abortions and doctors who performed them as child murderers. Sponsor of the legislation, Charles Canady, a Florida Republican, described the procedure of a late-term abortion:

> First, guided by ultrasound, the abortionist grabs the live baby's leg with forceps. Second, the baby's leg is pulled out into the birth canal. Third, the abortionist delivers the baby's entire body, except for the head. Fourth, then, the abortionist jams scissors into the baby's skull. The scissors are then opened to enlarge the hole. Fifth, the scissors are then removed and a suction catheter is inserted. The child's brains are sucked out causing the skull to collapse so the delivery of the child can be completed.[74]

Using this imagery, promoters of the ban not only emphasized the late stage of fetal development at which the procedure is used, but they also portrayed the procedure as an extreme perversion of the "natural" delivery process.

The imagery made the description of abortion as murder more compelling. Indeed, in this same speech, Canady portrayed the act as virtually indistinguishable from infanticide: "While every abortion sadly takes a human life, the partial-birth abortion method takes that life as the baby emerges from the mother's womb, while the baby is only partially in the birth canal. The difference between the partial-birth abortion procedure and homicide is a mere 3 inches."[75] By juxtaposing the image of women as caretakers with the image of women as conspirators in murder, arguments such as this present a stark choice, and they elevate the rights of the unborn with descriptors reserved for regulating interactions between citizens (i.e., committing homicide). While stoking the concerns of the religious right about the modern-day denigration of motherhood, this language also made imposing limits on abortion rights more generally acceptable.

Reminiscent of the "convenience" language used since the 1970s, pro-life advocates' approach again suggested that the reasons women chose to abort were frivolous and selfish. A National Conference of Catholic Bishops advertisement, for example, listed the reasons that a woman might use to justify a late-term abortion. The list included "won't fit into prom dress," "hates being fat," and "can't afford a baby and a new car."[76] In similar vein, Christopher Smith, Republican of New Jersey, told his colleagues, "A pregnancy is not a disease. Yet partial-birth abortions treat a partially delivered child as a tumor, as a wart, as a disease to be destroyed."[77]

This language resonated with the concern of the Christian right and other social conservatives that traditional values had been trampled by modern secularism. And, just like earlier references to "convenience," assertions about frivolous abortions had a populist undertone, suggesting a concern that elite materialism was corrupting traditional values and habits of the general populace. Many representatives used language that invoked traditional Judeo-Christian morality. Specific comments, such as a call for the "forgiveness of God," and a reference to Thomas Aquinas, accompanied more general comments about a popular moral consensus, such as a description of the "widespread agreement" that the medical procedure was an "unfortunate and sickening act."[78]

Some lawmakers continued to implicate abortion more directly in the problems associated with modern life. In making her case, North Carolina Republican Sue Myrick asserted, "I honestly believe that many of the societal problems we have today stem from the fact that we have no regard for human life. Partial-birth abortions, drive-by shootings, cop killings, they have all become a way of life. Mr. Chairman, call me old-fashioned, but I believe that every individual born into this world is special, needed and important."[79]

Much as pro-life representatives in the 1970s had linked abortion to what they saw as the moral degeneracy accompanying economic modernization, representatives in 1996 continued to position abortion as both a cause and a reflection of the loss of traditional values. In doing so, Republicans responded to the concerns of pro-life activists and social conservatives who had railed against the effects of modernization since the 1970s. However, as the new millennium approached, living in a more fully modern society, lawmakers had to more specifically pinpoint the elements of abortion rights that were indicative of modernity's excess. The right to abortion alone was insufficient to the task, but partial-birth abortion, when depicted as virtual infanticide, clearly ran contrary to traditional American values. This legislation allowed pro-life lawmakers to renegotiate the complexity of modernity in ways that preserved tradition and also spoke to constituents without such strong trepidations about modern life and social change.

ABORTION: NEW FODDER FOR THE PARTIES' GEOGRAPHICAL REORGANIZATION

In describing the electoral consequences of party elites' positions, scholars have argued that abortion has been instrumental in reshaping party coalitions. David Karol, for example, argues that party leaders shifted and clarified their position on abortion over time to entice new constituencies into their coalition.[80] Greg Adams has demonstrated that party polarization on abortion in Congress was *followed* by gradual but similar changes in the electorate, with voters responding to elite cues by shifting loyalties to the party with views most consistent with their own.[81] As Adams explains, people who identified themselves as Democrats only became more pro-choice than Republicans at the end of the 1980s, once the lingering presence of Southern Baptists and other pro-life groups in the Democratic Party coalition disappeared.[82] Christina Wolbrecht elaborates Adams's argument by describing how the Republican Party adapted its position on abortion and women's rights more generally to appeal to social conservatives and to develop the party's base in the South.[83]

These were logical directions for the parties to take, because the division on abortion largely reinforced the regional political divides that existed on other issues. After *Roe v. Wade*, Democrats in the 1970s found themselves divided, yet again, along regional lines. The abortion debate came to the national stage amidst the social upheavals that accompanied and drew sustenance from the economic and social changes of the postwar decades. Because of this, the polar ideologies that the debate generated were rooted in different socioeconomic experiences and the interpretations that accompanied those experiences. These were in turn embedded in different geographies. Support for abortion rights was greatest in the high-income, highly educated, urbanized states of the older industrialized Northeast and Pacific Coast, which had long histories of social progressivism. They were also states accustomed to establishing the economic and social priorities of the country. When the Democratic Party became pro-choice, it signaled its regional commitments.

Conversely, pro-life sentiment and a commitment to preserving traditional social values flourished in the states of the South and West as those two formerly agricultural regions rushed full-tilt through industrialization and modernization. Indeed, the metropolises of these regions were at the forefront of modernization, and this was a political opportunity for Republicans, who supported the economic changes that were driving regional growth. Not only did abortion further divide the Democrats, but in the ensuing decades the issue helped forge a new constituency in Republican growth regions. In abortion, Republicans had an issue that appealed to social conservatives in the South as well as in much of the West. By adopting a pro-life stance, the Republican Party claimed to offer an antidote to what they described as the cultural degeneration of modern life—an especially powerful message in the regions experiencing the most rapid modernization and social dislocation. It was fueled, moreover, by populist rhetorical traditions in those regions that railed against the imposition of national priorities by northeastern and Hollywood elites, liberal elites living on college campuses and in the big cities of the two coasts. By uniting with southern Democrats in the 1970s, Republicans not only secured passage of the Hyde Amendment, they demonstrated again to southerners that their party could represent the interests and value commitments of the region. Opposition to abortion was a coalition-building tool that worked well alongside other policy tools. In the same regions, the party could promote unfettered economic development with a policy like free trade while sympathizing, through abortion rhetoric, about the disquieting effects of modernization.

Particularly in the early years of the debate, Christian evangelical churches and the Catholic Church served as the institutions that organized opposition to abortion. Combined, these groups spanned the entire country and provided Republicans with an opportunity to mobilize a nationwide constituency by embracing pro-life. And indeed, Ronald Reagan's success realized this vision: by carving into a traditional Democratic constituency—white working-class Catholic voters—President Reagan and the Republican Party made gains in typically Democratic areas of the North.

While Republicans were unable to translate this into widespread, permanent gains in the North, the issue's potential for engaging Catholic voters in the North and evangelical voters in the East North Central states demonstrates why regional politics have remained salient. Not ossified and impermeable, regions can change politically as a result of the introduction of new issues. By bringing new cleavages to the surface for parties to exploit, new issues bring with them the potential for creating new regional alignments. An issue like abortion had the potential to leech constituencies from the Democrats, not just in the South, which in many ways had already been ceded, but also in areas, like the North, where the party was gaining strength. The issue thus had the potential to be dramatically destabilizing for Democrats and even more potent for Republicans.

By the 1990s, however, Republicans needed to reframe the abortion debate if it was to continue to pay political dividends. Pro-life violence in the 1980s had alienated much of the voting public, and more-moderate voters in the "new" South and West were not as wedded to traditional views as the party's religious right constituency. In a manner reminiscent of New Deal solutions, partial-birth ban legislation provided an avenue through which the Republican Party could resolve these internal tensions. In all likelihood, the Republican Party's future success with social conservatism will depend on their ability to generate similarly new ways of framing social issues.

CHAPTER 6

A HOUSE DIVIDED

THE GEOGRAPHY OF PARTIES AND CONFLICT

IN 1858, ABRAHAM LINCOLN famously described the country as "a house divided against itself." The Civil War that began shortly thereafter was easily the period of the country's greatest geographical strife. At the conclusion of the war, with the Union preserved and slavery abolished, the country was reborn in its "second founding." Unsurprisingly, though, the impress that the "War Between the States" left on the party system was a distinct sectional cleavage between the two major parties. With the important exception of the New Deal era, that basic geographic divide of the party system endured.

After the Civil War, the Democratic Party became, first and foremost, a southern institution, while the Republican Party emerged as the political machinery of the North. Throughout the nineteenth century, as the United States incorporated the Pacific Coast and the western interior, states' loyalties quickly became a source of contest, creating a dynamic of alliance and division between the regions that continues to characterize American party politics. While the basic geographical divide has remained the same, the manifestation of the divide within the party-region linkage has changed over time—reversed itself, in fact—since the nineteenth century. The North is no longer Republican bedrock but the bastion, along with Pacific Coast states, of the Democrats, and the solidly Democratic South, along with the West, has moved steadily closer to becoming solidly Republican. But the operative connection between region, national party building, and party conflict is still firmly intact. Fueling these geopolitics are the range of issues that have been disruptive since the founding: trade and economy, race and rights, morality and human nature, and the proper scope and size of the federal government.

Chapters 3, 4, and 5 traced the connection between regions and national parties as it evolved in the postwar era in the arenas of trade, welfare, and abortion policy making. Mirroring overall trends evident in congressional voting records, bipartisan agreement characterized the three issues until the mid-1970s, when voting in each area turned increasingly partisan. By the mid-1990s, all three issues had become highly divisive. The rise in party conflict held true both for longstanding legislative issues such as welfare and trade, which had experienced decreasing partisanship in the first postwar decades, and for abortion, a new national issue in the 1970s, but one that became intensely partisan over time.

The battles over trade, welfare, and abortion engaged different constituencies within the parties' coalitions, presented party leaders with different political imperatives, and, on occasion, cut through the regional bases of the North, South, West, and Pacific Coast in slightly different ways. Each of the policies also performed different political functions for the parties, both across time and when compared with the other policy issues. What emerges from analysis of these varied elements is an integrative story of the demise of the New Deal Democratic regime, a geographic redistribution of the parties, and a growing battle for control of national government and resources that pits a southern-and-western-based Republican Party against a Democratic Party pushed to the urban North and the Pacific Coast.

From the 1930s until the 1960s, trade liberalization served as a powerful tool with which New Deal Democratic leaders were able to unite the northern and southern halves of the party's coalition. In the early 1960s, backed by a robust economy and free trade's appeal as a device for fighting communism, President Kennedy not only maintained the New Deal interregional coalition with his trade policy but also secured the support of northern Republicans. Within a decade, however, regional economic changes generated divergent pressures. The northern industrial economy began to decline while the modernizing South and West became home to growing agribusiness, tourism, and high-tech and defense-related industries. Containment became a questionable international relations goal. While North and South had previously been in agreement on the importance of trade to Cold War ideology, in the lingering days of the

Vietnam conflict, they no longer agreed on the merits of a robust military state. Faced with these shifting regional fortunes and policy positions, Richard Nixon successfully executed an economic "southern strategy" by constructing a bipartisan free trade coalition that united the formerly protectionist Republican Party with southern Democrats. From that point forward, Republican promotion of free trade helped the party not only build their western base but also win the South. In contrast, Democrats used promotion of "fair trade" to bolster their traditional labor and industrial supporters in the North and, by the 1990s, to nurture a newer element in their coalition, environmentalists in both the North and the Pacific Coast states.

With its distributional consequences, trade is a tool that both parties have used at different moments to entice various geographically concentrated interests into cross-regional coalitions. But, linked to such all-purpose American values as democracy and free-market choice, the rhetoric of free trade has offered, since World War II, a particularly inviting ideological umbrella under which the parties (first Democrats and then Republicans) have united disparate interests around their foreign policy agendas. It is important to note that neither party has been so rigidly ideological as to prevent the purchasing of exemptions for specific regional interests that the party needed for building coalitions but which were disadvantaged by free trade, such as the powerful textile bloc in the southern states. Since World War II, protectionism has been the more difficult position upon which to construct and sustain a broad-based coalition, both because it is depicted as favoring specific groups and because, as the losing ideology, it appears to run counter to hallowed constitutional values. The Democratic Party's success in the North, and even more so in the more export-dependent Pacific Coast states, has been a function of its ability to link the demands of interests with previously conflicting agendas, primarily labor and environmentalists, under a slogan of "fair trade" that casts their efforts in the rhetoric of a common search for equity, a national value arguably on par with liberty.

Like trade, welfare policy since the New Deal was introduced has offered benefits to specific groups and so has also functioned as a regional coalition-building tool for leaders of both parties. Legislation that succeeded, such as the Democratic plan to expand AFDC in the 1960s and the Republican plan to restrict the program in the 1990s, did so because it accommodated diverse interests, built support across regions, and was cast (both times) in rhetoric that reinforced national liberal values of self-sufficiency and individualism. Yet welfare policy has also been used to divide parties along regional lines and, more recently, to de-fund and demobilize constituents in the opposition's re-gional base. In this sense, welfare demonstrates the ways in which politicians use policy not only for drawing divergent interests into a coalition but also as a weapon of offense in political warfare.

Twining race and economy, welfare has consistently provoked interre-gional conflicts. Under the New Deal Democratic regime, this conflict was ame-liorated because expansion of the national welfare program was accompanied by increased local discretion, to accommodate local interests in both North and South and to enable them to bypass national directives if necessary. In the early 1960s, even as the rhetoric of welfare was becoming racialized, the multifac-eted policy served the needs of both regions and thus enabled Democrats to maintain their coalition. Indeed, regional incentives in Kennedy's legislation were strong enough to induce the cooperation of northern Republicans as well.

Postwar changes in economy and racial demography affected the North and South differently, however, and as the impact of these changes escalated, the Democrats' interregional harmony became unsustainable. One conse-quence, in the early 1970s, was a debate over federalizing welfare that divided both parties along regional lines. With fractures emerging in the Democratic Party on a number of policy fronts, the issue played to a longstanding vulnera-bility in the party's coalition, and President Nixon and the Republicans clearly stood to gain from exploiting that division, even though the Republicans them-selves were not unified on the issue. This episode also fortified the link between Democrats in the older, urban areas of the North and Pacific Coast.

This regional cleavage of the 1970s persisted, and by the 1990s, Republicans were using welfare reform to help consolidate a new interregional coalition of business and social conservatives in the South and West. Republican leaders also used welfare reform legislation to debilitate the welfare infrastructure of the North and Pacific Coast, undercutting the Democrats' power base in these regions. The result was partisan battles aligned along a geographic divide that pit North and Pacific Coast against South and West.

The shape and definition of party politics in the matter of trade and wel-fare policy has turned in part on the regional distribution of material resources and political power. The country's trade policy has typically advantaged the re-gional interests of the dominant party while imposing costs on other regions. Welfare policy, too, has been entangled in fights over how the costs of support-ing the nation's poor will be distributed, and policy outcomes have reflected the interests of the winning region and party. Yet, in each of these cases, conflict became coherent and powerful in part because of historic regional animosities and because of distinct regional interpretations of the social and economic changes the regions were experiencing. Republican promotion of free trade and limited welfare were part of the party's call for limiting federal government activism, and this became attractive to the South and West in part because both regions were culturally receptive to resisting northern-dominated federal power. These cultural strains were activated by specific social and economic developments in the regions, including growing western dependence on exports and southern reaction to civil rights and racial change. In contrast, Democratic messages about equity and justice in the forms of fair trade and welfare support resonated in the North and Pacific Coast states, not just because of changing material conditions, but also in part because of regional histories of activating government on behalf of community welfare.

The case of abortion policy highlights the ideological contours of regional conflict even more plainly, although it, too, cannot be divorced from its material grounding. As much as the clash over abortion has been about a dissonance of worldviews, it has also been about conflict between regionally dispersed social groups over the role of traditional social structures and relations in modern America. But, more than just a proxy for economic or social group differences, the abortion conflict reflects regional disparities in the experience of modernization and in the dominant interpretive frameworks that have accompanied economic changes, including both how social and economic changes fit with prevailing regional self-understandings and how those self-understandings are affected by historic regional antagonisms.

When *Roe v. Wade* placed abortion on the national agenda in 1973, unambiguous party positions were not forthcoming, certainly not ones stemming from preexisting party ideologies. Bipartisanship prevailed. However, once the political stakes and the constituencies in the debate became clear, the national parties adopted positions that enabled them to cultivate distinct grassroots regional constituencies. The Republican Party nurtured conservative Christians in the South and West, while the Democratic Party appealed to social progressives on college campuses and in cities in the North and Pacific Coast.

The regions' different experiences with ongoing social and economic changes enabled these partisan efforts. Postwar advancements in technology, legal and organizational developments in health care, trends in the consumer economy, and changes in gender relations in both public and private spheres crystallized differently in the regions. During the rocky transition from an industrial to a postindustrial economy in the North and Pacific Coast, demand that social change keep pace with these developments created an environment increasingly supportive of abortion rights. At the same time, the South and West rocketed in the postwar decades from traditional agrarian to modern industrial and postindustrial economies, from small towns and farms to cities and then sprawling suburban metropolises. The social dislocation of this process, one spurred in large part by entrepreneurs from the North, generated a social backlash evident most clearly in the mushrooming of Christian evangelicalism. This fostered a regional environment that was ambivalent about, and at times hostile to, social changes, particularly those being promoted and exported by northerners. As James Cobb has written, "The South owed a good part of its entire regional identity to the existence of an intimidating and antithetical North—affluent, confident, and rational."[1] If the North was seen as promoting social change, the South was historically primed to be wary of embracing it.

For the political parties, particularly the Republicans, tapping into these social currents in the South and West provided a new avenue for stimulating regional support in a way that more or less reinforced existing regional developments within the parties. "Cultural issues" provided a glue for constituencies in the South and West that were ambivalent about where the party's conservative economic stances were taking the country. In this sense, these issues provided a counterweight to Democrats' traditional appeal to working- and middle-class citizens on economic issues, one that was especially attractive since Democrats no longer had a clear message about how to manage the global economy.

Because of the issue's significance to the Roman Catholic Church, abortion also appeared at the outset to give Republicans an opportunity to slice deeper into the geography of the Democratic base. In the 1980s Ronald Reagan captured traditional Democratic strongholds, such as portions of the East North Central states, which sent representatives to Congress that voted more like southerners and westerners on abortion policy. The issue failed to fully undermine Democratic strength in those areas, however; with the exception of abortion, the profile of the East North Central states more closely resembles the rest of the industrial North than South or West, and thus the magnitude of the political geographical implications of the issue seem to have reached their limit.

THE LOGIC OF REGION

American politics commonly assumes that the polity is national, an interpretation based on a teleological reading of the country's political history, a reading consistent with the liberal narrative of progress. From this perspective, the

Civil War produced the second founding, bridging the country's most significant geographic divide. From that point forward, celebrated historical markers trace the country's progression away from geographically derived inequalities and into a national polity of individual liberal citizens. Of perhaps greatest significance in this process, the New Deal jump-started a nationally integrated industrial economy and nationalized politics along class lines. The two world wars and the Cold War emphasized the country's ideological unity in opposition to an external enemy and spurred further economic development in the lagging regions of the South and West. Finally, civil rights achievements completed the task of bringing the South into the national fold. By this logic, regional differences and, therefore, politics based on regions were increasingly obsolete.

Yet, each of the country's regions has not only been historically constituted by different material and social conditions; they have each experienced and interpreted the economic and demographic changes of the last sixty years in different ways. With roots in both economy and culture, geographic distinctions are tenacious. The histories of trade, welfare, and abortion policy testify to these continued regional differences. While the politics and relevant interest groups associated with the issues are different, the issues have similar and mutually reinforcing stories—of differing regional developmental paths, national party responses to those differences, and resultant regionally driven national party conflicts.

That Congress is predicated on geographic representation accounts for some of the persistence of regions. There are structural incentives for building coalitions literally from the ground up. The more alike the constituent profiles of different areas, the easier it is to build a coalition between them, a tendency fortified when one party dominates a geographic area. While the conventional wisdom posits that district and party place cross-pressures on representatives, this is only true when parties are thought of strictly as entities that are above local concerns and that articulate, instead, national ideological commitments. But parties that are geographically concentrated relieve cross-pressures on representatives and function to amplify local concerns.

The process of growing party dominance in a geographic area, whether rapid or gradual, contains a self-perpetuating tendency. As a party becomes dominant within a state, its representatives deploy all of the advantages and resources of incumbency to nurture the prospects of fellow partisans in their state, privilege supportive constituencies, and establish the terms of discourse. Nowhere was this more evident than in Republican Tom DeLay's efforts to influence the congressional redistricting of Texas in the early 2000s. Within the state and within the region, the dominant party establishes the terms of debate for that area's electoral competition, making it difficult for opposition to succeed. For example, to compete in the North, most of today's Republicans advance positions and arguments that are more like those of northern Democrats than those of Republicans from other areas of the country. Another way of putting it is that Trent Lott would, in all likelihood, have a difficult time getting elected in Olympia Snowe's Maine. It is the message of geography, not party, that is paramount in getting elected.

A party's regional dominance can debilitate democratic choice, as V. O. Key aptly noted over half a century ago. To sustain power, the dominant party must suppress internal conflicts of interests. In the most extreme formulation, between the 1930s and the 1960s, disenfranchisement of African Americans proved critical to Democratic success in the South and thus was instrumental in the party's victory on the national stage. Less severe institutional methods, drawing from the resources and opportunities for making rules that come with holding office, still serve to demobilize potential opposition, as the 2003 Texas redistricting case made clear. In this sense, then, building the party within a region has the potential to reinforce regional winners and undermine the effectiveness of democratic choice within regions, at least in the short-term. In the long term, however, as the three policy cases illustrate, socioeconomic change and the potential for exploiting new and suppressed conflicts within regions prevent regional coalitions from ossifying. As regions experience social and economic change, their relationship to the parties shifts, keeping alive the prospects for healthy democratic conflict within regions.

To secure power and control of the levers of national government, parties must capture a majority of the country's political geography. And the key to building a successful and stable party coalition is to unite regions that are most easily linked, either because of similar histories or because of similarities in demography, economy, and ideology. In building national coalitions, parties often find it easiest to link states and regions with contiguous geographies, because they are more likely to have shared experiences. But this is not always the case. Both historical political fault lines (such as the demarcation of the old Confederacy) and historical and current socioeconomic fault lines deriving from geography (e.g., commercial waterways or agriculturally fertile topography) contribute to experiential similarities in areas and regions that are not contiguous. For example, as a result of patterns of development, Pacific Coast states, with their early industry, independent centers of finance, and histories of immigration, share more in common with the traditional industrial states of the North than the states of the Mountain West with which they are contiguous. And, of course, it is these general, historically grounded similarities between the North and the Pacific Coast upon which Democrats have capitalized in building their post–New Deal coalition.

As similarities between regions lessen, it becomes incumbent upon parties to forge linkages and bridge differences in their quest for majority status. This has driven parties to construct interregional coalitions and has required parties to establish positions that create similar objectives for or induce cooperation from those with different agendas—an inherently tenuous prospect. Perhaps the most impressive example of this sort of coalition building in the country's history (outside of the original founding) was the Democratic New Deal. By capturing the most populous areas of the country, the party under FDR built a formidable regime. To maintain this unique North-South coalition required more than the promotion of similar objectives, of course; it necessitated submerging critical longstanding differences, such as those surrounding race. Welfare policy and the attributes of federalism provide insight into how this was accomplished.

The ability of the Republican Party to eventually disrupt that coalition reveals both the inherent instability in cross-regional coalitions and, somewhat paradoxically, the vitality of regional coalition building to party politics. Parties must use inventiveness in policy compromise and negotiation and must also capitalize on opportunities to wedge apart the geography of the opposition's coalition. This is how Nixon and the Republicans profited from the varying regional impacts of economic change, civil rights, and Vietnam in the late 1960s and early 1970s. So, politics requires cross-regional coalitions, and building across regions requires politics.

Exploiting issues to consolidate power and to divide the opposition is, of course, not exclusive to the domain of geography. Republicans used race to create a cleavage between Democrats' traditional white ethnic base and the party's growing base among Latinos and African Americans throughout the country, and they used abortion to divide northern Catholics from secular, Jewish, and mainline Protestant groups. Yet, the objective is to use such issues to capture geography—districts, states, regions, even the votes that come with the electoral college. When Republicans use abortion to obtain the support of midwestern Catholics, this is only an interim goal. The larger objective is to use abortion, alone or in combination with other issues, to wean away enough of the Democrats' geography to tip the partisan balance.

In making and breaking cross-regional coalitions, both parties have continued to promote, exploit, and reinforce geographic differences. Of the various political moments studied here, explicit political attention to region was perhaps most obvious in the Republicans' coalition-breaking efforts of the 1970s, yet it is evident in both of the other time periods examined. The New Deal regime's success in maintaining a cross-regional coalition lasted only as long as policy accommodated regional differences—in the process reinforcing them. Sometimes this reinforcement is a costly price for votes; sometimes it is a goal in itself. Recent Republican success has been predicated on the use of policy incentives and rhetoric that emphasize similarities between the South and West while playing to historic regional animosities toward the North.

In a political system in which parties are a primary means for organizing power and electoral rewards are based on geographic control, parties have an incentive to build regional coalitions. The alternatives are simply not as viable. Coalitions based solely on material conditions are hard to sustain because of the weakness of class politics in the United States. Those based solely on ideology founder because the ideas associated with classical liberalism are pervasive in America and each party claims allegiance to core cultural values; the hurly-burly of mass election campaign battles does not easily accommodate the nuance needed to make meaningful distinctions between the parties. Geographic coalition building, on the other hand, draws on both material conditions and ideas about those conditions. Figuring out where and how best to bridge the country's primary geographical fault lines as they emerge is one of the tasks of parties intent on building majority coalitions.

REGIONAL PARTY POLITICS IN THE GLOBAL AGE

One of the most often cited political aphorisms of late is that place-based differences are disappearing. The left sees technology and economic interdependencies shrinking the globe and erasing historic distinctions. The right sees Anglo-American ideas about democracy and free market economy being embraced worldwide. From either vantage point, the easy mobility of goods, people, capital, and ideas makes notions of sustained regional differences outdated. But, is there an inevitable march toward convergence or toward progress, as American cultural mythologizing (from both left and right) would suggest? If the recent past is prologue to the future, the answer is, Not necessarily. This book argues against popular wisdom, citing how modernizing changes and new ideas during the last fifty years have been differently incorporated by, and indeed have reinforced, America's distinctive regions.

Instead of anticipating the disappearance of geographic-based differences, let us ask how emergent trends and events are being received differently in the country's regions and what possibilities or constraints these differences place on the political parties. Beginning with the premise that regions differ from each other and that they refract national and international developments differently enables us to think in new ways about national party developments and the prospects for bipartisanship.

Recently, regional differences have produced a partisan stalemate. Because the parties now command the allegiances of opposite halves of the country, majority status rests on a razor's edge and party conflict is the norm. Neither party is likely to risk its current coalition unless it believes that majority status will be achieved only by doing so. Yet, because regions are dynamic and because parties are made up of strategic actors, today's configuration of partisanship will eventually give way to new regional alignments and a new era of bipartisanship. What developments, trends, or issues might serve as catalysts for this?

One development is the continuing deindustrialization of the economy and outsourcing of jobs. As industries and towns in the New Economy regions of the South and West experience deindustrialization akin to that which hit the North thirty years ago, the issue may become ripe for exploitation by a Democratic majority. The party, for example, fared well in the 2006 congressional elections by stressing economic and trade issues in areas of the Midwest and South hard hit by job and industry losses. If Democrats begin to compete in the South on these issues, Republicans will either have to embrace similar policies, giving rise to a new trade bipartisanship, or the Republican coalition in the South will be destabilized. While the defensive posture on trade of some southern Republicans in recent years suggests the possibility of a new bipartisan protectionism, neoliberal policies are nonetheless still broadly embraced throughout much of the South and West, and it will likely take a crisis for the economy to stimulate a regional realignment on that issue.

Even if a cross-regional consensus around managing the vicissitudes of globalization could be found, for either party to benefit from it, regional differences on social issues would have to be navigated. This is not only because, as the case of abortion reveals, regions have different social policy preferences, but also because these differences are increasingly being codified into state laws and state constitutions. For example, the nine continental states currently permitting civil unions, domestic partnerships, or marriage for same sex couples are in the North or Pacific Coast, while the great majority of constitutional prohibitions against gay marriage are in states in the South or West. Historically, federalism, and the state discretion that it allows, has been called upon to mediate various social policy preferences. This, of course, was how the national Democratic Party handled issues pertaining to race for much of the New Deal era. When Democrats regained congressional majority in the 2006 elections, they did so in part by again suppressing social issues. Gay marriage was downplayed in election campaigns, and successful Democrats in the South and West, such as Representative Heath Schuler in North Carolina and Senator Jon Tester in Montana, combined the party's traditional economic policies with socially conservative stances on issues such as abortion and gun control. To sustain their congressional majority, Democrats may find it electorally advantageous to push social issues to the states and allow for regional differences.[2]

Regardless of how parties respond to new developments in their long-standing economic and cultural battles, they will have to simultaneously attend to new and recently highlighted issues that have the potential to alter the old lines of conflict. For example, party regional alignments may be affected by trends in immigration (especially Latino immigration, which has been regionally concentrated in the Southwest) and by the conflicts this engenders. Though Latinos have voted in the past at lower rates than other major demographic groups, recent efforts at immigration reform might mobilize them. The effect this will have on the parties' regional alignments, however, is uncertain. On the one hand, mobilization could provide Democrats with an important inroad in the region, especially given the party's past efforts on behalf of working-class and minority constituents. If so, Republicans may attempt to defend their regional territory by exploiting Anglo backlash and calling for greater real and symbolic efforts to limit entry into the United States, as House Republicans did in 2005. Whether this would lead to a regional realignment or a rigidification of the existing alignment depends on the strength of the issue vis-à-vis other issues and on how parties respond to other issues.

On the other hand, the social and religious conservatism of most Latino voters makes them a reasonable bloc for the Republican Party to target, given its social conservatism and its strength in the Southwest. Striking a moderate response on immigration reform (e.g., emphasizing a generous guest worker program and paths to citizenship) is one strategy by which the party could further court Latinos. Such a strategy would also likely appeal to the many regional businesses that benefit from having a larger labor pool, and these businesspeople are another key regional constituency for Republicans.

The other issue that may affect existing regional dynamics is the War on Terror. While reaction against the Bush administration's handling of the war in Iraq was apparent nationwide in the 2006 elections, it is not clear how this will extend to the broader War on Terror. Both the West and the South still benefit from the defense state and thus may remain committed to the Republican Party's foreign policy agenda of unilateral militarization. Yet, the 2006 election evinced a fissure in the party's cross-regional coalition. Republicans in recent decades have built their coalition in part by decrying what they claimed was the overreach of the New Deal federal government into the lives of ordinary citizens. This resonated both with civil libertarians in the West and states' rights advocates in the South. But the Bush administration's simultaneous build-up of the administrative state in service of fighting the War on Terror and its curtailment of civil liberties in investigating terrorism resulted in defections of western libertarians from the party in 2006 more than states' rights advocates in the South. This realignment hints at a potential division between the libertarian reaction against centralized power and the states' rights reaction; while both regions have accommodated federal government activity in service of their economic interests, the South has also, at times, been more willing to use national government power to enforce its vision of society. Policies that highlight the division between the two, including social policy, could prove problematic for the cross-regional Republican coalition. In an indirect example of this, Sandra Day O'Connor, a Republican-appointed Supreme Court Justice and a westerner, angered social conservatives with her votes to reaffirm abortion rights and oppose the display of the Ten Commandments.

It is impossible to predict how these issues and trends will congeal within the American political system and to what effect. What is certain is that the regions have different stakes in the outcomes of the most significant issues on the horizon. Paying attention to their regional effects is the first step in understanding how the national party coalitions will evolve, and when and in what form bipartisanship will be found.

THE STATE OF DISUNION: THE COSTS OF REGIONAL ANTAGONISM

Vigorous partisanship is often said to be a sign of democratic health, but if the political partisanship falls along regional lines, is that healthy? Should we worry that the contestants are increasingly hailing from consistently opposing parts of the country? In the aggregate, regionally based partisanship appears still to be based on the exercise of democratic choice, as taken advantage of by the political parties. The winning party's program still seems to be that which satisfies the interests and ideas of a majority of the country. But, the alignment of party with region could become problematic if election results come to mean winning and losing regions. Potentially unsettling is the prospect of alienation from national governance of an entire region of the country if one party and its regional constituents come to dominate national government through successive elections and to choose a partisan approach to governing. A potential by-product of the constitution and the two-party system, this is an enduring possibility in American politics.

As the quotation from Cato at the outset of Chapter 1 indicates, anti-federalists wary of the constitutional undertaking saw tremendous variation among the states and were suspicious of efforts to impose a large, powerful, singular governing structure onto that geographic diversity. Believing homogeneity necessary for a well-functioning republic and finding it present in reverse proportion to the size of the republic, anti-federalists warned that "in a republic, the manners, sentiments, and interests of the people should be similar. If this is not the case, there will be a constant clashing of opinions; and the representatives of one part will be continually striving against those of the other."[3] The federalists countered that it was this very feature of the constitutional design and the large new republic that would be the safeguard against tyranny, yet they had their own concerns about the strength of local attachments. Noting the extent to which the sovereignty of the states was preserved by the Constitution, Madison speculated that the tendency toward disunion, characteristic of earlier confederations, would be a bigger threat to the new country than would national government tyranny.[4]

Hamilton, in assessing the predominance of local attachments, concurred with the others and pinned his hopes for the union on the successful administration of the national government. From the federalist standpoint, the selection processes and institutional practices of the national government would produce governance that would stand in contrast to the corruption that plagued many state governments. And when citizens saw that the national government was better administered than the state governments, this would help them overcome their local biases—competence over familiarity, in other words. But the Constitution holds a tension in the architecture it prescribes for the government. Meritorious administration, of the sort for which Hamilton hoped, requires majority decision making, yet those in the minority are certain to disagree on the merit of the outcomes produced. Minority representatives will not only feel aggrieved by the majority outcome, their grievance, if they have done their constituents' bidding, will naturally contrast the national outcome (i.e., the democratically endorsed public interest) with their own local interest, which is geographically based. In other words, these representatives—and their constituents—will bend toward the tendency in human nature to value the familiar, local interest over the general good produced by national majority decision making. To the extent that a two-party system—which the founders did not foresee—is geographically differentiated and produces consistently defined majorities and minorities, the dissonance for the minority party between local attachment and the national (majority) body is all the more entrenched. Citizens in the minority may not have reason to fault the national government for corruption in the traditional sense, but they are likely to see its aims and purposes as bankrupt and to fear that central power will be used for illegitimate purposes. (To the extent that the national government, once the two-party system was inaugurated, did become a source of patronage and regular corruption scandals, these fears of maladministration have been nurtured.) "Successful administration" becomes a matter of geographic perspective.

In view of the increasingly region-based partisanship we are seeing, a reassessment of national party politics in America seems in order. For mid-twentieth-century "responsible-party" theorists, national two-party conflict was healthy, indeed essential, for democracy. The ideal was clearly defined: Opposed parties present the electorate with a choice about what is best for the entire country. The presumption is that all voters have the opportunity to rationally evaluate party alternatives and, through the relatively straightforward act of majority decision making, endorse one course of action for the country over another. The out-party stands ready to offer critiques, point out abuses, and provide new alternatives. The outcome is thus a reasonable approximation of collective national deliberation in the act of self-governance.[5]

In a geographically divided political system, however, this presumption does not necessarily stand, and thus the product of democratic endorsement is not necessarily the same as the product of national deliberation. Elections that are competitive throughout the country suggest that when a national majority forms, it reflects the sort of rational voter endorsement of one course of action over another in the manner described above. It suggests more or less equivalent contests of ideas occurring simultaneously throughout the nation in each individual polling location. In the two-party system, the partisan regime that is the result is understood as the product of equally politically empowered voters rationally evaluating and authorizing (or reauthorizing) the majority party's governing philosophy. With the fears he expressed in Federalist 10 about majority tyranny, Madison might have found this sustained partisan regime, one that overrides institutional checks, somewhat worrisome; there is a greater likelihood that there will be a consistent and aggrieved minority that believes its will is being trampled by the majority. Yet, the beneficial effects of parties for democracy, in terms of connecting voters to their government, make this prospect of a sustained and coherent majority an acceptable risk, especially since the minority party can, theoretically at least, appeal to reason to win over rational voters—they can engage in the contest of ideas.[6]

However, if elections are largely uncompetitive between the parties—if one party regularly, easily wins in one region and another party regularly, easily wins in another region—the outcome will be very different. In this case, the partisan regime that results suggests not deliberative national voter endorsement but the dominance of one geographic area, with its interests and interpretations, over another in ways that both Madison and responsible-party theorists would surely find troubling. Without the fair competition of ideas so prized by democratic and responsible-party theory, this would be more akin to a factious majority's government by conquest. It is, in other words, the twinning of Cato's fears of geographic animosities and Madison's fears of a factious majority. The result is one section continually striving against the other over the nature and purpose of the Union, with the winning region qua party regime free to impose its interpretation.

The very Constitution that created union also preserved geographic difference, and politicians in the two-party system tend to organize around those differences. In this sense, the Constitution itself, when combined with the two-party system, militates against Hamilton's hopes for a national organ that would trump local affiliations. The dominant regions and party may feel that the national government they have produced is successfully and justly administered, but the minority regions and party will disagree. Over successive elections, the region or regions out of power are more likely to develop a sustained suspicion of the national project and its legitimacy, in turn likely to result in an erosion of national cohesion and unity. This has been the state of American politics for much of the country's history, and it is increasingly the state of American politics today.

APPENDIX A

RESEARCH METHOD AND CASE SELECTION

THE RESEARCH in this book involves actors at virtually all levels of the party system: presidents, congressional representatives, interest groups, and voters. The analytical focus, however, is on the House of Representatives. Studies of party conflict typically focus on the House because, of all of the national institutions, the House most closely approximates the general electorate. It is thus safe to assume that regional differences observed in the House represent regional differences in the electorate.[1] The analysis in the book relies primarily on information from House roll calls and debates.

Most existing studies of congressional party conflict rely heavily on aggregate data analysis. This book, instead, uses the vehicle of historical case studies of policy conflict in order to examine in greater depth the causal linkages between party conflict outcomes and the factors propelling these outcomes. Narrowing the lens to focus on conflict in specific issue areas (disaggregating) introduces a degree of control in that it reduces, though by no means eliminates, the uncertainty associated with aggregate analyses.[2]

A case study does not an argument make, however. The votes in any one area, in all likelihood, do not constitute a particularly large proportion of congressional votes; and therefore, explaining this pattern of conflict provides only partial leverage on the question of party conflict more generally. Moreover, the politics of trade are different from the politics of abortion. Because of this, cases were selected to represent the range of foreign, economic, and social policy issues over which the parties have fought in recent decades.

Trade, welfare, and abortion policy cases serve as proxies for larger groups of policies.[3] Trade policy resembles other economic regulatory policy. Like other economic policies, it has explicit distributional consequences and invites competition between economic groups and associations. For the case of welfare, I focus specifically on the now defunct program Aid to Families with Dependent Children (AFDC). This is a proxy for the general category of social welfare policy. Many of the more general means-tested social welfare services and provisions were, in fact, linked programmatically to AFDC. As a case study, AFDC combines the distributional politics of regions with their racial politics.

The dominant scholarship on regions in recent decades has treated regions as proxies for political economy divisions. While both trade and welfare have noneconomic dimensions to their regional politics (namely, foreign policy ideology in the former and racial politics in the latter), abortion is the case that demonstrates the cultural dimensions of regional politics most explicitly. It is the case that most clearly reveals regions to be more than just vehicles for political economy differences but, rather, political entities with distinct material and cultural properties.

The case of abortion fulfills another function as well. Since this policy was introduced into national political debate in the 1970s, in the middle of the period under study, it provides a useful illustration of how parties incorporate new issues into existing regional dynamics. Specifically, abortion reveals the potential for new issues to redefine the regional landscape in ways that have profound implications for party coalitions and interparty conflict dynamics. The extent to which an issue succeeds in transforming the party system depends in large part on how the parties construct and define the issue for their regional audiences.

Within each of the policy cases, both quantitative and qualitative indicators demonstrate the role of geography in legislative party conflict. Roll call data illustrate party and regional differences on the three issues, and statistical analyses establish geographical voting patterns. Statistical analyses of state-level data on economic, demographic, and party factors help explain variation in the geography of support for issues.

These quantitative assessments are meaningful, however, because they are embedded in a historical account of the developmental paths of the regions as well as representatives' substantive debates on the issues studied. The research here draws broadly on the *Congressional Record,* newspaper articles, political journals such as the *Congressional Quarterly Weekly Report* and the *National Journal,* and government produced documents and data, such as that accumulated by the Census Bureau and other executive agencies. Information has also been culled from memoranda, correspondence, surveys, press statements, and internal party documents that exist in the archival holdings of Republican Party leader Robert Michel, Democratic leader Carl Albert, and Nixon aide Harry Dent. In addition to roll call data, public opinion and electoral data from the Interuniversity Consortium for Political and Social Research (ICPSR) and the National Election Studies have been used. A wealth of secondary source material on regions, parties, the policy areas, and the presidencies of Kennedy, Nixon, and Clinton supplement the primary data. Combined, these sources provide the basis for the historical narrative of each of the chapters.

APPENDIX B

CONGRESSIONAL VOTE ANALYSIS

I RELY ON measures of party voting and especially party difference to establish the degree of partisanship over time. Scholars studying party conflict in Congress commonly use both. The party voting index is simply the percentage of all votes cast in a congress that are party votes (defined as a vote in which a majority of Democrats vote against a majority of Republicans). Calculating the party difference index is done by deriving the absolute value of the difference between the percentage of Republicans and the percentage of Democrats in support of each measure. The mean difference is then calculated for that congress. One of the shortcomings of the party vote measure is that it does not discriminate between instances when the party majorities are separated by only a few percentage points and those when they are widely separated. Thus, a vote in which 51 percent of Republicans voted yea along with 49 percent of Democrats is treated the same as a vote in which 98 percent of Republicans voted yea with 11 percent of Democrats (both are party votes). The party difference statistic helps to remedy this in that it provides a sense of the degree of polarization between the parties. I rely more heavily on party difference scores across time, though the two trend lines (party voting and party difference) typically move in tandem.[1]

Analyzing the voting trends specific to each issue treated in this book (trade, welfare, and abortion) required some interpretation in the vote selection process, because the nature and the definition of issues change over time. The particular selection process for each issue is indicated in notes to each chapter, but *generally*: on trade, I used only omnibus trade legislation (not industry-specific trade bills); on welfare, I used only program-specific reform legislation, in this case, AFDC (not broad social welfare spending or multipurpose legislation); and on abortion, I used all abortion-related votes. My goal with each was to isolate the issue under consideration in its purest form, free from the "noise" that might accompany the legislation if it were piggybacked on other issues or legislative goals.

Once this level of selection was completed, it was necessary to control for idiosyncrasies in voting procedures and amendments. On any one issue, in any given year or congress under analysis, multiple votes were typically cast. To get the truest sense of legislative support for the bill under consideration, I identified similar votes on the issue under study in each congress using factor analysis. Those votes that loaded at .6 or higher were selected. This weeded out votes that represented idiosyncratic behavior; the votes typically discarded were universal or extremely lopsided votes. After this was completed, I recoded the direction of the votes to make them consistent (e.g., on welfare, a "1" indicates support for expanding or maintaining welfare and a "0" indicates opposition to welfare expansion or maintenance). Announced and paired votes were included in the tallies.

Next, to maximize the information from these votes, I constructed an "index of support" for each representative who voted on at least half of the selected votes; I calculated the percentage of votes cast in which he or she favored the selected policy position (e.g., the percentage of votes in which the "pro–welfare expansion" position was supported). The result is that, for instance, a representative in the 104th Congress who voted in favor of maintaining AFDC on every one of the factor-loaded votes would receive an index score of 100 percent, while a representative who voted in favor of AFDC on half of the votes, would receive a score of 50 percent. The goal is to capture intensity of support, and the presumption is that greater consistency indicates greater intensity.

This "index of support" is the primary measure used to demonstrate party, region, and state support for policy in the three issues under analysis. Means were calculated for each level of aggregation, and these are used to convey the general sentiment (or central tendency) of the party, region, or state. In the case of abortion, the variation was, in particular instances, as significant for explaining patterns of support as the mean; this information is included as part of the analysis when necessary for accurate interpretation. Significant variations are also indicated through the narrative analysis.

It should be noted that an alternative method of analysis, using a single "key" vote for each piece of legislation (typically the vote prior to the final vote, as it was often the most conflict ridden) was initially used on the first issue analyzed (trade), and this method generated similar and even more robust findings. Though it is a slightly less straightforward measure, I opted for the index because it maximizes use of available information and avoids the potential selection bias of the analyst that is involved in deciding which vote is "key." The possibility for selection bias would have been greater for welfare, and especially abortion, because these issues had a larger number and a greater variety of votes cast. I supplement parts of my discussion, however, particularly on trade, with quantitative and narrative data on key votes. When this key vote information is provided in the text, the corollary index results are reported in the notes.

With the exception of the 1998 trade vote on fast-track authority, and unless otherwise noted, all vote calculations were derived from roll call data available from the Interuniversity Consortium for Political and Social Research (ICPSR) for respective years. The data for the 1998 fast-track vote were drawn from roll call data for the 105th House generously made available by Keith Poole and Howard Rosenthal at their website voteview.com.

The heart of my analytic method lies in how votes are distributed—by party and by region—and in a narrative analysis of the remarks made by political actors, given the historical and regional context. I supplement the primarily qualitative analysis with additional quantitative analyses in each chapter, including ordinary least squares regression analyses of factors contributing to state support for specific policy positions. These analyses are intended to be supplementary, illustrating the issues and concerns in the substantive policy debates and in the historical era under study. For the regression analyses, the dependent variable is the state index of support score for the policy position in question. The independent variables represent the themes discussed in connection with that issue. They represent a mix of economic, demographic, and geographic variables that are cited in the issue debates and the regional literature as politically consequential.

In addition to the economic and demographic variables, I tested regional dummy variables in each of the regressions. On the advice of an anonymous reviewer, variables for South, West, and Pacific Coast were included in the regression models, with the North excluded as a base category. When significant, I reported the results in the model (Tables 3.2, 4.2, and 5.2). If F-test results indicated that the dummy variable coefficients were individually and collectively insignificant, then they were not reported in the final model results (Tables 4.3 and 5.5). The purpose of testing regional dummy variables was to capture the effect of geography above and beyond the models' specified economic and demographic variables, which themselves differed regionally. The assumption is that, with key economic and demographic factors controlled, the regional variables will reflect the independent effect of regional political cultures. However, the interpretation that the regional variable reflects culture should be treated with caution. It is possible that other economic or demographic factors not included in the regression analyses exist that also vary by region, and that these are manifest in the regional dummy variables. In short, the regional dummy variables are, at best, a crude and imprecise measure of political culture, and all that can be claimed definitively is that there is something common to the region, something not captured by the other variables, that has an effect on state support for the policy in question.

INTRODUCTION

1   Anne E. Kornblut, "Seeking 'Common Ground,'" *Boston Globe*, December 14, 2000.

2   As evidence of the popularity of the phrase, when the Linguistic Society of America held their annual meeting in 2005, members voted for "red state, blue state, purple state" as the phrase that had most dominated national discussion in 2004. "Top Phrase of 2004: 'Red State, Blue State, Purple State,'" CNN. Accessed at www.cnn.com/2005/US/01/10/top.phrase.ap/ on February 5, 2005.

3   E. J. Dionne, "One Nation Deeply Divided," *Washington Post*, November 7, 2003; Michael Barone, "The 49 Percent Nation," *National Journal*, June 9, 2001; David Brooks, "One Nation: Slightly Divisible," *Atlantic Monthly*, December 2001; David Von Drehle, "Political Split Is Pervasive," *Washington Post*, April 25, 2004.

4   A third category of analysis, behavioral studies, focuses on explaining general patterns of rising and falling partisanship in Congress across time. These offer generic insights into the conditions associated with growth in conflict, but they are less useful, for my purposes, as causal explanations. These aggregate data studies typically establish the correlation of party conflict with other institutional factors, such as divided government, party turnover, distinct party platforms, or size of the majority, that are the product of more primary electoral factors. Samuel C. Patterson and Gregory A. Caldeira, "Party Voting in the United States Congress," *British Journal of Political Science* 18 (January 1988): 111–131; David Brady, Joseph Cooper, and Patricia Hurley, "The Decline of Party in the U.S. House of Representatives, 1887–1986," *Legislative Studies Quarterly* 4 (1979): 381–407; William Lowry and Charles Shipan, "Party Differentiation in Congress," *Legislative Studies Quarterly* 27 (2002): 33–60.
    New research is emerging which argues that polarization, rather than reflecting the equal divergence of the parties away from the center, is an artifact of Republicans' rightward shift, with Democrats occupying more or less the same ideological ground as in past decades. Jacob Hacker and Paul Pierson, *Off Center: The Republican Revolution and the Erosion of American Democracy* (New Haven: Yale University Press, 2005); Nolan McCarty, Keith Poole, and Howard Rosenthal, *Polarized America: The Dance of Ideology and Unequal Riches* (Cambridge: MIT Press, 2006).

5   John Aldrich, *Why Parties: The Origins and Transformation of Political Parties in America* (Chicago: University of Chicago Press, 1995); Gary W. Cox and Matthew D. McCubbins, *Legislative Leviathan* (Berkeley: University of California Press, 1993); Richard Fenno, *Home Style* (Boston: Little, Brown, 1978); Morris P. Fiorina, *Representatives, Roll Calls, and Constituencies* (Lexington, MA: Lexington Books, 1974); Benjamin Ginsberg, "Elections and Public Policy," *American Political Science Review* 70, no. 1 (March 1976): 41–49; John Kingdon, *Congressmen's Voting Decisions*, 3rd ed. (Ann Arbor: University of Michigan Press, 1989); Keith Poole and Howard Rosenthal, *Congress: A Political-Economic History of Roll Call Voting* (New York: Oxford University Press, 1997); David Rohde, *Parties and Leaders in the Postreform House* (Chicago: University of Chicago Press, 1991).

6   Rohde, *Parties and Leaders in the Postreform House*; Barbara Sinclair, *Legislators, Leaders, and Lawmaking: The U.S. House of Representatives in the Postreform Era* (Baltimore: Johns Hopkins University Press,

1995); Larry Sabato, *The Party's Just Begun: Shaping Political Parties for America's Future* (Glenview, IL: Scott, Foresman, 1988); David Price, *Bringing Back the Parties* (Washington DC: Congressional Quarterly Press, 1984); Paul Herrnson, *Party Campaigning in the 1980s* (Cambridge: Harvard University Press, 1988).

7   See Rohde, *Parties and Leaders in the Postreform House,* 46–47.

8   Rohde, *Parties and Leaders in the Postreform House;* Aldrich, *Why Parties,* esp. ch. 7.

9   Harry V. Jaffa, "The Nature and Origin of the American Party System," in *Political Parties, U.S.A.,* ed. Robert A. Goldwin, (Chicago: Rand McNally, 1964); Herbert Storing, "Federalists and Anti-Federalists: The Ratification Debate," in *Toward a More Perfect Union: Writings of Herbert Storing,* ed. Joseph M. Bessette (Washington DC: AEI Press, 1995).

10   John Gerring, "Party Ideology in America: The National Republican Chapter, 1828–1924," *Studies in American Political Development* 11 (Spring 1997): 46; Gerring, *American Party Ideologies, 1828–1992* (Cambridge: Cambridge University Press, 1998).

11   On the relationship between economic factors, economic policy, and party polarization, see John Coleman, *Party Decline in America: Policy, Politics, and the Fiscal State* (Princeton: Princeton University Press, 1996); McCarty, Poole, and Rosenthal, *Polarized America;* Jeffrey Stonecash, *Class and Party in American Politics* (Boulder, CO: Westview Press, 2000); and Jeffrey Stonecash, *Diverging Parties* (Boulder, CO: Westview Press, 2002).

12   John Kenneth White, *The Values Divide* (Chatham, NJ: Chatham House, 2003).

13   Samuel L. Huntington, *American Politics and the Promise of Disharmony* (Cambridge, MA: Belknap Press, 1981).

14   James W. Ceaser, "True Blue vs. Deep Red: The Ideas that Move American Politics," paper prepared for the 2006 Bradley Symposium, sponsored by the Hudson Institute in Washington, DC. Also, James W. Ceaser, *Nature and History in American Political Development* (Cambridge: Harvard University Press, 2006).

15   In addition to White, *The Values Divide;* Huntington, *American Politics;* and Ceaser, *Nature and History;* see also Gerring, *American Party Ideologies;* E. J. Dionne, *Why Americans Hate Politics* (New York: Simon and Schuster, 1991); James Davison Hunter, *Culture War: The Struggle to Define America* (New York: Basic Books, 1991); James Morone, *Hellfire Nation: The Politics of Sin in American History* (New Haven: Yale University Press, 2003); Rogers Smith, *Civic Ideals: Conflicting Visions of Citizenship in American History* (New Haven: Yale University Press, 1997); Christopher Lasch, *The Revolt of the Elites and the Betrayal of Democracy* (New York: W. W. Norton, 1995); Michael Lind, *The Next American Nation: The New Nationalism and the Fourth American Revolution* (New York: Free Press, 1995); Thomas Byrne Edsall with Mary D. Edsall, *Chain Reaction: The Impact of Race, Rights, and Taxes on American Politics* (New York: W. W. Norton, 1992); Everett Carll Ladd, Jr., "Liberalism Upside Down: The Inversion of the New Deal Order," *Political Science Quarterly* 91, no. 4 (Winter 1976–77): 577–600; and Ronald Inglehart, "The Renaissance of Political Culture," *American Political Science Review* 82 (December 1988): 1203–1230.

There is debate about whether contemporary cultural divisions cut across the economic class divisions of the New Deal era (as would be suggested by a realignment) or rather reinforce them. On the persistence of economic class divisions between the parties, see Stonecash, *Class and Party.* If it is the latter, that cultural divisions reinforce class divisions, what is noteworthy is that the rhetoric of economic class has been supplanted by cultural disputes. While this is an extremely important debate, the important point to be drawn here is that social or cultural politics, as a source of partisan dispute, rose in significance after the 1960s.

16   V. O. Key, *Politics, Parties, and Pressure Groups*, 5th ed. (New York: Thomas Y. Crowell Co., 1964 [1942]), 229.

17   Entrenching New Deal policies in the administrative state in ways that, ironically, displaced vigorous party politics was another of Roosevelt's accomplishments. Sidney Milkis, *The President and the Parties* (New York: Oxford, 1993). On the legislation before them, however, members of Congress still exercised the choice to cooperate or not based on regional incentives. See Ira Katznelson, Daniel Kryder, and Kim Geiger, "Limiting Liberalism: The Southern Veto in Congress, 1933–1950," *Political Science Quarterly* 108, no. 2 (Summer 1993): 283–306.

18   The consensus school in American politics is broad. Traceable back at least to Alexis de Tocqueville, it is most associated with scholars writing in the aftermath of World War II, including Louis Hartz, Richard Hofstadter, Daniel Bell, and Seymour Martin Lipset. Later scholars in history and political science historicized this intellectual current (along with pluralism, also ascendant after World War II), attributing its dominance at the time to the influence of several factors, including the broad success of the New Deal (and the related lack of Depression-inspired revolution, especially in contrast to the conflicts that consumed Europe in the first half of the twentieth century), the general prosperity of the postwar decades, and the national devotion to Cold War containment policy.

19   Stephen Skowronek, *The Politics Presidents Make: Leadership from John Adams to George Bush* (Cambridge: Belknap Press of Harvard University Press, 1993).

20   James Sundquist's description of the shift from the "placid" years of New Deal consensus to the conflicts of the 1960s generated by the rise of new cross-cutting cleavages, though not overtly focused on the regional dimensions, provides an excellent summary of the issues and party politics at the time. For Sundquist, the events of these years did not lead to a realignment of the sort that had occurred in earlier periods of American history; rather, it led to dealignment and potentially (he was writing in 1983) a revitalization of the New Deal system; with a longer historical perspective, it is clear that the destabilization of the 1960s contributed to a secular realignment of the parties, in ways that subsequent chapters of this book explain. See Sundquist, *Dynamics of the Party System: Alignment and Realignment of Political Parties in the United States*, rev. ed. (Washington DC: Brookings Institution, 1983), esp. chs. 15–18.

21   See Matthew Lassiter, *The Silent Majority: Suburban Politics in the Sunbelt South* (Princeton: Princeton University Press, 2005) for a persuasive account of Republican use of multiple policy ideas in the South.

22   The phrase "emerging Republican majority" was coined by Republican strategist Kevin Phillips, who predicted the rise to national dominance of a Republican Party built in the suburbs and small communities of the South and West. Phillips, *The Emerging Republican Majority* (New Rochelle, NY: Arlington House, 1969).

23   These four regions—the South, interior West ("West"), North, and Pacific Coast—are the primary geographic units of my analysis, and the set of states in each region is consistent throughout the book. Chapter 1 provides regional definitions, along with a map, and explains the logic of the divisions. The only exception to these definitions is when I quote another source that uses the same term (e.g., North) to refer to a slightly different set of states; these instances are clearly noted as such. The four regions are broad categories, however, and it is important to note at the outset that the aggregation obscures important differences within regions. (For an excellent analysis of the regional trends *within* states, see James Gimpel and Jason Schuknecht, *Patchwork Nation: Sectionalism and Political Change in American Politics* [Ann Arbor: University of Michigan Press, 2004]). Because, on occasion, there are analytically important distinctions and variations within the four regions, I also provide data and analysis of subregions (the Southeast and Southwest in the South; the Mountain and West North Central states in the West; the East North Central, Mid-Atlantic, and New England states in the North). In particular, the chapter on abortion includes discussion of subregional differences in the North, between the "Northeast," including the Mid-Atlantic and New England subregions, and the East North Central states. I have taken pains to limit the potential terminological confusion, but using multiple levels of analysis (including, in some instances, cities and states) is necessary to accurately capturing the nuances of large-scale party change.

24   See Appendix A for a discussion of case selection.

CHAPTER 1 RECASTING REGION

1   Cato III, *Essays on the Constitution of the United States*, ed. Paul Leicester Ford (Buffalo: William S. Hein and Co., 2003 [1892]).

2   James Sterling Young, *The Washington Community, 1800–1828* (New York: Columbia University Press, 1966), ch. 5.

3   On the relationship of sections to parties, see V. O. Key, *Politics, Parties, and Pressure Groups*, 5th ed. (New York: Thomas Y. Crowell Co., 1964 [1942]); Walter Dean Burnham, *Critical Elections and the Mainsprings of American Politics* (New York: Norton, 1970); J. Clark Archer and Peter Taylor, *Section and Party* (New York: John Wiley and Sons, 1981); and Fred M. Shelley, J. Clark Archer, Fiona M. Davidson, and Stanley D. Brunn, *Political Geography of the United States* (New York: Guilford Press, 1996). For a sampling of work on sectional influences in politics in specific late-nineteenth- and early-twentieth-century periods, see Paul Kleppner, *Continuity and Change in Electoral Politics: 1893–1928* (Westport, CT: Greenwood Press, 1986); Richard Bensel, *Yankee Leviathan: The Origins of Central State Authority in America, 1859–1877* (New York: Cambridge University Press, 1991); Elizabeth Sanders, *Roots of Reform: Farmers, Workers, and the American State, 1877–1917* (Chicago: University of Chicago Press, 1999); Theda Skocpol, *Protecting Soldiers and Mothers: The Political Origins of Social Policy in the United States* (Cambridge: Harvard University Press, 1995); Paul Kleppner, *The Third Electoral System, 1853–1892: Parties, Voters, and Political Cultures* (Raleigh-Durham: University of North Carolina Press, 1979); and Richard Valelly, *The Two Reconstructions* (Chicago: University of Chicago Press, 2004).

4   V. O. Key, *Southern Politics in State and Nation* (New York: Alfred A. Knopf, 1949); E. E. Schattschneider, *The Semisovereign People: A Realist's View of Democracy in America* (Hinsdale, IL: Dryden Press, 1975 [1960]).

5   While it is fairly commonplace for political economists to claim Turner's heritage, his writings, taken as a whole, evince a more complex relationship between geography, on the one hand, and the economic interests and cultural attitudes that directly inform politics, on the other. Frederick Jackson Turner, *The Significance of Sections in American History* (New York: Holt and Rinehart and Winston, 1932); and, esp., Turner, *The Frontier in American History* (New York: Henry Holt and Co., 1921). For the political economy tradition, see John Agnew, *The United States in the World-Economy: A Regional Geography* (New York: Cambridge University Press, 1987); Stanley D. Brunn, *Geography and Politics in America* (New York: Harper and Row, 1974); Harvey Perloff, *Regions, Resources, and Economic Growth* (Baltimore: Johns Hopkins Press, 1960); John House, ed., *United States Public Policy: A Geographical View* (Oxford: Clarendon Press, 1983); Ann Markusen, *Regions* (Totowa, NJ: Rowman and Littlefield, 1987); Richard Bensel, *Sectionalism and American Political Development, 1880–1980* (Madison: University of Wisconsin Press, 1984); Peter Trubowitz, *Defining the National Interest: Conflict and Change in American Foreign Policy* (Chicago: University of Chicago Press, 1998).

6   Bensel, *Sectionalism.*

7   The Pacific Coast states have also been described as having a "mixed" economy of core and periphery activities during the earlier years of the region's development. Sanders, *Roots of Reform.*

8   See Harvey Perloff and Vera Dodds, *How a Region Grows: Area Development in the U.S. Economy,* Supplementary Paper No. 17 (New York: Committee for Economic Development, 1963); Perloff, *Regions, Resources, and Economic Growth.*

9   Perloff and Dodds, *How a Region Grows,* 15.

10   Ibid., 16, 18, Tables 1 and 2.

11   Samuel C. Patterson and Gregory A. Caldeira, "Party Voting in the United States Congress," *British Journal of Political Science* 18 (January 1988): 111–131; David Brady, Joseph Cooper, and Patricia Hurley, "The Decline of Party in the U.S. House of Representatives, 1887–1986," *Legislative Studies Quarterly* 4 (August 1979): 381–407; William R. Lowry and Charles R. Shipan, "Party Differentiation in Congress," *Legislative Studies Quarterly* 27 (February 2002): 33–60.

12   Bensel, *Sectionalism;* also, Burnham, *Critical Elections;* Key, *Southern Politics;* Schattschneider, *The Semisovereign People;* Trubowitz, *Defining the National Interest;* and Peter Trubowitz and Nicole Mellow, "Going Bipartisan: Politics by Other Means," *Political Science Quarterly* 120, no. 3 (Fall 2005): 433–453.

13   See, esp., Agnew, *United States in the World-Economy;* Markusen, *Regions;* Bensel, *Sectionalism;* Trubowitz, *Defining the National Interest;* Ann Markusen, Scott Campbell, Peter Hall, and Sabrina Deitrick, *The Rise of the Gunbelt and the Military Remapping of America* (New York: Oxford University Press, 1991); Larry Sawyers and William Tabb, eds., *Sunbelt/Snowbelt: Urban Development and Regional Restructuring* (New York: Oxford University Press, 1984).

14   The idea that a "culture war" dominates American politics has spawned its own set of disputes. Accounts that question the validity of the war tend to focus on the centrism of mass public opinion on key matters, such as abortion, race, and gun control, in contrast to the more extreme issue positions taken by activists and many party elites. For a sampling of this debate, see James Davison Hunter, *Culture War: The Struggle to Define America* (New York: Basic Books, 1991); John Kenneth White, *The Values Divide* (Chatham, NJ: Chatham House, 2003); E. J. Dionne, *Why Americans Hate Politics* (New York: Simon and Schuster, 1991); Paul DiMaggio, John Evans, and Bethany Bryson, "Have Americans' Social Attitudes Become More Polarized?" *American Journal of Sociology* 102, no. 3 (November 1996): 690–755; Morris Fiorina, Samuel Abrams, and Jeremy Pope, *Culture War? The Myth of a Polarized America* (New York: Pearson Longman, 2004); and Alan Wolfe, *One Nation, After All: What Americans Really Think about God, Country, Family, Racism, Welfare, Immigration, Homosexuality, Work, the Right, and Left, and Each Other* (New York: Viking Press, 1998).

15   Thomas Frank, *What's the Matter with Kansas? How Conservatives Won the Heart of America* (New York: Metropolitan Books, 2003). On the persistence of low-income and working-class support for the Democratic Party, see Jeffrey Stonecash, *Class and Party in American Politics* (Boulder, CO: Westview Press, 2000).

16   Lisa McGirr, *Suburban Warriors: The Origins of the New American Right* (Princeton: Princeton University Press, 2001).

17   Alexis de Tocqueville, *Democracy in America,* trans., Harvey Mansfield and Delba Winthrop (Chicago: University of Chicago Press, 2000); 1:1:3. One of the best-known portraits of American regional cultures, but one that is also broadly contested, is Daniel Elazar, *American Federalism: A*

View from the States (New York: Thomas Y. Crowell and Co., 1972). Elazar described "individualistic states" in lower New England, the Mid-Atlantic, and the Plains, "traditionalist states" in the South, and "moralistic states" in the North, Pacific Coast, and Rocky Mountains as each reflecting varying combinations of commonwealth and marketplace values. See also, Elazar, *American Mosaic: The Impact of Space, Time, and Culture on American Politics* (Boulder CO: Westview Press, 1993). For alternative cultural readings, see David Hackett Fisher, *Albion's Seed: Four British Folkways in America* (New York: Oxford University Press, 1989); Anne Norton, *Alternative Americas: A Reading of Antebellum Political Culture* (Chicago: University of Chicago Press, 1986); Kleppner, *The Third Electoral System;* Susan-Mary Grant and Peter J. Parish, eds., *Legacy of Disunion: The Enduring Significance of the American Civil War* (Baton Rouge: Louisiana State University Press, 2003). There is also a large number of monographs of distinctive regional and subregional cultures. For examples, see, C. Vann Woodward, *The Burden of Southern History,* 3rd ed. (Baton Rouge: Louisiana State University Press, 1993); W. J. Cash, *The Mind of the South* (New York: Vintage Book, 1991 [1941]); James C. Cobb, *Redefining Southern Culture: Mind and Identity in the Modern South* (Athens: University of Georgia Press, 1999); John Shelton Reed, *Minding the South* (Columbia: University of Missouri Press, 2003); David M. Wrobel, *Promised Lands: Promotion, Memory, and the Creation of the American West* (Lawrence: University Press of Kansas, 2002); David M. Wrobel and Michael Steiner, *Many Wests: Place, Culture, and Regional Identity* (Lawrence: University Press of Kansas, 1997); Elliot West, *The Way to the West: Essays on the Central Plains* (Albuquerque: University of New Mexico Press, 1995); Walter Nugent, *Into the West: The Story of Its People* (New York: Vintage, 2001); Mark Voss-Hubbard, *Beyond Party: Cultures of Antipartisanship in Northern Politics before the Civil War* (Baltimore: Johns Hopkins University Press, 2001); Jean H. Baker, *Affairs of Party: The Political Culture of Northern Democrats in the Mid-Nineteenth Century* (New York: Fordham University Press, 1998); Gerald Gamm, *The Making of New Deal Democrats* (Chicago: University of Chicago Press, 1989). It is easier to find claims of distinctive, post–Civil War southern and western regional cultures than it is to find treatments of a northern regional culture. This might be attributable to the relatively early ethnic and religious pluralism of the North as a result of immigration; it also might be that "northern culture" is simply equated with national culture because of the historic political and economic dominance of northern elites.

18   Hunter, *Culture War,* chs. 3–4. Also see Clyde Wilcox, *Onward Christian Soldiers? The Religious Right in American Politics,* 2nd ed. (Boulder, CO: Westview Press, 2000).

19   Lisa Wedeen, "Conceptualizing Culture: Possibilities for Political Science," *American Political Science Review* 96, no. 4 (December 2002): 721.

20   Norton, *Alternative Americas,* 5.

21   George W. Pierson, "The Obstinate Concept of New England: A Study in Denudation," *New England Quarterly,* 28, no. 1 (March 1955): 3–17.

22   Kent Ryden, "Writing the Midwest: History, Literature, and Regional Identity," *Geographical Review* 89, no. 4 (October 1999): 511–532. Ryden argues that the Midwest's identity derives more from the "little" histories than do other regions.

23   For example, Woodward, in the chapter "The Search for Southern Identity" in *The Burden of Southern History* writes of the resilience of a distinctive southern identity despite the region's "economic and social revolution" of the mid-twentieth century. For Woodward, replacing the South's racist traditions as markers of regional distinctiveness was the shared history, or "collective experience" of southerners; the historic experience of poverty, failure, and living with moral corruption (slavery and its legacy) were southern departures from "American" national identity. Cash describes the basic continuity of the "mind of the South" over time, yet juxtaposes this continuity with detailed descriptions of the clashes between southerners, over the virtues of the "old" and "new" South or between traditional practices and modern beliefs, as they struggled over the region's evolution. See also Cash, *The Mind of the South*.

24   When it comes to specifying the geography of regions, there is greater, though by no means perfect, agreement among political economists than there is among cultural historians. When discussing cultural geography, scholars talk persuasively about American political culture (e.g., Louis Hartz, *The Liberal Tradition in America* [New York: Harcourt, Brace, Jovanovich, 1955] and Samuel L. Huntington, *American Politics and the Promise of Disharmony* [Cambridge, MA: Belknap Press, 1981]), about the political cultures of North, South, and West (e.g., Norton, *Alternative Americas*), and about the political cultures of even smaller subregions, such as the Midwest or New England (e.g., Ryden "Writing the Midwest" and Pierson, "The Obstinate Concept of New England").

25   Bruce Schulman, *From Cotton Belt to Sunbelt: Federal Policy, Economic Development, and the Transformation of the South, 1938–1980* (New York: Oxford University, 1991).

26   Many accounts, primarily popular ones, do investigate today's red and blue divides, as a reflection of the culture wars. These include an impressionistic account of divergent lifestyles and battles over "authenticity" by David Brooks, Thomas Frank's account of the substitution of religious conservatism for economic radicalism in the heartland, and Fiorina et al.'s empirical account of moderate public opinion versus elite polarization. While interesting, these accounts rarely dig beneath the surface to get at the substance of cultural disputes. Instead, the clash of ideas is dismissed as misplaced economic ire (Frank) or as the battles of political class purists that straightjacket unenthusiastic voters with limited ballot options (Fiorina et al.). These works are not especially useful for my purposes in understanding regions as cultural entities. As James Ceaser has pointed out in a rejoinder to Fiorina, even if it is true that polarization is a product only of the political class, since this class more or less shapes the country's political life, it is not to be dismissed but rather to be substantively investigated. See David Brooks, "One Nation: Slightly Divisible," *Atlantic Monthly*, December 2001; Frank, *What's the Matter with Kansas*; Fiorina, Abrams, and Pope, *Culture War?*, and James W. Ceaser, "True Blue vs. Deep Red: The Ideas that Move American Politics," paper prepared for the 2006 Bradley Symposium, sponsored by the Hudson Institute in Washington DC.

27   Benedict Anderson, *Imagined Communities*, rev. ed. (New York: Verso, 1991), 7.

28   Anthony Smith, "Culture, Community, and Territory: The Politics of Ethnicity and Nationalism," *International Affairs* 72, no. 2 (July 1996): 445–458.

29   For recent interpretations of this tension, see James Morone, *Hellfire Nation: The Politics of Sin in American History* (New Haven: Yale University Press, 2003); Rogers Smith, *Civic Ideals: Conflicting Visions of Citizenship in American History* (New Haven: Yale University Press, 1997); and Samuel Huntington, *Who Are We? The Challenges to American National Identity* (New York: Simon and Schuster, 2004).

30   For more on America as an interpretive project, see J. David Greenstone, "Political Culture and American Political Development: Liberty, Union, and the Liberal Bipolarity," *Studies in American Political Development* 1 (1986): 1–49. Also Morone, *Hellfire Nation*; Norton, *Alternative Americas*.

31   Anderson, *Imagined Communities*, 201.

32   James Gimpel and Jason Schuknecht, *Patchwork Nation: Sectionalism and Political Change in American Politics* (Ann Arbor: University of Michigan Press, 2004).

33   Ibid., 3.

34 Peter Katzenstein, *A World of Regions: Asia and Europe in the American Imperium* (Ithaca: Cornell University Press, 2005).

35 Pierson, "The Obstinate Concept of New England," 5.

36 Turner, *The Frontier in American History,* 205–206.

37 Katzenstein, *A World of Regions,* 12.

38 As previously noted, there is disagreement among both political economists and cultural historians on the most relevant regional demarcations. For example, Bensel (*Sectionalism*) privileges two regions while Trubowitz (*Defining the National Interest*) emphasizes three. Norton (*Alternative Americas*) describes three as does Elazar (*American Federalism*), although his differ from Norton's. I have chosen to utilize broad distinctions in making my demarcations: the North and Pacific Coast have significantly different economic histories from the South and West, as Bensel would point out, but there are also important distinctions between North and Pacific Coast (Sanders, *Roots of Reform*) and South and West (Trubowitz). From a cultural perspective, North, South, and West are generally acknowledged to be distinct (Norton, Elazar), though the Pacific Coast has been described as sharing attributes with states both in the North and in the West (Elazar).

39 The *North* includes: (a) Connecticut, Maine, Massachusetts, New Hampshire, Rhode Island, and Vermont (collectively New England); (b) Delaware, Maryland, New Jersey, New York, and Pennsylvania (collectively Mid-Atlantic); and (c) Illinois, Indiana, Michigan, Ohio, and Wisconsin (collectively East North Central). The *Pacific Coast* includes California, Oregon, and Washington. The *South* includes: (a) Alabama, Florida, Georgia, Kentucky, Mississippi, North Carolina, South Carolina, Tennessee, Virginia, and West Virginia (collectively, Southeast); and (b) Arkansas, Louisiana, Oklahoma, and Texas (collectively, Southwest). The *West* includes: (a) Arizona, Colorado, Idaho, Montana, Nevada, New Mexico, Utah, and Wyoming (collectively, Mountain States); and (b) Iowa, Kansas, Minnesota, Missouri, Nebraska, North Dakota, and South Dakota (collectively, West North Central). Alaska and Hawaii, which became states after World War II, are not included in the analysis.

40 George Washington, *The Farewell Address* (1796). Reprinted online at www.yale.edu/lawweb/ avalon/washing.htm.

CHAPTER 2 REGIME CHANGE

1 E. J. Dionne, *Why Americans Hate Politics* (New York: Simon and Schuster, 1991), 152. In Stephen Skowronek's model of party regimes, a Republican like Eisenhower tried to "preempt" the New Deal but was ultimately unsuccessful in disrupting the dominant ideas and interests. Stephen Skowronek, *The Politics Presidents Make: Leadership from John Adams to George Bush* (Cambridge: Belknap Press of Harvard University Press, 1993).

2 For a cogent discussion about the long-term trend in American politics toward an emerging Republican majority up through the 2004 election, see Michael Nelson, "The Setting: George W. Bush, Majority President," in *The Elections of 2004*, ed. Michael Nelson (Washington DC: Congressional Quarterly Press, 2005).

3 See Appendix B for an explanation of how these measures are calculated.

4 As quoted in John B. Judis and Ruy Teixeira, *The Emerging Democratic Majority* (New York: Scribner's, 2002), 30.

5   See, for example, David Mayhew, "Congressional Elections: The Case of the Vanishing Marginals," 6 *Polity* (1974): 295–317.

6   Another avenue to party influence in a delegation, evident particularly in the South, is party conversion by a sitting representative.

7   Since the decennial reapportionments reflect population movement from the Democratic North to the Republican South and West, one might expect this migration to redistribute Democrats to those regions. Research suggests, in fact, that transplants tend either to adapt to the new political or partisan culture to which they have moved or to be moving to areas that better reflect their own political leanings, a tendency which amplifies the regional concentrations of the party system. See James Gimpel and Jason Schuknecht, *Patchwork Nation: Sectionalism and Political Change in American Politics* (Ann Arbor: University of Michigan Press, 2004); and Lisa McGirr, *Suburban Warriors: The Origins of the New American Right* (Princeton: Princeton University Press, 2001).

8   Walter Dean Burnham, "The Future of American Politics: Two Scenarios," paper presented at American Politics in a New Millennium, conference, Mexico City, April 2002.

9   American National Election Studies data, cumulative data file, 1948–2000.

10   The percentage of households considered low-income increased from 20.7 percent in 1969 to 22.2 percent in 1996, while the Gini coefficient increased by 20.1 percent from 1968 to 2001. U.S. Census Bureau, www.census.gov/hhes/income/mednhhld/ta5.html.

11   Harold Stanley and Richard Niemi, *Vital Statistics on American Politics* (Washington, DC: CQ Press, 2004).

12   Bruce Schulman, *From Cotton Belt to Sunbelt: Federal Policy, Economic Development, and the Transformation of the South, 1938–1980* (Durham, NC: Duke University Press, 1994); Gavin Wright, *Old South, New South: Revolutions in the Southern Economy since the Civil War* (Baton Rouge: Louisiana State University Press, 1996).

13   Gurney Breckenfeld, "Business Loves the Sunbelt (and vice versa)," *Fortune* (June 1977): 133. Quoted in Bruce Schulman, *The Seventies: The Great Shift in American Culture, Society, and Politics* (New York: Free Press, 2001), 110.

14   Memorandum No. 29 from John Barriere to Speaker Carl Albert, March 6, 1972. Carl Albert Papers, Legislative Series, Box 238, File 9. Albert's papers are held in the Congressional Archives of the Carl Albert Center at the University of Oklahoma in Norman. All references are to this collection. Democratic leaders also sought to diffuse those issues, such as race and civil rights, which would force party members to choose between the demands of their constituents and those of their party brethren in other regions. Memorandum No. 1 ("Mississippi Challenge") from Barriere to Albert, January 19, 1971. Carl Albert Papers, Legislative Series, Box 238, File 7.

15   Robert Michel Papers, Speech and Trip File, 10/17/81. Michel's papers are a part of the Dirksen Congressional Center collection, housed in Pekin, Illinois. References to the Michel Papers are to this collection.

16   Ibid. It should be noted, though, that the western states included the Pacific Coast states.

17   Quoted in Elizabeth Drew, *Whatever It Takes: The Real Struggle for Political Power in America* (New York: Viking Press, 1997), 251.

18   McGirr, *Suburban Warriors*.

19   Peter Trubowitz, *Defining the National Interest: Conflict and Change in American Foreign Policy* (Chicago: University of Chicago Press, 1998), ch. 4.

20   Ibid. Also, Ann Markusen, Scott Campbell, Peter Hall, and Sabrina Deitrick, *The Rise of the Gunbelt and the Military Remapping of America* (New York: Oxford University Press, 1991).

21   Southern Democrats regularly opposed legislation on civil rights and labor starting in the 1940s, but they generally supported federal welfare spending. As Chapter 4 makes clear, this support typically came with contingencies related to race. Ira Katznelson, Daniel Kryder, and Kim Geiger, "Limiting Liberalism: The Southern Veto in Congress, 1933–1950," *Political Science Quarterly* 108, no. 2 (Summer 1993): 283–306.

22   Kari Frederickson, *The Dixiecrat Revolt and the End of the Solid South, 1932–1968* (Chapel Hill: University of North Carolina Press, 2001), 227.

23   For an excellent analysis of the divisions within the Nixon administration on how best to appeal to the South, and the administration's successes and failures in using race to target the region, see Matthew Lassiter, *The Silent Majority: Suburban Politics in the Sunbelt South* (Princeton: Princeton University Press, 2005).

24   Kenneth O'Reilly, *Nixon's Piano: Presidents and Racial Politics from Washington to Clinton* (New York: Free Press, 1995), 285.

25   Frederickson, *The Dixiecrat Revolt*; Thomas Byrne Edsall and Mary D. Edsall, *Chain Reaction: The Impact of Race, Rights, and Taxes on American Politics* (New York: W. W. Norton, 1991); Paul Frymer, *Uneasy Alliances: Race and Party Competition in America* (Princeton: Princeton University Press, 1999).

26   Nicole Mellow, "Voting Behavior: The 2004 Election and the Roots of Republican Success," in *The Elections of 2004*, ed. Michael Nelson (Washington DC: Congressional Quarterly Press, 2005), 80. Also see Robert Huckfeldt and Carol Weitzel Kohfeld, *Race and the Decline of Class in American Politics* (Urbana: University of Illinois Press, 1989).

27   Transcript of Morton's remarks in Everett Dirksen Papers, Republican Congressional Leadership File, Box 37, May 9, 1963. The Dirksen Papers are held in the Dirksen Congressional Center in Pekin, Illinois. References to the Dirksen Papers are to this collection.

28   Both Phillips quotes in Garry Wills, *Nixon Agonistes: The Crisis of the Self-Made Man* (1970; Boston: Houghton Mifflin, 2002), 265.

29   Lee Atwater, "The South in 1984," an unpublished analysis of southern politics prepared for the Reagan/Bush campaign. Cited in Edsall and Edsall, *Chain Reaction*, 221.

30   While race is treated separately from other social issues, such as those relating to family and gender, they are not exclusive. The compounding of them helped provoke strenuous backlash. This is made clearer in Chapters 4 and 5.

31   The correlation of higher education and the size of the professional class with social progressivism and support for the Democratic Party, along with the country's greater racial and ethnic diversity, are keys to Judis and Teixeira's argument about an "emerging Democratic majority," especially in "ideopolises," or new, information-focused cities. What is increasingly clear, however, is that ideopolises do not necessarily transform the regions in which they sit nor are they immune to regional influences. See Judis and Teixeira, *The Emerging Democratic Majority*.

32   Memo, Pat Caddell to President Carter, December 10, 1976; Press Files: Jody Powell; in Jimmy Carter Library. As cited in Judis and Teixeira, *The Emerging Democratic Majority*, 120.

33 U.S. Census Bureau, *Statistical Abstract of the United States, 2004–2005* (Washington DC: Government Printing Office, 2005), Table 216.

34 John C. Green, "The Christian Right and the 1996 Elections: An Overview," in *God at the Grass Roots, 1996: The Christian Right in American Elections,* ed. Mark J. Rozell and Clyde Wilcox (Lanham, MD: Rowman and Littlefield, 1997), 3. Also see Christina Wolbrecht, *The Politics of Women's Rights: Parties, Positions, and Change* (Princeton: Princeton University Press, 2000); and Greg Adams, "Abortion: Evidence of an Issue Evolution," *American Journal of Political Science* 41 (1997): 718–737; Stanley B. Greenberg, *The Two Americas: Our Current Political Deadlock and How to Beat It* (New York: St. Martin's, 2004).

35 Drew, *Whatever It Takes,* 24. The quote is from Reed's book.

36 Quoted in ibid., 22.

37 Carl Albert Papers, Legislative Series, Box 128, File 23B.

CHAPTER 3 SUNBELT RISING

1 Figure 3.1 presents the mean party difference scores for all trade and tariff votes by Congress from 1947 through 1998 (see Chapter 2 and Appendix B for a discussion of party difference calculations). Scores were calculated from individual vote data provided by Keith Poole and Howard Rosenthal at their website voteview.com.

2 Figure 3.2 shows mean support for free trade in each party on general or omnibus trade legislation from 1949 through 1998, including the three pieces of legislation analyzed in-depth in this chapter. This figure is based on an "index of support" for free trade using votes cast on the following pieces of major trade legislation: HR 1211 (81st House), HR 1612 (82nd), HR 5894 (83rd), HR 1 (84th), HR 12591 (85th), HR 11970 (87th), HR 18970 (91st), HR 10710 (93rd), HR 6023 (98th), HR 4800 (99th), HR 3 (100th), HRES 101 (102nd), HR 3450 (103rd), and HR 2621 (105th). General trade bills were chosen because they are more likely to capture genuine or principled free trade sentiment than bills targeting specific, often geographically concentrated, industries (e.g., steel). General trade bills are also, therefore, a harder test of the geographic argument. See Appendix B for explanation of how the index of support measure was created for the examples of trade, welfare, and abortion.

3 *1962 Congressional Quarterly Almanac,* vol. 18 (Washington DC: Congressional Quarterly News Features, 1963), 250.

4 Judith Goldstein, for example, writes that, "between 1947 and 1962, the entire complexion of the trade issue changed" as "trade policy lost much of its partisan character." See Goldstein, *Ideas, Interests, and American Trade Policy* (Ithaca: Cornell University Press, 1993), 164. Similarly, I. M. Destler writes that, "in the quarter-century after World War II, neither party, while out of office, singled out trade policy as a primary point of difference with the administration in power." See Destler, *American Trade Politics,* 2nd ed. (Washington DC: Twentieth Century Fund, 1992), 31.

5 *Congressional Quarterly Weekly Report,* June 29, 1962, 1083.

6 The postwar programs and policies included, for example, the Marshall Plan, the General Agreement on Tariffs and Trade, the North Atlantic Treaty Organization, and a growing commitment to providing foreign military and economic aid. Along with legislation on trade liberalization, these were part of what Peter Trubowitz has called America's "cold war internationalism." See Trubowitz, "Sectionalism and American Foreign Policy: The Political Geography of Consensus and Conflict," *International Studies Quarterly* 36 (1992): 173–190.

7   *1962 Congressional Quarterly Almanac*, 264.

8   Committee for a National Trade Policy, "Big 'E' for Exports," in *Trade Talk* (February 14, 1962). Carl Albert Papers, Legislative Series, Box 56, File 3.

9   *1962 Congressional Quarterly Almanac*, 882.

10   Ibid., 250.

11   All four regions supported the TEA. Even on the most controversial vote, the Mason motion to recommit the bill (one of the data sources for Table 3.1), chi-square analysis confirms that support for free trade was independent of representatives' regional affiliations. None of the four regions was significantly different from the others in the degree to which lawmakers demonstrated commitment to free trade (Pearson's chi-square = 2.72, p = .44). When the legislation is analyzed using trade index scores for the Congress, analysis of variance (ANOVA) results confirm no significant differences in regional means (F = .50, p = .69).

12   A good source for the political economic developments of the South is Bruce Schulman, *From Cotton Belt to Sunbelt: Federal Policy, Economic Development, and the Transformation of the South, 1938–1980* (New York: Oxford University Press, 1991). See also, Gavin Wright, *Old South, New South: Revolution in the Southern Economy since the Civil War* (New York: Basic Books, 1986).

13   Memo of June 25, 1962, from Tom Kenan to Democratic Whip Carl Albert on prospects for the bill's passage. According to Kenan, the earlier agreement was critical to securing the needed support of textile states. From the Albert Papers, Legislative Series, Box 56, File 2.

14   On the South's brand of individualism, see John Shelton Reed, *Minding the South* (Columbia: University of Missouri Press, 2003), 22–27.

15   Goldstein, *Ideas, Interests, and American Trade Policy*, 164, n. 70.

16   The skill with which Mills steered his committee's legislation is noted in John F. Manley, "Wilbur D. Mills: A Study in Congressional Influence," *American Political Science Review* 63 (June 1969).

17   The map of state support for free trade in 1962 relies on index support scores for the 1962 Trade Expansion Act. All subsequent maps also use index scores for the policy being examined in each case. In this instance, the national average support score for the TEA was 64 percent. States that were above average (64 to 92 percent) were within one standard deviation above the mean, while states well above average (>92 percent) were more than one standard deviation above the mean.

18   *Congressional Record*, 87th Cong., 2nd sess., 1962, 108, pt. 9, 11926.

19   Calculated from state figures provided in the document, "Workers, Farmers, Consumers, and Industries of Every State Benefit from Our Export Trade," Carl Albert Papers, Legislative Series, Box 55, File 34.

20   Ibid.

21   *Congressional Record*, 87th Cong., 2nd sess., 1962, 108, pt. 9, 11950.

22   Ibid., 11953.

23   John Agnew, *The United States in the World-Economy: A Regional Geography* (New York: Cambridge University Press, 1987), 125–126.

24   See Nicol Rae, *The Decline and Fall of Liberal Republicans from 1952 to the Present* (New York: Oxford University Press, 1989), esp. ch. 1.

25   *Congressional Record*, 87th Cong., 2nd sess., 1962, 108, pt. 9, 12014–12015.

26   *1961 Statistical Abstract of the United States* (Washington DC: Government Printing Office).

27   Robert Pastor, *Congress and the Politics of U.S. Foreign Economic Policy* (Berkeley: University of California Press, 1980), 104–107.

28   *1962 Congressional Quarterly Almanac*, 257–258.

29   Analyzing changes in the Republican Party in *The Decline and Fall of Liberal Republicans*, Rae writes that the 1964 election, in which Barry Goldwater captured the Republican nomination, "appears to have been . . . a decisive stage in the realignment of factional forces within the GOP, to the disadvantage of the liberal wing" (76).

30   James Sundquist, *Dynamics of the Party System: Alignment and Realignment of Political Parties in the United States*, rev. ed. (Washington DC: Brookings Institution, 1983), 332–337. Also see Rae, *Decline and Fall of Liberal Republicans*. This strain of Republicanism was also found to some extent in rural areas of the Northeast; note that Maine's support of the TEA was well below average (see Figure 3.3.)

31   Ralph Smuckler, "The Region of Isolationism," *American Political Science Review* 47, no. 2 (June 1953): 386–401. Also see Rae, *Decline and Fall of Liberal Republicans*.

32   Memo fron Kenan to Albert. Carl Albert Papers, Legislative Series, Box 56, File 2.

33   See Goldstein, *Ideas, Interests, and American Trade Policy*, 154–161.

34   This is a point repeatedly returned to by Representatives Hoeven and Kyl of Iowa. *Congressional Record*, 87th Cong., 2nd sess., 108, pt. 9, 11997–12003.

35   Ibid., 12008.

36   Ibid., 11991.

37   Rep. Hollifield of California, *Congressional Record*, 87th Cong., 2nd sess., 108, pt. 9, 11958.

38   Barry Bluestone and Bennet Harrison, *The Deindustrialization of America: Plant Closings, Community Abandonment, and the Dismantling of Basic Industry* (New York: Basic Books, 1982). Also see Agnew, *United States in the World-Economy*, ch. 4.

39   Memorandum communication. Carl Albert Papers, Legislative Series, Box 238, File 8.

40   For world trade share, see Bluestone and Harrison, *Deindustrialization of America*, 140. OECD share figures calculated from data in Goldstein, *Ideas, Interests, and American Trade Policy*, 168, Table 4.3.

41   *Congressional Quarterly Weekly Report*, May 19, 1973, 1215.

42   Earlier in the year, the Democratic caucus, under the influence of the Democratic Study Group, had amended House rules to allow members to more easily and successfully petition for legislation to be considered under an open rule. Pressure for this change, like others, had come largely from northern Democrats who found their policy initiatives frustrated by the tight control exercised over legislation by committee chairs, typically southern Democrats.

43 This was the assessment made by Ways and Means Committee member, Sam Gibbons (D-FL). *Congressional Quarterly Weekly Report,* December 15, 1973, 3257.

44 Charles Culhane, "Labor Shifts Tactics on Administration Bill, Seeks Concessions on Imports, Multinationals," *National Journal,* July 28, 1973, 1095–1096.

45 Western Democrats were split evenly on the vote.

46 Based on chi-square analysis of representatives' region and vote choice on the modified closed rule (Pearson's chi-square = 22.78, p = .000). While differences existed between expected and observed values for northern and southern lawmakers, there was no difference in observed and expected values among western and Pacific Coast representatives.

47 Chi-square analysis of region and vote choice among Republicans results in a Pearson's chi-square = 2.62, p = .453. Analysis of Democrats shows a highly significant relationship between region and vote choice (Pearson's chi-square = 55.43, p = .000). When the index of support for free trade is used, ANOVA results confirm the pattern of differences in regional means. Significant differences existed between regional means for all representatives (F = 6.77, p = .000), but when party is controlled, it becomes clear that divisions are between Democrats (F = 25.35, p = .000) and not Republicans (F = 1.38, p = .25).

48 OLS analysis: The unit of analysis is the state. The dependent variable is the state mean index scores for Democrats. Independent variables include measures of ideology and interest composition. *Unemployment* is the average of the 1970 and 1971 rates. *Export Dependence* is the share of shipments produced in each state that was exported in 1969. *Size of Agricultural Sector in State* is the total 1972 per capita farm employment. *South, West,*and *Pacific Coast* are regional dummy variables (with the North excluded as a base category) designed to capture regional effects independent of key economic and demographic factors. See Appendix B for additional discussion of regression analysis and variables.

49 These are 1971 data from *1972 Statistical Abstract* (Washington DC: Government Printing Office).

50 Schulman, *From Cotton Belt to Sunbelt* and *The Seventies;* Reed, *Minding the South;* Daniel Elazar, *American Federalism: A View from the States* (New York: Thomas Y. Crowell Co., 1972). The West is at the edge of conventional significance (p = .08).

51 See Bluestone and Harrison, *Deindustrialization of America.*

52 Ibid.

53 In the North, average state employment growth from 1960 to 1970 was 27 percent. In the South, this number was 41 percent, in the West, 35 percent, and in the Pacific Coast states, 38 percent. Calculated from information in the *1972 Statistical Abstract* (Washington DC: Government Printing Office).

54 Department of Labor statistics from March 1973 provided in "The Employment Outlook," a document of the Democratic Party's Steering and Policy Committee. Carl Albert Papers, Legislative Series, Box 182, File 3. The Bureau of Labor Statistics of the Department of Labor defines "major labor market areas" as the standard Metropolitan Statistical Areas (MSAs) that are designated each decade by the Office of Management and Budget.

55 This was a point emphatically made by Democrat John Dent of Pennsylvania during floor debate. See *Congressional Quarterly Weekly Report,* December 15, 1973, 3257.

56 Culhane, "Labor Shifts Tactics," 1091.

57 *National Journal*, November 24, 1973, 1752.

58 *Congressional Record*, 93rd Cong., 1st sess., 1973, 119, pt. 31, 40531–40532.

59 Ibid., 40492.

60 David Rohde, "Partisanship, Leadership, and Congressional Assertiveness in Foreign and Defense Policy," in *The New Politics of American Foreign Policy*, ed. David A. Deese (New York: St. Martin's Press, 1994), 76–101.

61 When President Nixon assumed office in 1968, he promoted a foreign policy premised on the idea of détente, and he sought greater political and diplomatic ties with countries such as China and the Soviet Union. One of the most controversial provisions of Nixon's original trade proposal was to extend MFN status to Communist countries, a provision sought in order to implement a trade agreement signed with the Soviet Union in the previous year. While there was much debate about the wisdom of including this provision, Nixon was persuaded to keep it in at first because he was convinced that détente was popular with the country and that this might help ensure passage of the trade bill (Pastor, *Congress and Foreign Economic Policy*, 144). While he no doubt thought détente would be an effective blunt to criticisms launched by northern Democrats against Vietnam and general Cold War ideology, as it was manifested in the trade bill, this did not turn out to be the case.

62 *Congressional Record*, 93rd Cong., 1st sess., 108, pt. 9, 40807.

63 Ibid., 40792–40793.

64 Pastor, *Congress and Foreign Economic Policy*, 122, n. 60.

65 Robert L. Paarlberg, *Fixing Farm Trade: Policy Options for the United States* (Cambridge, MA: Ballinger Publishing, 1988), 8–15.

66 Richard Frank, "Industry Seeks Greater Voice in Trade Talks to Influence Decisions on Its Products," *National Journal*, October 20, 1973, 1568.

67 *Congressional Record*, 93rd Cong., 1st sess., 119, pt. 31, 40489.

68 Ibid., 40492.

69 *Congressional Record*, 93rd Cong., 1st sess., 119, pt. 31, 40498.

70 Pacific Coast states fell somewhere in the middle of northern protectionism and southern and western free trade positions, largely because of the mix or diversity of the economies of their states at the time, which combined agriculture and new industry growth with older big city manufacturing. Pacific Coast Democrats were more protectionist (like northern Democrats), while Republicans were unified with their party overall.

71 Destler, *American Trade Politics*, 46.

72 William K. Tabb, "Urban Development and Regional Restructuring, an Overview," in *Sunbelt/Snowbelt: Urban Development and Regional Restructuring*, ed. Larry Sawyers and William K. Tabb (New York: Oxford University Press, 1984), 10.

73 Pastor, *Congress and Foreign Economic Policy*, 180–181 and 122, n. 64.

74 This is confirmed by ANOVA results of comparing regional means of the index of support

for free trade. Significant differences exist in the regional means overall ($F = 10.12$, $p = .000$) and within the parties. Regional differences between Democrats were significant ($F = 6.958$, $p = .001$), and differences between Republicans were significant at the $p = .069$ level ($F = 2.39$).

75 Destler, *American Trade Politics*, 175–176.

76 See Martha L. Gibson, *Conflict amid Consensus in American Trade Policy* (Washington DC: Georgetown University Press, 2000), 172.

77 *Congressional Record*, 105th Cong., 2nd sess., 1998, 144, no. 130, H8792. Diverse numbers were used to support the claim that NAFTA had created jobs as well as the claim it had destroyed jobs.

78 Ibid., H8781.

79 Ibid., H8792.

80 Ibid., H8797.

81 This was true not just for Democrats. In a 1993 meeting of Republican freshmen Congress members with Lee Iacocca, Representative Mike Castle from Delaware, citing a United Auto Workers advertisement, complained that he was supportive of NAFTA but found the issue to be too much of "a political problem." Robert Michel Papers, Legislative Series, Shelly White Files, Box 1, File: NAFTA Meeting Notes.

82 *1997 Statistical Abstract* (Washington DC: Government Printing Office). Averages calculated from state-level information on union membership.

83 Gibson, *Conflict amid Consensus*, 173.

84 This concern has been widely documented. See, for example, ibid., 174.

85 *Congressional Record*, 105th Cong., 2nd sess., 144, pt. 130, H8790.

86 The League of Conservation Voters, for example, has state offices in more than two-thirds of northern and Pacific Coast states but in less than half of southern and western states. Similarly, the Public Interest Research Group has local branches in 85 percent of northern and Pacific Coast states but 31 percent of western and southern states. Information taken from the groups' websites: www.lcv.org and www.pirg.org. Accessed on February 12, 2001.

87 Data from the 1996 American National Election Survey of the Interuniversity Consortium for Political and Social Research (ICPSR). Among those who identified as Republicans, 4.7 percent strongly agreed with the statement that tougher regulations on business are needed to protect the environment. Among Democrats, this number was 20.4 percent. Chi-square analysis of tri-regional differences among Democrats on this statement (which indicates that northern and Pacific Coast Democrats were more supportive than southern and western) results in a Pearson's chi-square = 7.83 ($p = .019$).

88 Fred M. Shelley, J. Clark Archer, Fiona M. Davidson, and Stanley D. Brunn, *Political Geography of the United States* (New York: Guilford Press, 1996), 257–264.

89 Calculated from figures on 1996 gross state product, by industry, in the *1997 Statistical Abstract* (Washington DC: Government Printing Office).

90 U.S. Senate Republican Policy Committee, "Talking Points: NAFTA in Brief," September 20, 1993. Robert Michel Papers, Legislative File, Karen Buttaro Files, Box 14, File: NAFTA Offsets (1991–1993).

91 Calculated from state export figures for 1990 and 1996 in the *1997 Statistical Abstract*.

92 Based on export and import figures in the *1997 Statistical Abstract* for various industries and products, including chemicals, aerospace, and scientific instruments, to name a few. Overall, the 1996 merchandise trade deficit was $166.6 billion while the total trade deficit in goods and services was $114.2 billion. Figures from *1997 Statistical Abstract*.

93 *1997 Statistical Abstract*.

94 *Congressional Record*, 105th Cong., 2nd sess., 144, pt. 130, H8784.

95 Ibid., H8787.

96 *2002 Congressional Quarterly Almanac*.

97 *2005 Congressional Quarterly Almanac*.

98 Molly Hennessy-Fiske, "Free Trade at the Fore of Races," *Los Angeles Times*, September 25, 2006, A19.

CHAPTER 4 CHANGE COMES TO THE COTTON BELT

1 Mean party difference scores were calculated from data provided by Keith Poole and Howard Rosenthal at the website, voteview.com and identified by Poole and Rosenthal as social welfare, broadly defined, using a coding schema originally developed by Aage Clausen. A range of issues (e.g., Social Security, public housing, urban renewal, education, welfare, and unemployment) is included. It should be noted that much of this legislation was tied programmatically to AFDC.

2 Results are based on "index of support" scores for major postwar welfare legislation. Data here and elsewhere in the chapter, unless otherwise noted, are based on specific AFDC legislation, including: HR 6000 (81st Congress); HR 4249 (85th); HR 10606 (87th); HR 16311 (91st); HR 1 (striking Title IV) (92nd); HR 7200 (95th); HR 4904 (96th); HR 1720 (100th); and HR 4 / HR 3734 (104th). Not included are votes that affected AFDC but which were considered part of general Social Security Amendment legislation, such as the 1967 WIN program legislation.

3 On the "era of normalcy" extending from 1939 to 1962, see Steven M. Teles, *Whose Welfare? AFDC and Elite Politics* (Lawrence: University Press of Kansas, 1996), 34–37; on the lack of partisanship, see Gilbert Steiner as quoted in Edward D. Berkowitz, *America's Welfare State: From Roosevelt to Reagan* (Baltimore: Johns Hopkins University Press, 1991), 101; and on the security of welfare programs, see Fay Lomax Cook and Edith J. Barrett, *Support for the American Welfare State: The Views of Congress and the Public* (New York: Columbia University Press, 1992), 4.

4 *Congressional Quarterly Weekly Report*, February 2, 1962, 188–189.

5 Kennedy's proposal included other measures, most notably ones to reduce child abuse. Also included were incentives to states to reduce or eliminate residency requirements for recipients and to increase payments to adult recipients. The name change, from Aid to Dependent Children (ADC) to Aid to Families with Dependent Children (AFDC), also happened at this time.

6 "'Preventive' Welfare Bill Moves toward Enactment," *Congressional Quarterly Weekly Report*, June 22, 1962, 1059.

7 *Congressional Report*, 87th Cong., 2nd sess., 1962, 108, pt. 3, 4281.

8   Among Democrats, mean southern support for welfare expansion on the index was 94 percent, while in the other three regions, Democrat support was 100 percent. Among Republicans, the percentages were 38 and 44 (western and Pacific Coast, respectively) and 50 and 52 (northern and southern, respectively).

9   *Congressional Quarterly Weekly Report,* June 22, 1962, 1059. A fourth trend highlighted in the report was growing rates of divorce and desertion, which left more families headed by single women. Because Social Security now covered widows of most workers, ADC payments were concentrated among families headed by women who had either been divorced or were never married. Just before passage of the Social Security Act in 1935, 85 percent of the women supported by states' "mothers' pensions" received benefits because they had been widowed; by 1962, only 7 percent of ADC caseloads involved children receiving benefits because of the death of the father. See Berkowitz, *America's Welfare State,* 100–101.

10   Nicholas Lemann, *The Promised Land: The Great Black Migration and How It Changed America* (New York: Vintage Books, 1992), 6.

11   Jill Quadagno, "From Old-Age Assistance to Supplemental Security Income: The Political Economy of Relief in the South, 1935–1972," in *The Politics of Social Policy in the United States,* ed. Margaret Weir, Anna Shola Orloff, and Theda Skocpol (Princeton: Princeton University Press, 1988), 252–253. Also, Lemann, *The Promised Land,* ch. 1; and Gavin Wright, *Old South, New South: Revolution in the Southern Economy since the Civil War* (New York: Basic Books, 1986), 230–257.

12   From 1940 to 1960, the African American population in the South (still, by far, the region with the largest black population) grew by 1.4 million, while the black population in the North grew by 3.9 million. The rise in the sparsely populated West and Pacific Coast regions was roughly 800,000, which was concentrated in California. See Teles, *Whose Welfare?* 26.

13   Theda Skocpol, "The Limits of the New Deal System and the Roots of Contemporary Welfare Dilemmas," in *The Politics of Social Policy in the United States,* ed. Margaret Weir, Anna Shola Orloff, and Theda Skocpol (Princeton: Princeton University Press, 1988), 304.

14   U.S. Department of Labor, Bureau of Labor Statistics, *1970 Handbook of Labor Statistics* (Washington DC: Government Printing Office, 1970).

15   Lemann, *The Promised Land,* 201.

16   Teles, *Whose Welfare?* 24–26. The majority of families on ADC, however, continued to be white.

17   Ibid.

18   Frances Fox Piven and Richard A. Cloward, *Regulating the Poor: The Functions of Public Welfare,* updated edition (New York: Vintage Books, 1993), 132.

19   On the racial impact of the new emphasis on work, see Robert C. Lieberman, *Shifting the Color Line: Race and the American Welfare State* (Cambridge: Harvard University Press, 1998), 161.

20   On Kennedy's ties to business and the implications for antipoverty policy, see Charles Noble, *Welfare as We Knew It: A Political History of the American Welfare State* (New York: Oxford University Press, 1997). For the nature of corporate support of social welfare policy in the postwar years, see Skocpol, "The Limits of the New Deal System."

21   Berkowitz, *America's Welfare State,* 106.

22   OLS analysis: The unit of analysis is the state. The dependent variable is the percentage of a state's representatives voting against the motion to recommit the bill to committee (a key vote). Since support on the index measure was so strong throughout the country, the OLS analysis focuses on state support for *rejecting* the motion to recommit, which was the most controversial of the three votes considered. The motion to recommit focused on striking increases in the adult assistance (OAA) portion of the bill, and it is impossible to fully ascertain whether a vote for the motion represents concern about just that part of the legislation or was an attempt to defeat the legislation overall. (However, including a measure of the size of a state's OAA population was not significant, suggesting that this was not a factor in the decision calculus.) Size of ADC program is simply the percentage of a state's total population receiving ADC benefits. Democratic is percentage of the state's congressional delegation that is Democratic. The regional variables are dummy variables, with the North excluded.

23   *Congressional Record*, 87th Cong., 2nd sess., 1962, 108, pt. 3, 4282.

24   Ibid., 4272.

25   For an excellent account of how Democratic and Republican presidents from FDR onward used federal resources and urban policy to cultivate different constituencies, see John Mollenkopf, *The Contested City* (Princeton: Princeton University Press, 1983).

26   Steven P. Erie, *Rainbow's End: Irish-Americans and the Dilemmas of Urban Machine Politics, 1840–1985* (Berkeley: University of California Press, 1988), 165–170.

27   Piven and Cloward, *Regulating the Poor*, 242.

28   Erie, *Rainbow's End*, 165–170.

29   Ibid., 167–169.

30   Lieberman, *Shifting the Color Line*, 142–146.

31   "Welfare Revisions," *Congressional Quarterly Weekly Report*, February 16, 1962, 254.

32   Ibid.

33   See, for example, Frances Fox Piven and Richard A. Cloward, "Popular Power and the Welfare State," in *Remaking the Welfare State: Retrenchment and Social Policy in the United States and Europe*, ed. Michael Brown (Philadelphia: Temple University Press, 1988).

34   *Congressional Record*, 87th Cong., 2nd sess., 1962, 108, pt. 3, 4282.

35   Assessing Kennedy's campaign strategy and the election results, Theodore H. White wrote that victory in several of the key large industrial northern states was likely made possible by Kennedy's appeal to urban black voters. See Piven and Cloward, *Regulating the Poor*, 254–255 and fn. 4.

36   Piven and Cloward, *Regulating the Poor*, 255–256; also Paul Frymer, *Uneasy Alliances: Race and Party Competition in America* (Princeton: Princeton University Press, 1999).

37   Richard Reeves, *President Kennedy: Profile of Power* (New York: Simon and Schuster, 1993), 269.

38   While 2.2 percent of the population in the average state in the South relied on OAA, 1.4 percent relied on OAA in the Pacific Coast states, 1.3 percent in the West, and .7 percent in the North (derived from state old-age assistance recipients and population figures in the *1961 Statistical Abstract* and the *Department of Health, Education, and Welfare's 1961 Annual Report*).

39   On the South's growing support for the old-age assistance program, see Quadagno, "Old-Age Assistance," 252–262.

40   *Congressional Record,* 87th Cong., 2nd sess., 1962, 108, pt. 3, 4281.

41   This "deal" has been well documented. See, for example, Lieberman, *Shifting the Color Line,* ch. 4. On the 1962 case specifically, see 161–166. Also see Noble, *Welfare as We Knew It,* 92.

42   *Congressional Record,* 87th Cong., 2nd sess., 1962, 108, pt. 3, 4278.

43   Piven and Cloward, *Regulating the Poor,* 205–209.

44   For an account of the Louisiana case as well as a similarly controversial case in Newburgh, New York, see Berkowitz, *America's Welfare State,* 101–105.

45   Lieberman, *Shifting the Color Line,* 163–164. Also see Mills comments (*Congressional Record,* 87th Cong., 2nd sess., 1962, 108, pt. 3, 4628).

46   The other mechanisms were, of course, the systematic curtailment of social and political rights.

47   Lee J. Alston and Joseph P. Ferrie, *Southern Paternalism and the American Welfare State: Economics, Politics, and Institutions in the South, 1865–1965* (Boston: Cambridge University Press, 1999), esp. chs. 1 and 6.

48   Jill Quadagno, *The Color of Welfare: How Racism Undermined the War on Poverty* (New York: Oxford University Press, 1994), 128.

49   Alston and Ferrie, *Southern Paternalism,* ch. 6.

50   Ibid., 121.

51   Quoted from congressional hearings on HR 16311 in Quadagno, *The Color of Welfare,* 128.

52   George Thomas Kurian, ed., *Datapedia of the United States, 1790–2005: America Year by Year,* 2nd ed. (Lanham, MD: Bernan, 2001), Series H, 346–367. Various explanations, focusing on social and economic demographic changes as well as political factors, have been offered for the sudden expansion of welfare rolls in the 1960s. A full discussion is beyond the scope of this chapter, but a review of some of the explanations can be found in Piven and Cloward, *Regulating the Poor.*

53   Piven and Cloward, *Regulating the Poor,* 188, Table 2. The regional categories are theirs. It is important to note that these authors include the Pacific Coast states in the West, and much of western growth is driven by the significant increases in California.

54   Ibid.

55   Piven and Cloward note in *Regulating the Poor* (261), "The hallmark of the Great Society programs was the direct relationship between the national government and the ghettoes, a relationship in which both state and local governments were undercut." Also see Lemann, *The Promised Land,* ch. 3; Theodore Lowi's, *The End of Liberalism: The Second Republic of the United States,* 2nd ed. (New York: W. W. Norton, 1979), ch. 8; and Margaret Weir's, "The Federal Government and Unemployment: The Frustration of Policy Innovation from the New Deal to the Great Society," in *The Politics of Social Policy in the United States,* ed. Margaret Weir, Anna Shola Orloff, and Theda Skocpol (Princeton: Princeton University Press, 1988).

56   It is important to note that the percentage of AFDC recipients who were black had grown the most in the decades before the 1960s expansion of the rolls. Throughout the 1960s, the majority of families on AFDC continued to be white. See Teles, *Whose Welfare?* 25, fig. 2.4.

57   Nixon's welfare proposal also included provisions to federalize the adult assistance programs that provided benefits to older and disabled individuals and to set a minimum monthly payment level of $110 per recipient. See "Features and Issues of Welfare Reform," in John K. Iglehart and Dom Bonafede, "Welfare Report: Nixon's Family Assistance Plan Faces Showdown on Senate Floor," *National Journal*, December 5, 1970, 2639.

58   Ibid.

59   Berkowitz, *America's Welfare State*, 122–130.

60   Based on index scores.

61   As reported in Table 4.1, the mean index of support for 1970 welfare federalization among representatives in the North was 74 percent. In the Pacific Coast, it was 81 percent; in the West, 54 percent; and in the South, just 24 percent. Analysis of variance (ANOVA) indicates that these are significant differences, yielding an F statistic of 43.14 (p = .000), with N = 408. Regional divisions within the parties yield similar results. Among Democrats, the mean in the North was 87 percent, the Pacific Coast was 88 percent, West was 62 percent, and South was 22 percent (F statistic of 56.22, p = .000, N = 227). Among Republicans, the mean in the North was 62 percent, Pacific Coast was 69 percent, West was 48 percent, and South was 28 percent (F statistic of 5.62, p = .001, N = 181).

62   It should be noted that, even in the House debates at the time, a few individuals disputed the connection between benefit levels and migration, and they introduced evidence to demonstrate the fallacy of the hypothesis that higher levels spurred migration (*Congressional Record*, 91st Cong., 2nd sess., 1970, 116, pt. 9, 12069). Moreover, black migration from the South was slowing and came to an end in 1970, although it is possible that few people were aware of the decline at the time (Lemann, *The Promised Land*, 211). Neither disputation squelched the popularity of the argument, however.

63   *Congressional Record*, 91st Cong., 2nd sess., 1970, 116, pt. 9, 12083.

64   The mean among states in the North in terms of average monthly payment for a family of four in 1968 was $186; for states in the Pacific Coast, this figure was $169. Among states in the South, the mean was $94, and in the West, it was $154. Calculated from figures on the average monthly payment per family in 1968 in the *1969 Statistical Abstract* (Washington DC: Government Printing Office).

65   *Congressional Record*, 91st Cong., 2nd sess., 1970, 116, pt. 9, 12078.

66   It is worth recalling that in 1970 New York City's fiscal crisis (the apex of which occurred in 1975) was only a few years away. Passage of California's Proposition 13 (the public tax revolt that led to drastically lower local revenues for cities and counties) was eight years away.

67   *Congressional Record*, 91st Cong., 2nd sess., 1970, 116, pt. 9, 12028.

68   In *City Limits* (Chicago: University of Chicago Press, 1981), Paul Peterson argues that precisely because most localities rely on policy inducements to compete for economic development and revenue, they will shirk in areas such as redistribution. For this reason, he argues, redistributive policy should be left to the federal government.

69   *Congressional Record*, 91st Cong., 2nd sess., 1970, 116, pt. 9, 12034.

70   Estimates of the Department of Health, Education, and Welfare. See Jill Quadagno, "Race, Class, and Gender in the U.S. Welfare State: Nixon's Failed Family Assistance Plan," *American Sociological Review* 55 (1990), 23.

71   California's governor, Ronald Reagan, was an exception. See Iglehart and Bonafede, "Welfare Report," 2637. Support from governors in states with large welfare burdens was initially slow in coming because it was thought that the proposed program did not do enough to provide relief to large industrial states. See, for example, John Iglehart, "Administration's Welfare Reform Bill Heads for House Committee Approval," *National Journal,* February 21, 1970, 378.

72   Iglehart and Bonafede, "Welfare Report," 2638–2640. Fiscal relief was to be provided by FAP in several ways. By providing a uniform national payment of $1,600 per family of four, FAP would ensure federal coverage of a sizeable portion, the entire portion in some states, of the benefits paid to AFDC families. While the FAP payment would raise the benefits for AFDC families in eight states (all southern) where annual benefit levels were low, the remaining states would be required to supplement the federal payment up to existing AFDC benefit levels or the poverty level (whichever was lower). No supplement was required for working families. The Ways and Means Committee amended the bill to establish a 30 percent federal match for these supplementary costs, further augmenting federal financial responsibility for welfare. The committee increased the federal portion of costs in several other areas as well, including costs associated with day care and with certain administrative services.

73   *Congressional Record,* 91st Cong., 2nd sess., 1970, 116, pt. 9, 12076.

74   Lemann, *The Promised Land,* 190.

75   From a 1973 letter to Melvin Laird, Moynihan's successor in the Nixon administration, as quoted in ibid., 213.

76   As early as 1967, leaders of large corporations were participating in conferences on the American welfare system and promoting the idea of a negative income tax similar to that embodied in FAP. See Quadagno, "Race, Class, and Gender in Welfare," p. 16. Welfare provision as a method for quelling unrest and regulating poor and working-class individuals more generally is the central argument made by Piven and Cloward, *Regulating the Poor.*

77   Quadagno, "Race, Class, and Gender in Welfare," 19.

78   *Congressional Record,* 91st Cong., 2nd sess., 1970, 116, pt. 9, 11902.

79   Quadagno, "Race, Class, and Gender in Welfare," 19–20.

80   *Congressional Record,* 91st Cong., 2nd sess., 1970, 116, pt. 18, 24615.

81   Labor's endorsement was slow to emerge but it did. See Daniel Patrick Moynihan, *The Politics of a Guaranteed Income: The Nixon Administration and the Family Assistance Plan* (New York: Vintage Books, 1973), 270–277. Also, resistance to FAP among northern Democrats who felt that the benefit amounts were insufficient was a position taken also by the National Welfare Rights Organization.

82   *Congressional Record,* 91st Cong., 2nd sess., 1970, 116, pt. 9, 11902. Business opposition to FAP was centered in the U.S. Chamber of Commerce.

83   Ibid., 11871.

84   This was the charge made by the American Conservative Union, for example. Iglehart and Bonafede, "Welfare Report."

85   *Congressional Record,* 91st Cong., 2nd sess., 1970, 116, pt. 9, 11886.

86   Ibid.

87   Lemann, *The Promised Land*, 50–51. Also see Alston and Ferrie, *Southern Paternalism*, ch. 6; and Gilbert C. Fite, *Cotton Fields No More: Southern Agriculture, 1865–1980* (Lexington: University Press of Kentucky, 1984), esp. ch. 10.

88   Fite, *Cotton Fields No More*, 208–209.

89   Alston and Ferrie, *Southern Paternalism*, ch. 6.

90   See, for example, Bruce Schulman, *From Cotton Belt to Sunbelt: Federal Policy, Economic Development, and the Transformation of the South, 1938–1980* (New York: Oxford University Press, 1991), 159–161.

91   Ibid., esp. ch. 7.

92   Fite, *Cotton Fields No More*, 209.

93   This would include, for example, efforts to slow down the pace of desegregation or weaken civil rights statutes. Many of these actions were made through appeals to President Nixon. See, for example, Dewey W. Grantham, *The Life and Death of the Solid South: A Political History* (Lexington: University Press of Kentucky, 1988). Also see Bruce H. Kalk, "Wormley's Hotel Revisited: Richard Nixon's Southern Strategy and the End of the Second Reconstruction," *North Carolina Historical Review* (January 1994): 85–105.

94   Fite, *Cotton Fields No More*, 221.

95   Alston and Ferrie, *Southern Paternalism*, 141.

96   Adam Smith, "The City as the OK Corral," *Esquire* (July 1985): 64.

97   *Congressional Record*, 91st Cong., 2nd sess., 1970, 116, pt. 9, 12041.

98   In *The Silent Majority: Suburban Politics in the Sunbelt South* (Princeton: Princeton University Press, 2005), Matthew Lassiter describes this connection especially with regard to desegregation efforts, noting, for example, that organizations such as the NAACP and the Southern Regional Council (an organization dedicated to fighting racial injustice) were labeled "communist-inspired organizations" by rural state legislators (84). And author Rick Perlstein, in *Before the Storm: Barry Goldwater and the Unmaking of the American Consensus* (New York: Hill and Wang, 2001), 14, attributes growing conservative successes in the postwar decades, in part, to these sorts of arguments. For example, the early political success of Jim Johnson, founder of the Arkansas White Citizens Council and later a justice of the Arkansas Supreme Court, is traced to his willingness to make arguments about the "Communist plan" to exploit blacks and foment uprising among them.

99   *Congressional Record*, 91st Cong., 2nd sess., 1970, 116, pt. 9, 12077.

100   Ibid., 12041.

101   The percentage of individuals falling below the national low-income level in 1969 was 23 percent, on average, for states in the South as compared to 14 percent in the West, 10 percent in the North, and 11 percent in the Pacific Coast (*1972 Statistical Abstract* [Washington DC: Government Printing Office]).

102   Jill Quadagno, *The Color of Welfare*, 129.

103   Moynihan, *The Politics of a Guaranteed Income*, 388.

104   There is speculation about Mills's motivations in promoting the president's proposal, about which he had initially voiced reservations. On the one hand, Mills is purported to have

experienced a personal "conversion" to the cause of FAP, particularly its inclusion of the working poor, and on the other, the charge was made that he changed tactics, allowing the bill to go forward, because he believed it would be defeated once the public realized the extent of the expenses involved. On the first, see Moynihan, *The Politics of a Guaranteed Income*, 428–429. On the second, see Dona C. Hamilton, *The Dual Agenda: Race and Social Welfare Policies of Civil Rights Organizations* (New York: Columbia University Press, 1997), 184.

105 *Congressional Record*, 91st Cong., 2nd sess., 1970, 116, pt. 9, 11880.

106 Moynihan, *The Politics of a Guaranteed Income*, 385.

107 OLS analysis: The unit of analysis is the state. The dependent variable is the state mean index score of support for federalization of welfare. Size of welfare burden is the ratio of total 1968 spending on AFDC to the total state and local revenue in 1967. Size of African American population is the percentage of a state's total population that was identified as black in 1970. Democratic is the percentage of the state's representatives that are Democrats.

108 Interestingly, a low-income variable (size of the low-income population) was tested in this model in place of the size of the black population variable and was found to be insignificant. Nonetheless, the two variables are correlated at $r = .64$.

109 Frymer, *Uneasy Alliances*.

110 Figures are regional means, derived from information on expenditures on AFDC in states in 1961 and 1968. Data from U.S. Health, Education, and Welfare, *Annual Report, 1961* (Washington DC: Government Printing Office, 1962) and *1969 Statistical Abstract*.

111 Bruce Schulman, *The Seventies: The Great Shift in American Culture, Society, and Politics* (New York: Free Press, 2001), 34; Richard Reeves, *President Nixon: Alone in the White House* (New York: Simon and Schuster, 2001), 111.

112 Reeves, *President Nixon*, 111.

113 H. R. Haldeman, *The Haldeman Diaries: Inside the Nixon White House* (New York: G. P. Putnam's Sons, 1994), 181.

114 "Editorial/Column Analysis of the President's Welfare Proposals, August 20, 1969," attachment accompanying a memorandum from Kenneth J. Cole, Jr. circulated to forty-six individuals. Harry S. Dent Papers, Special Collections, Clemson University Libraries, Box 4, Folder 103.

115 Ibid. Italics added.

116 Kalk, "Wormley's Hotel Revisited," 88. Also Grantham, *Life and Death of the Solid South*, 178. For the relationship between Strom Thurmond and Nixon, see Garry Wills, *Nixon Agonistes: The Crisis of the Self-Made Man* (New York: Signet, 1970), 251–256. For the controversy within the Nixon administration between a strategy of exploiting racial backlash in the South and a strategy of embracing more centrist, moderate policies, see Lassiter, *The Silent Majority*.

117 Both points of view in this discussion (as well as many others) can be found in the essays in Brown, *Remaking the Welfare State*.

118 Evidence of the persistence of regional differences, generally and within the parties, is revealed in calculating the regional means of individual welfare index support scores for each congress and, separately, for both parties in each congress. ANOVA results yield significant regional differences ($p < .05$) in each of the congresses with significant welfare reform legislative efforts (81st, 85th, 87th, 91st, 92nd, 96th, 100th, 104th), with the exception of the 85th and

104th (where $p = .07$ in both). Analysis of variance of regional means among Democrats yields significant differences in every congress. Among Republicans, there are significant differences beginning in the 91st Congress (consideration of FAP), continuing to the 104th Congress (104th Republicans, $p = .09$).

119 A straightforward account of the development, debate, politics, and passage of the 1996 welfare reform bill are provided in Anne Marie Cammisa, *From Rhetoric to Reform? Welfare Policy in American Politics* (Boulder, CO: Westview Press, 1998).

120 Standard deviation is 18 percent for Democrats and 5 percent for Republicans.

121 As evidence of the strength of the Republican assault on this issue, however, the magnitude of the differences between the regions was less in this congress than in those just prior or just after.

122 See Table 4.1.

123 Southern Republicans deviate most from their party's position. Many of these defectors represented areas with large immigrant constituencies worried that their benefits would be eliminated.

124 Eliza Newlin Carney, "Welfare Reform: The Loose Caboose," *National Journal*, September 23 1995, 2341–2343.

125 R. Kent Weaver, "Ending Welfare as We Know It," in *The Social Divide: Political Parties and the Future of Activist Government*, ed. Margaret Weir (Washington DC: Brookings Institution, 1998), 372.

126 *Congressional Record*, 104th Cong., 1st sess., 1995, 141, pt. 52, H3346. Many Republicans made reference to President Johnson's War on Poverty when condemning the $5 trillion spent in the ensuing thirty years. It should be noted that Representative Goss appears to have misspoke on the timing of the launch of the War on Poverty (it began in the 1960s).

127 Noble, *Welfare as We Knew It*, ch. 6.

128 See Schulman, *From Cotton Belt to Sunbelt*; John Agnew, *The United States in the World-Economy: A Regional Geography* (New York: Cambridge University Press, 1987), ch. 4; Richard Bensel, *Sectionalism and American Political Development, 1880–1980* (Madison: University of Wisconsin Press, 1984).

129 Mancur Olson, "The Causes and Quality of Southern Growth," in *The Economics of Southern Growth*, ed. E. Blaine Liner and Lawrence K. Lynch, report of conference sponsored by Southern Growth Policies Board and Economic Development Administration of the U.S. Department of Commerce, 1977, p. 129.

130 Fred M. Shelley, J. Clark Archer, Fiona M. Davidson, and Stanley D. Brunn, *Political Geography of the United States* (New York: Guilford Press, 1996), 133–134. The ability of local and state government to keep costs down is a feature of both timing and preference. Economic development of the South and West took place at a time when the federal government was investing more funds in infrastructure development than when the industrial core states were experiencing economic development. At the same time, many areas of federal spending (such as social welfare programs) require state and local financial matches, and many states chose federal dollars to promote industrial development while passing up federal aid in the area of social welfare. See Schulman, *From Cotton Belt to Sunbelt*; and Wright, *Old South, New South*, 257–263.

131 Calculated from state figures for AFDC spending in Table 8.23 in the House Committee on Ways and Means, *1996 Greenbook* and from 1996 state figures for number of persons below poverty level in the *1999 Statistical Abstract* (Washington DC: Government Printing Office).

132   Schulman, *From Cotton Belt to Sunbelt*, 215–217.

133   Elizabeth Drew, *Whatever It Takes: The Real Struggle for Political Power in America* (New York: Viking, 1997), 99.

134   *Congressional Record*, 104th Cong., 2nd sess., 1996, 142, pt. 106, H7801.

135   See, for example, Malcolm Gladwell, "Remaking Welfare: In States' Experiments, a Cutting Contest," *Washington Post*, March 10, 1995, A1.

136   Wade Henderson, director of the Washington bureau of the NAACP, quoted in Jeff Shear, "Looking for a Voice," *National Journal*, March 16, 1996, 595.

137   Mark H. Greenberg, staff attorney for the Center for Law and Socil Policy, quoted in ibid.

138   Mollenkopf, *The Contested City*, ch. 6.

139   Ibid. Also see Schulman, *From Cotton Belt to Sunbelt*, chs. 6 and 7. FAP is an obvious case in point.

140   John Meacham, "A Defiant South Secedes Again," *Newsweek*, January 16, 1995, 20.

141   See Steven V. Roberts, "Church Meets State: The Religious Right," *U.S. News and World Report*, April 24, 1995, 26–30.

142   See, for example, Michael P. Malone and Richard W. Etulain, *The American West: A Twentieth-Century History* (Lincoln: University of Nebraska Press, 1989), 193–205.

143   As quoted in Roberts, "Church Meets State," 26.

144   Weaver, "Ending Welfare as We Know It," 376–377. It is worthwhile to note that, aside from the racialization of welfare in general, the focus on illegitimacy, in particular, plays upon racial themes. While illegitimacy rates have risen among both black and white Americans, rates for African Americans have historically been higher and have risen more; thus, punitive measures, such as family caps and denying benefits to teenage mothers, would disproportionately affect black families. Given that the U.S. and state governments and various organizations have periodically promoted population control measures particularly for ethnic and racial minorities, the implications of the illegitimacy focus should not be lightly dismissed.

145   Dan Balz and Ronald Brownstein, *Storming the Gates: Protest Politics and the Republican Revival* (New York: Little, Brown, 1996), 281.

146   On Gingrich's goal of debilitating the New Deal political infrastructure and the role of welfare reform, see Elizabeth Drew, *Showdown: The Struggle between the Gingrich Congress and the Clinton White House* (New York: Simon and Schuster, 1996).

147   Shear, "Looking for a Voice."

148   Eliza Newlin Carney, "Taking Over," *National Journal*, June 10, 1995, 1383–1387. Also see Weaver, "Ending Welfare as We Know It," 376.

149   *Congressional Record*, 104th Cong., 2nd sess., 1996, 142, pt. 106, H7815.

150   Ibid., pt. 105, H7749.

151   Hamilton, *The Dual Agenda*, 195.

152   *Congressional Record*, 104th Cong., 2nd sess., 1996, 142, pt. 105, H7750.

153   Ibid., 1st sess., 1995, 141, pt. 52, H3348.

CHAPTER 5 THE POLITICAL RESURRECTION OF THE BIBLE BELT

1   Groups mobilizing on both sides of the abortion issue have self-identified and been identified in public discourse by an assortment of morally fraught labels. While mindful of the significance of linguistic choices, I will, for simplicity's sake, use the common labels of "pro-choice" and "pro-life" throughout this chapter to describe those who support abortion rights and those who are opposed to them, respectively.

2   Calculations for Figure 5.1 are based on vote data made available by Keith Poole and Howard Rosenthal at the website voteview.com. Votes were selected using Poole and Rosenthal's issue categorization, which includes all votes on abortion and on care for deformed newborns.

3   Data for Figure 5.2 and throughout this chapter (unless otherwise noted) are based on index scores of support for abortion rights generated for each representative. In the cases of trade and welfare, significant pieces of legislation from throughout the postwar era were selected for the index analysis (omnibus trade and AFDC only bills). On abortion, this type of variation in legislation (between big and small or general and specific bills) is not as apparent. In each Congress, there was typically a large number of abortion bills, many or all of which were significant. Because of this, all of the votes identified with Poole and Rosenthal's abortion issue categorization were used as the basis for the index; factor analysis was then conducted to isolate similar votes and construct the index (see Appendix B).

4   Lawrence H. Tribe, *Abortion: The Clash of Absolutes* (New York: W. W. Norton, 1990).

5   Not only is the mean Republican position lower on the issues of welfare and trade (protectionism) than abortion rights, the standard deviations associated with those issues are smaller, suggesting greater unity and intensity of opposition on those issues.

6   It should be noted that the drop-off in support for abortion rights in all regions in the 104th House (1995–96) reflects the impact of a new type of abortion legislation, proposals to limit late-term abortions (the "partial-birth" ban).

7   The Partial Birth Abortion Ban Act of 2003 was subsequently enacted by Republicans in Congress, signed by President Bush, and upheld by the Supreme Court in 2007.

8   On the history of the Hyde Amendment, see Joyce Gelb and Marion Lief Palley, *Women and Public Policies: Reassessing Gender Politics* (Charlottesville: University Press of Virginia, 1996), ch. 6; Barbara Hinkson Craig and David M. O'Brien, *Abortion and American Politics* (Chatham, NJ: Chatham House, 1993), ch. 4; and Kenneth J. Meier and Deborah R. McFarlane, "Abortion Politics and Abortion Funding Policy," in *Understanding the New Politics of Abortion*, ed. Malcolm L. Goggin (Newbury Park, CA: Sage Publications, 1993).

9   There were two floor votes initially taken in the House on the Hyde Amendment on June 24, 1976. The second vote, to agree to the Hyde Amendment, passed by a slightly narrower margin than the first (199 to 165 versus the earlier vote's 207 to 167).

10   The range is most clearly demonstrated in the fairly large standard deviations within the parties; standard deviations are 45 and 40 percent for Democrats and Republicans, respectively.

11   Because there were only 135 Republicans voting on the issue in the House at the time, southern Democratic support was imperative to passage.

12   The bloc of relatively high support from the northernmost southern states is somewhat anomalous for this time period. Abortion rights support in Virginia, South Carolina, Tennessee,

and West Virginia dropped over the next few congresses; only in North Carolina did support for abortion rights remain high until the 1990s.

13   Spiro Agnew, Republican dinner speech in Houston, Texas, May 22, 1970.

14   OLS analysis: The unit of analysis is the state. The dependent variable is the mean abortion rights index score for representatives in each state. The size of a state's conservative Christian population includes membership in the following churches: Church of God, Mormons, Church of Christ, Church of the Nazarene, Mennonites, Conservative Baptist Association, Missouri Synod Lutheran, Free Will Baptists, Pentecostal Holiness, Salvation Army, Seventh-Day Adventist, Southern Baptist, and Wisconsin Synod Lutheran. Percent of women in the labor force is a frequently used proxy measure to signify women's political mobilization (see Susan Hansen, "Differences in Public Policies toward Abortion: Electoral and Policy Context," in *Understanding the New Politics of Abortion,* ed. Malcolm Goggin (Newbury Park, CA: Sage Publications, 1993). College education is the percentage of the state population with at least four years of college education. The percentage of the state population that is Catholic was initially used in the model but presented multicollinearity problems with the size of the Christian conservative population. Using percent of Catholic representatives is one way around this problem, as it is highly correlated ($r = .744$) with the percentage of Catholics in the state but is not collinear with other factors in the model. Some care is needed in interpretation, however, as it has been suggested that a legislator's religion is an important source of his or her own ideological position (separate perhaps from the representative function). See, for example, Chris Fastnow, J. Tobin Grant, and Thomas Rudolph, "Holy Roll Calls: Religious Tradition and Voting Behavior in the U.S. House," *Social Science Quarterly* 80, no. 4 (December 1999): 687–701. Regional variables are dummy variables.

15   On the doubling of the rate, see Gelb and Palley, *Women and Public Policies,* 16. Note that the figure 49.6 is the percentage of women who worked in 1969, not degree of labor force participation, which was 41.1 percent. U.S. Bureau of the Census, *1970 Census of Population,* vol. 1, *Character of the Population,* part 1, *U.S. Summary,* sec. 2, table 342.

16   Christina Wolbrecht, *The Politics of Women's Rights: Parties, Positions, and Change* (Princeton: Princeton University Press, 2000), 151.

17   U.S. Census Bureau, No. HS-13: Live Births, Deaths, Infant Deaths, and Maternal Deaths: 1900 to 2001. Accessed online at www.census.gov/statab/www/minihs.html on June 21, 2005.

18   Rate is per 1,000 married women 15 years and over. U.S. Department of Health and Human Services, National Center for Health Statistics, *Monthly Vital Statistics Report,* vol. 34, no. 9, supplement, December 26, 1985, table 1.

19   Kristin Luker, *Abortion and the Politics of Motherhood* (Berkeley: University of California Press, 1984).

20   Luker, *Abortion and the Politics of Motherhood,* 117–118. Italics in original.

21   While Spiro Agnew and others in the Nixon administration railed against the "liberal elites" in this class, advisors to Jimmy Carter, such as Pat Caddell, targeted them as the source of a new Democratic constituency that cared less about economic issues and more about social ones.

22   Jane Mansbridge, *Why We Lost the ERA* (Chicago: University of Chicago Press, 1986), 107–108.

23   Luker, *Abortion and the Politics of Motherhood,* ch. 7.

24   Hansen, "Differences in Public Policies toward Abortion," 226.

25   Ronald Inglehart, "The Silent Revolution in Europe: Intergenerational Change in Post-Industrial Societies," *American Political Science Review* 65 (December 1971): 991–1017; Inglehart, "Post-Materialism in an Environment of Insecurity," *American Political Science Review* 75 (December 1981): 880–900.

26   In *Bobos in Paradise: The New Upper Class and How They Got There* (New York: Simon and Schuster, 2000), David Brooks criticizes the "ruling class" generation that grew out of this as the "bohemian bourgeoisie" (or Bobos).

27   Congressional Record, 94th Cong., 2nd sess., 1976, 122, pt. 24, 30898.

28   See Edward Carmines and James Stimson, *Issue Evolution: Race and the Transformation of American Politics* (Princeton: Princeton University Press, 1989). For the link to Democratic support of women's rights, see Wolbrecht, *The Politics of Women's Rights,* esp. ch. 5.

29   Luker, *Abortion and the Politics of Motherhood,* 126.

30   *New York Times,* November 27, 1977, sec. 4, 4, as quoted in Craig and O'Brien, *Abortion and American Politics,* 44.

31   Craig and O'Brien, *Abortion and American Politics,* 43–45.

32   Above average abortion rights support, or opposition to the Hyde Amendment, in Virginia, North Carolina, South Carolina, and Tennessee is seemingly incongruous with the favorable ratings that most lawmakers in these four states received from the American Conservative Union (ACU) in these years. (Lawmakers in the fifth southern state with an above average score, West Virginia, generally did not receive favorable scores from the ACU.) Virginia Republican Manley Butler, for example, received a 97 percent favorable score from the ACU in 1975 and a 78 percent score in 1976, yet on the Hyde Amendment, he voted "unfavorably" according to the ACU, that is, against the amendment (his vote on the Hyde Amendment contributed to the lowering of his conservative score from 97 to 78). Determining individual motivations is difficult, because representatives from these states were silent in the floor debates, and there are multiple possible reasons for their apparently anomalous behavior. On the one hand, highly dependent on federal Medicaid dollars, southern states were unlikely to be able to replace the missing funds if the amendment were to pass, and Virginia and the Carolinas had among the highest rates of Medicaid-funded abortions in the South. This, then, could be the reason for their opposition to the Hyde Amendment. Yet, if this were the only factor, one would expect southern states with equally high or higher rates of Medicaid-funded abortions, such as Texas and Georgia, to be as opposed to the funding ban, and this was not the case. Alternatively, as Johanna Schoen and others have pointed out, issues of reproductive control in places like North Carolina and Virginia generated a complex politics that made for unusual bedfellows—those supporting women's reproductive control and those interested in exercising greater control over poor, especially African American, women's reproductive lives. Both sets of actors had a stake in obtaining federal government funds to pay for poor women's abortions. These local politics were also occurring in an international context in which issues of the earth's finite resources and population control were being debated. See Johanna Schoen, *Choice and Coercion: Birth Control, Sterilization, and Abortion in Public Health and Welfare* (Chapel Hill: University of North Carolina Press, 2005); also Dorothy Roberts, *Killing the Black Body: Race, Reproduction, and the Meaning of Liberty* (New York: Pantheon Books, 1997). For Medicaid-abortion rates, see Richard Lincoln, Brigitte Doring-Bradley, Barbara Lindheim, and Maureen Cotterill, "The Court, the Congress, and the President: Turning Back the Clock on the Pregnant Poor," *Family Planning Perspectives* 9, no. 5 (September–October 1977): 207–214.

Generally, while first and foremost a referendum on abortion rights, the debate on the Hyde Amendment intersected with debates about healthcare inequities, increasing poverty, and welfare—debates that, like those on AFDC, were racially charged. Social conservatives favoring the Hyde Amendment's Medicaid funding ban at times appealed to racial progressives by accusing abortion rights supporters of engaging in racial genocide. For example, the bill's sponsor, Illinois Republican Henry Hyde, argued, "All of us should have a particular sensitivity to the concept of the word genocide. In New York City, last year for every 1,000 minority births, there were 1,304 minority abortions. That is one way to get rid of the poverty problem, get rid of poor people. Let us call that pooricide." Hyde then proceeded to quote Jesse Jackson. Similarly, Texas Republican Ron Paul, also a supporter of the Hyde Amendment (and recipient of a 90% favorable score from the ACU), argued, "The sickest argument for abortion is that the poor black population needs to be reduced. Keep them off the welfare rolls some conservatives argue. Even liberals have argued with me that since I oppose the welfare state this would fit into my desires." It is possible that, in raising the spectre of racial genocide, social conservatives, not typically at the forefront of racial justice battles, were simply trying to divide abortion rights supporters. Even so, the fact that several representatives made this sort of argument suggests that the claim had some currency and that there were multiple reasons for wanting the federal government to pay for poor women's abortions. In other words, it suggests that one reason some people favored federal payments for abortions was because they wanted to reduce births to poor and especially minority women, not because they were interested in enhancing women's rights. *Congressional Record*, 94th Cong., 2nd sess., 1976, 122, pt. 21, 26785–26787.

33   *Congressional Record*, 94th Cong., 2nd sess., 1976, 122, pt. 23, 29049.

34   Clyde Wilcox, *Onward Christian Soldiers*, 2nd ed. (Boulder, CO: Westview Press, 2000), 52. Wilcox writes that, while the white evangelical community was the traditional target of the Christian right, the movement has in recent years also targeted conservative Catholics, mainline Protestants, and African Americans (45–55).

35   Bob Holbrook, "Baptists Reject Abortion Practice," letter to the editor of the *Shreveport Times* from the coordinator of Texas Baptists for Life, reprinted, at the request of Louisiana Democrat Joe Waggonner, in *Congressional Record*, 94th Cong., 2nd sess., 1976, 122, pt. 21, 26447.

36   "Is Abortion a Catholic Issue?" editorial, *Christianity Today*, January 16, 1976, reprinted in *Congressional Record*, 94th Cong., 2nd sess., 1976, 122, pt. 5, 5728, observes that, in the states where Mormons had political clout, their opponents called abortion a "Mormon issue."

37   *Dictionary of Christianity in America*, ed. David Reid, Robert Linder, Bruce Shelley, and Harry Stout (Downers Grove, IL: Inter-Varsity Press, 1990), 817–819. Also see, John C. Green, "The Christian Right and the 1996 Elections: An Overview," in *God at the Grass Roots, 1996: The Christian Right in American Elections*, ed. Mark J. Rozell and Clyde Wilcox (Lanham, Md: Rowman and Littlefield, 1997), 2–5.

38   *Dictionary of Christianity.*

39   Ibid.

40   Glenn H. Utter and John W. Storey, *The Religious Right: A Reference Handbook*, 2nd ed. (Santa Barbara: ABC Clio, 2001), 133. Kristen Luker's interview data reinforces survey data. Ninety-one percent of the pro-life activists she interviewed said that religion (not necessarily a fundamentalist religion) was either important or very important in their lives, while three-quarters of

pro-choice activists said that formal religion was either unimportant or irrelevant to them. Luker, *Abortion and the Politics of Motherhood*, 196–197.

41   James C. Cobb, *Redefining Southern Culture: Mind and Identity in the Modern South* (Athens: University of Georgia Press, 1999), 190–193. Also, Carl Abbott, *The Metropolitan Frontier: Cities in the Modern American West* (Tucson: University of Arizona Press, 1993). In contrasting southern modernization with that of the North, Cobb notes that the South's more geographically diffused form of industrialization was possible because of the late timing of modernization, which enabled the region to take advantage of federal assistance with electricity, highways, etc. This, he argues, resulted in an experience with and response to modernization different from the North's.

42   For a full discussion of economic modernization in the South, see Cobb, *Redefining Southern Culture*; and Bruce Schulman, *From Cotton Belt to Sunbelt: Federal Policy, Economic Development, and the Transformation of the South, 1938–1980* (New York: Oxford University, 1991). On the West, see Abbott, *The Metropolitan Frontier*; Michael Malone and Richard Etulain, *The American West: A Twentieth-Century History* (Lincoln: University of Nebraska Press, 1989); and Lisa McGirr, *Suburban Warriors: The Origins of the New American Right* (Princeton: Princeton University Press, 2001).

43   Oran P. Smith, *The Rise of Baptist Republicanism* (New York: New York University Press, 1997), 84.

44   McGirr, *Suburban Warriors*. Also see Bruce Schulman, *The Seventies: The Great Shift in American Culture, Society, and Politics* (New York: Free Press, 2001), esp. ch. 4.

45   Marshall Frady, "Gone with the Wind," *Newsweek*, July 28, 1975, 11, as described in Cobb, *Redefining Southern Culture*, 194.

46   Cobb, *Redefining Southern Culture*. Addressing the South in *The Seventies*, Schulman describes the related rise in regional pride, or as he calls it "redneck chic," that took hold among southern suburbanites who lauded the South's ruralism.

47   *Congressional Record*, 94th Cong., 2nd sess., 1976, 122, pt. 16, 20410. Italics mine.

48   Ibid.

49   Ibid., pt. 9, 11481.

50   Ibid., pt. 23, 29049.

51   Barbara Vobejda, "Harsh Details Shift Tenor of Abortion Fight; Both Sides Bend Facts on Late-Term Procedure," *Washington Post*, September 17, 1996, A1.

52   In three of the northernmost western states—North Dakota, South Dakota, and Montana—there was strong support for abortion rights. This regional anomaly reflects Democratic strength; each of these three sparsely populated states had one representative and all three were Democrats. Interestingly, only the Montana Democrat, Pat Williams, was broadly progressive; he was replaced by a Republican representative after his retirement in 1997. The North Dakota representative, Earl Pomeroy, is a "Blue Dog," moderately conservative Democrat who received a 35% rating by NARAL for his frequency of agreement with their organization, suggesting that the "above average" support in the 104th is, indeed, anomalous. Tim Johnson, the South Dakota Democrat (now in the Senate), is also generally conservative, receiving a 15% NARAL rating for his Senate votes. (The Republican currently representing Montana in the House, Denny Rehberg, has a 0% NARAL rating.) See ratings at www.naral.org.

53   See Greg D. Adams, "Abortion: Evidence of an Issue Evolution," *American Journal of Political Science* 41, no. 3 (July 1997): 718–737. Also see Craig and O'Brien, *Abortion and American Politics*, ch. 7.

54 *Contract with America* available at www.house.gov/house/Contract/CONTRACT.html.

55 Kevin Merida, "Antiabortion Measures Debated; House Republicans Push for New Restrictions in Several Areas," *Washington Post,* June 14, 1995, A4.

56 From the text of HR 1833, section 1531. *Congressional Record,* 104th Cong., 1st sess., 1995, 141, pt. 171, H11604. Italics mine.

57 Vobejda, "Harsh Details Shift Tenor."

58 Ibid.

59 Edwin Chen, "Congress Braces for Renewed Salvos in 'Culture War' Politics: Budget Deal Blurred Parties' Differences. Returning to Debate on Social Issues Offers Chance to Stress Their Clashing Visions," *Los Angeles Times,* May 14, 1997, A16.

60 The index for abortion voting generally in the 104th House includes 23 votes. The standard deviation for Democrats on the general index is 38 percent and for Republicans 28 percent. The index for partial-birth ban legislation includes six votes. Standard deviations are 43 and 23 percent, respectively.

61 Statistics are from state percentages of individuals who favored abortion in all cases, 1988–1992, in Matthew Wetstein, *Abortion Rates in the United States: The Influence of Opinion and Policy* (Albany: State University of New York Press, 1996), 87.

62 OLS analysis: The dependent variable is the mean state abortion rights index score, in general (model 1) and on partial-birth ban voting only (model 2). The conservative Christian population measure is similar to that used in the 1976 model. NARAL (National Abortion Rights Action League) strength is based on membership per 1,000 people in each of the states in 1990. Percent of Catholic representatives was not significant in the regressions and so was dropped from the results. The NARAL membership data was generously provided by Kenneth Meier and Deborah McFarlane (personal correspondence, June 2, 2002).

63 This is not to imply that the women's labor force participation and NARAL activity are interchangeable. The first describes an economic condition that is associated with support for abortion rights and the second an interest group political demand that is associated with support for abortion rights. The difference between the two is suggested by the difference in the correlation between state NARAL membership and the percentage of the state female population in the workforce ($r = .334$, $p = .02$) and that of state NARAL membership with the percentage of state female population over 25 with a BA ($r = .863$, $p = .000$). This suggests that women with more education, more likely professional women, are stronger NARAL supporters than the general population of working women.

64 Gelb and Palley, *Women and Public Policies,* 151.

65 For some demographic data about abortions in the early to mid-1990s, see "GOP Convention '96: Abortion in America," *Los Angeles Times,* August 12, 1996, A15. For some 2006 data, see Alan Guttmacher Institute, "Facts on Induced Abortions in the United States," at www.guttmacher.org/pubs.

66 *Congressional Record,* 104th Cong., 2nd sess., 1996, 142, pt. 44, H2900.

67 Ibid., 1st sess., 1995, 141, pt. 171, H11614. Italics mine.

68 Vobejda, "Harsh Details Shift Tenor."

69 Ibid.

70 *Congressional Record*, 104th Cong., 2nd sess., 1996, 142, pt. 44, H2908.

71 Elizabeth Drew, *Showdown: The Struggle between the Gingrich Congress and the Clinton White House* (New York: Simon and Schuster, 1996), 45.

72 Alison Mitchell, "A Calculation in Tears," *New York Times*, April 12, 1996, A1.

73 Helen Dewar, "Senate Sustains Clinton Veto of Late-Term Abortion Ban," *Washington Post*, September 27, 1996, A4.

74 *Congressional Record*, 104th Cong., 1st sess., 1995, 141, pt. 171, H11606.

75 Ibid., H11605.

76 Vobejda, "Harsh Details Shift Tenor."

77 *Congressional Record*, 104th Cong., 2nd sess., 1996, 142, pt. 44, H2910.

78 *Congressional Record*, 104th Cong., 1st sess., 1995, 141, pt. 171. On the first, see the comments of Oklahoma Republican Thomas Coburn, H11615; on the second, see the comments of Bob Dornan, Republican of California, H11614; and on the third, see Florida Republican Ileana Ros-Lehtinen, H11609.

79 Ibid., H11612–H11613.

80 David Karol, "How and Why Parties Change Positions on Issues: Party Policy Change as Coalition Management in American Politics," paper presented at the annual meeting of the American Political Science Association, San Francisco, CA, 2001.

81 Adams, "Abortion: Evidence of an Issue Evolution."

82 Ibid., 730–731.

83 Wolbrecht, *The Politics of Women's Rights*.

CHAPTER 6 A HOUSE DIVIDED

1 James C. Cobb, *Redefining Southern Culture: Mind and Identity in the Modern South* (Athens: University of Georgia Press, 1999), 209.

2 Allowing state differences on gay marriage may prove to be constitutionally problematic, given that rights granted in one state are not recognized in another. To the extent that such differences influence individual decisions about where to live, these state laws (and other state social policy laws) reinforce regional differences.

3 Brutus I, 2.9.16, as quoted in Herbert Storing, "Federalists and Anti-Federalists: The Ratification Debate," in *Toward a More Perfect Union: Writings of Herbert Storing*, ed. Joseph M. Bessette (Washington D.C: AEI Press, 1995).

4 *The Federalist*, 45.

5 American Political Science Association's Committee on Political Parties, *Toward a More Responsible Two-Party System*, (New York: Rinehart, 1950).

6 For a provocative argument about the state of contemporary politics and efforts by the cur-

rent Republican majority to thwart or undermine minority contestation, see Jacob Hacker and Paul Pierson, *Off Center: The Republican Revolution and the Erosion of American Democracy* (New Haven: Yale University Press, 2005).

APPENDIX A RESEARCH METHOD AND CASE SELECTION

1   The assumption is that representatives are primarily interested in reelection and that, to ensure this, they adopt positions consistent with their constituents' interests. As a result, the behavioral patterns and arguments made by House representatives are consistent with the polity at large; they serve, in essence, as a proxy for the polity. On this subject, see David Mayhew, *Congress: The Electoral Connection* (New Haven: Yale University Press, 1974). This assumption is shared by other recent regional analyses, including Richard Bensel, *Sectionalism and American Political Development, 1880–1980* (Madison: University of Wisconsin Press, 1984); and Peter Trubowitz, *Defining the National Interest: Conflict and Change in American Foreign Policy* (Chicago: University of Chicago Press, 1998).

2   A growing number of scholars have begun to explore party dynamics in relation to single issue areas. See Greg D. Adams, "Abortion: Evidence of an Issue Evolution," *American Journal of Political Science* 41, no. 3 (July 1997): 718–737; Christina Wolbrecht, *The Politics of Women's Rights: Parties, Positions, and Change* (Princeton: Princeton University Press, 2000); and Charles Shipan and William Lowry, "Environmental Policy and Party Divergence in Congress," *Political Research Quarterly* 54, no. 2 (2001): 245–263.

3   Scholars have long categorized policies by such descriptive features as type of issue and scope and nature of the conflict. My formulation bears similarity to three of Aage Clausen's five categories of policy: governmental management (trade as representative of), social welfare (Aid to Families with Dependent Children program), and civil liberties (abortion). Aage Clausen, *How Congressmen Decide: A Policy Focus* (New York: St. Martin's Press, 1973).

APPENDIX B CONGRESSIONAL VOTE ANALYSIS

1   For a discussion of various measures of legislative behavior, see Lee F. Anderson, Meredith W. Watts, Jr., and Allen R. Wilcox, *Legislative Roll-Call Analysis,* (Evanston, IL: Northwestern University Press, 1966).

Page numbers in *italic* refer to figures and tables.